What Others Are Saying about This Book . . .

"In her gripping memoir Jennifer Myers offers a startling account of how the pursuit of an elusive American dream can lead us to the depths of the American criminal underbelly. Her book is as much about being human in a hyper-materialistic society as it is about drug culture. When the DEA finally knocks on Myers' door, she and the reader both see the moment for what it truly is—not so much an arrest as a rescue." **—Tony D'Souza, author of** *Whiteman* **and** *Mule*

"Jennifer Myers has written a powerful story of transformation and resilience. Riveting and compelling, this is a must-read." **—Jodie Lawston, Ph.D., Women's Studies Program, California State University San Marcos, CA; author of** *Sisters Outside: Radical Activists Working for Women Prisoners;* **co-editor of** *Razor Wire Women*

"*Trafficking the Good Life* is a powerful, compelling story of one woman's journey to hell and back. With honesty, clarity, pathos and humor, Jennifer Myers helps us understand, with real empathy, her downfall, rehabilitation, and resurrection." **—Gloria Killian, Executive Director, the Action Committee for Women in Prison; Exoneree; co-author of** *Full Circle*

"I want all my clients to read this book. Beneath the drug story is a universal theme all women can relate to: the desperate search for self, and the ultimate journey to finding the true feminine voice that longs to emerge in what often feels like a world of additions. I hope parents will read this book before their children reach grade school. *Trafficking the Good Life* is insightful, educational, and, ultimately, a journey to the heart." **—Moe Ross, addictions specialist; Director, Northwest Community Counseling Services and Hollyhock Retreat Center**

D1158785

"An enthralling first-hand account of lives turned upside down by incarceration and imprisonment. If you want insight into the human condition in general, and the condition of incarceration in particular, read this honest and dramatic portrayal." —**Dennis Sobin, Director, Safe Streets Arts Foundation**

"Most people grow up believing that everyone in prison is a rapist, child molester, or murderer. Jennifer Myers proves them wrong. Her personal journey to prison is a chilling lesson in how our love affair with incarceration sends thousands of nonviolent offenders to prison for decades." —**Julie Stewart, President and Founder, Families Against Mandatory Minimums (FAMM)**

"Freedom, true freedom, isn't something anyone can give you or take away; freedom comes from within. *Trafficking the Good Life* is a precious reminder of these truths as Jennifer Myers both inspires and entertains us in her riveting story of drug trafficking, incarceration, and redemption." —**Darrin Zeer, bestselling author of *Office Yoga;* CNN's "America's Relaxation Expert"**

"Myers' narrative is a painfully raw and stunningly honest exploration of a woman finding her way through a very masculine world filled with frightening consequences. It is a powerful story of redemption—of how one woman finds her voice by facing the choices she has made and learning a truth that is hers and hers alone." —**Dr. Linda Savage, author of *Reclaiming Goddess Sexuality: The Power of the Feminine Way***

"Myers risks it all as she exposes her soul. Her poignant, brutal honesty will touch your heart." —**Azim Khamisa, best-selling author, *Azim's Bardo: From Murder to Forgiveness***

TRAFFICKING
THE GOOD LIFE

JENNIFER MYERS

BETTIE YOUNGS BOOKS

Copyright © 2012 by Jennifer Myers

All rights reserved, including the right to reproduce this work in any form whatsoever, without permission in writing from the publisher, except for brief passages in connection with a review.

Disclaimer: This is a true story, and the characters and events are real. However, in some cases, the names, descriptions, and locations have been changed, and some events have been altered, combined, or condensed for storytelling purposes, but the overall chronology is an accurate depiction of the author's experience.

About the Cover: The art on the front cover, *Crying Wind,* was created by artist Brian Driggers while he was incarcerated. With limited access to art supplies inside prison, Brian used instant coffee and beet juice for paint, and hair taken from his head as a brush.

Cover Photograph by Brian Driggers
Cover Design by Tatomir Pitariu
Text Design by Jane Hagaman
Senior Editor: Donna Kennedy
Author photo of Jennifer Myers by Martin Mann, Martin Mann
    Photography
Publisher: Bettie Youngs Book Publishers

Bettie Youngs Books are distributed worldwide. If you are unable to order this book from your local bookseller or online or from Espresso, you may order directly from the publisher.
BETTIE YOUNGS BOOK PUBLISHERS
www.BettieYoungsBooks.com
info@BettieYoungsBooks.com

ISBN: 978-1-936332-67-0
ePub: 978-1-936332-68-7

Library of Congress Control Number: 2012941208

1. Myers, Jennifer. 2. Incarceration. 3. Marijuana. 4. Women. 5. Self-image. 6. Spirituality. 7. Prison. 8. Faith. 9. Relationships.

Printed in the United States of America.

Dedication

For mom, who was my best friend

Without realizing it, the individual composes
his life according to the laws of beauty,
even in times of greatest distress.

—Milan Kundera

CONTENTS

FOREWORD

Two hundred sixty-seven miles. I knew that because I'd checked the distance and route online. Two hundred sixty-seven miles was all that separated Jen from the prison to which she'd been committed. We had to have her there by noon the following day and although the navigation system estimated that it would take a bit over five hours I knew, for Jen, the journey was going to seem infinite. I knew because years earlier I'd made that same journey, in fact, like Jen, I'm still on it.

After being released from federal prison in 1996, I made my living working with people facing a period of federal incarceration. Through this work I came to know them, their families, their colleagues, their priests, rabbis, and imams. I've done what I could to ease the terror of the process that had, most often through their own bad acts, threatened to engulf them.

I've watched these men and women cry, yell, scream, hurt, question, and heal. I've watched each of them evolve as the events and people around them shaped that part of their lives. I've often considered myself privileged, blessed in fact, being a part of this agonizing process because through it I've seen lives, perhaps even souls, evolve.

In *Trafficking the Good Life* Jennifer Myers, in what I can only describe as heroic vulnerability, shares this incredibly intimate journey of evolution with her readers. How does a "good girl" from Ohio end up trafficking marijuana across the country? What traits allow a well-raised person to justify illegal activity? How can a person lead such a compartmentalized life? Can a person grow through this process? Is there redemption?

In her crisp, accessible prose, Jennifer brings readers along on her journey. Jennifer expertly weaves her narrative through the disparate worlds of marijuana trafficking, federal incarceration, spiritual development, and the internal struggles brought about through exposure to each of these worlds. Without excuse, Jennifer shares her rationalizations, triumphs, and defeats.

Her candor, in fact, the entirety of *Trafficking the Good Life* is evocative. It's moving, thought provoking, and should be read by anybody truly interested in exploring the human side of our federal judicial process. Beyond that *Trafficking the Good Life* is a journal celebrating the process of growth through adversity. Not always linear, often messy and, at times painful, the journey Jennifer shares with her readers is one that most of us will identify with.

Quite often while working with the families of those facing federal prosecution and incarceration, I've been frustrated with my inability to provide them insight as to why: Why did their loved one make the decisions they did? Why did they break the law? How did this happen? In *Trafficking the Good Life* Jennifer Myers sheds light on these questions and, perhaps more importantly, sheds lights on that part within all of us tempted to traffic our way to the good life.

Although we only had to drive 267 miles to bring Jennifer to prison, her journey back has been immeasurable. *Trafficking the Good Life* is a testament to that journey.

David Novak, author of
DownTime: A Guide to Federal Incarceration

ACKNOWLEDGMENTS

To those at the beginning who believed in me: Sarah Gallogly for her beautiful editing and inspiring words; Laurie Baum for her editing, insights, and astrological gifts.

To those who joined along the way: Bruce McAllister, wizard of the written word, who brought wisdom, unlimited patience, and knowledge of the publishing business. Without you, I would have given up long ago; endless thanks for introducing me to Donna Kennedy, editor extraordinaire. Her encouragement and loving scalpel released the magic of my words and relaxed my inner critic. I've found not only an editor, but a friend.

To my gifted and knowledgeable publisher, Bettie Youngs of *Bettie Youngs Book Publishers*, who saw the beauty in my story. I wouldn't be here without you. And to her staff, especially Elisabeth Rinaldi for her sensitive line editing and to Jane Hagaman for the interior design and Adrian Pitariu for the overall cover design, all of you, thank you!

To my artist, Brian Driggers, I'm so glad I found you. The art on the front cover, *Crying Wind,* was created by Brian while he was incarcerated. With limited access to art supplies inside prison, Brian used instant coffee and beet juice for paint, and hair taken from his head as a brush. Thanks for your creativity and vision.

To my supportive friends who listened on the phone night after night: Karen, Chris, Stella, Linda, Maria, Laura, Wendy, Sonia, and Lane. To Moe, who opened inner doors, and to Chicago friends

Brian and Bess. To my intuitive friends at Kindred Journeys, Mystical Dragon, Awakenings, and Psychic Eye. To Claudia for her bright light and beach walks; Calista, who weathered my complaints with honesty and grace. To teachers Darrell, Sheri, and Mata for their consciousness while I was in prison; to Barbara for writing to me every day; and Ian, who helped with all the details and never left my side.

To Ms. Utterback and the group who encouraged me to write my story. To the women still in prison and to those who became my friends forever.

To my SGI community and Buddhist friends—yes, that includes you, Noriko, my entire district, and Denease. Thank you, Rise, for always reminding me of who I am and for keeping me on my feet. To Armand for your gifted insight and for creating a space for healing, and to Lynne—and all the other women in the work—for guiding the way.

To my family: my mom, who was my biggest fan and who still pushes miracles my way. (I miss you so much.) And to my dad and my brother for their infinite patience and support.

To my feline friends: Kimmy, who had my back while I wrote (I miss you, too), and Otis, who shows me how to love.

To Mic for her creativity and soft heart, and finally, to Tim, who was my partner (and sponsor) on this incredible journey. You'll always be home to me. Words cannot express my gratitude.

And lastly, to the inner provider and shining light who gives me conviction and courage, and guides me even when I lose the way.

PROLOGUE

"Jennifer Myers, I'm from the DEA. You've been indicted by the Eastern District of Michigan."

I froze, barely breathing. Fear swept through my body. At his words everything began to fade away—my life, my dreams, my future.

I knew why he was here. I was being arrested for my part in a major marijuana-trafficking ring, and I'd no one else to blame but myself.

Nothing could change it. Not my budding career in real estate or my dance success in Chicago, not even my good girl past. My mom, a high school math teacher, had taught me to be nice, to care what other people thought. Now I was letting everyone down. I had defiled my Girl Scout uniform and the cookies I'd sold on the street, my captain's cheerleading outfit, and the dance costumes I'd cherished. In one instant, my "good life" was gone. Even the spiritual work I'd done to transform my life was corrupted.

I couldn't tear my eyes away from this man I didn't know. In shock, every detail about him came alive.

The man was short and compact. He reminded me of the fraternity boys I'd known in college. They wore baseball caps, slept in late, and emitted a particular musky smell. I didn't see a gun, and he looked too young to carry one, but I knew one was there. I'd only seen two guns in my life: the rifle my dad had fired to scare the groundhog and the one I'd held trapshooting with Casey. Not even in my marijuana trafficking had I seen guns.

We three stood in the doorway of my boss's office: me, a thirty-five-year-old Ohio State grad dressed in ridiculous light blue sweats for lunchtime Pilates standing next to this stranger, and Stephen, my boss.

Stephen looked at me with love, pain and betrayal in his eyes. When he hired me as a manager at his real estate company, there had been only one condition: I must give up my illegal business.

I'd promised.

We'd met four years ago at a transformational workshop. He'd trusted me to work as a manager in his company, and I'd made a promise I thought I could keep. But my spiritual quest had done nothing to erase my addiction to the money the drugs brought in.

Had I lied?

Yes, I had. Because I didn't have the strength to let go of the trips.

Reeling, I stepped back but didn't look away. He had been betrayed in more ways than one. He'd loved me romantically, and I hadn't returned it.

The moment passed and Stephen leapt into action. He asked me for my parents' phone number. No words were registering with me. "Jen, you have to give me your parents' number!"

What was their number? No. They couldn't know about this. But they had *to know about this. Jesus.*

I couldn't speak or think.

The man led me into the kitchen where two other DEA agents stood, one a woman. She was there to frisk me—to touch me everywhere—looking for who knows what. I felt her small hands running down my sides. My body automatically responded with goose bumps. Inside I was heaving, storing up tears that wouldn't have a chance to come for a long time.

I yelled for Stephen to get my purse.

"Where is it, Jen?"

He was frantic, searching. The female agent leaned me against the counter and brought my hands behind my back. I was staring at the tan Formica.

"There, *under there.*"

I was praying. *Click.* I felt for the first time the grip of the handcuffs too tight around my wrists. I closed my eyes and pictured the white barn of my childhood, the safe place I always thought of when I was scared. *Purse. Got to find my purse.*

"The green one," I heard myself say.

Stephen picked up the purse and the woman spoke: "If you give her anything she is not supposed to have, you could be an accomplice."

With a wild look, Stephen dropped the bag.

I couldn't pick it up myself, but it was open. I told him to pull my wallet out.

"It's a business card," I said. "An attorney. I need his number."

The attorney . . . and Ian needs to know. Call Ian, I thought to myself. *Zoey. Who's going to feed Zoey? They're taking me for how long? And where? How am I going to contact Dane?* The agents wanted to confiscate my car. "Where's your key?"

My Land Rover Discovery was parked in the back beyond the peaceful pond where Stephen's koi swam. "What peace?" a voice babbled in my head. Stephen was raging, my heart was thundering, and my coworkers had faded into the background.

"I'm calling my attorney on the phone!" Stephen shouted. "You're not taking her car."

"Sir, we *can* legally take her car."

The sound of Stephen's voice diminished as they led me outside. I walked head down, not looking at anyone. Like a mobster in old photographs. But even in my handcuffs, I was too numb and scared even to feel the shame. I guess I belonged to the government. Wasn't that what the judgment from the Eastern District of Michigan had meant? My fingers touched each other, bound together in their steel. My wrists hurt. Inside, there was no steel.

"Do you have any needles, sharp objects, or weapons in your purse?" the male agent who carried my purse asked.

What?

Do I have anything sharp in my purse?

"I don't know." He reached into my Marc Jacobs bag, the one I loved. I'd bought it as a feeling-sorry-for-myself gift after Casey ended our relationship. The purse had cost thousands, and I'd had the money—from the drugs.

The agent quickly drew his hand back.

"I'm going to ask you again. Do you have any needles or weapons in your purse?"

At that moment I truly felt it: I was a criminal.

But I'm not a criminal. I'm a good girl. Everyone thinks I'm a good girl.

He reached back into my purse and pulled out folded papers.

Oh no, I thought. *How could I be so stupid?*

He called the other agents over. "Look! What is this?" I tried to tell my story, but he was already dialing a number on his cell.

"We've got something. Looks like a rental agreement to a storage unit."

I wanted to shout, "It's a mistake!" But, I didn't have the energy to argue. Instead, defeated, my head hung low.

All of the agents were so young—not even thirty—and this annoyed me. I needed the juice of annoyance.

The female agent pushed me into a Ford Taurus. Gold. No markings. Neither the agents nor the cars looked official. Everything was ordinary, but nothing was ordinary. I wanted to scream. I stared at the J on my zipper. "J" for Juicy, not "Jennifer" or "Jen." Now "J" for "judge" and "Just so, ain't life a bitch," not "justice."

The female agent got into the driver's side and backed into the other agent's Mustang. I was jolted forward from the impact. I couldn't resist turning my head. They'd had an accident, dented the cars. Their embarrassment relaxed me for a moment. These were just kids playing dress-up, playing the DEA game. This was their job, and I was just another criminal who needed to be arrested, the one scheduled for 2 p.m. They didn't have to remember my name. It was on the piece of paper.

They swarmed around the back where the car was damaged. "Hey, grab the camera. We have to take pictures."

They were fast but followed protocol as I sat in the passenger seat. I wanted to laugh at their silliness. Otherwise, what was really happening to me would be too real.

During the drive, I stared out the window. The agent talked, but I didn't respond. I'd shifted my weight onto my left hip to make room for my arms cuffed behind my back when, suddenly, the car exited off the ramp and downhill into a driveway.

We were in a basement. Steel lattice panels covered the windows; light barely peeked in. Empty police cars lined the parking structure like soldiers, waiting to be assigned.

I felt hidden, lost—already forgotten.

We took an elevator up and then proceeded down a hall, empty but for the tall man walking toward us.

"Hi, Lori."

His eyes laughed, which felt degrading to me.

Who is Lori?

My flip-flops echoed on tiled floor. My arms ached. Then I remembered the conversation. "I'm Bob," Rob had said to the driver as the Atlas Van truck stopped beside our Tucson storage unit, "and this is Lori." The name had come out of that five-minute encounter. Now the court docket stated that I had an alias, "Lori." It was sick. I wanted to cry.

In a small room with a telephone, the agents uncuffed me. Someone in Detroit wanted to talk to me. I stared at my wrist, hating the phone.

I've hurt myself.

The grooves on each wrist were slightly welted, perfectly light pink. I added them to the new list in my mind, with a crossed-off item at the top:

The first time I was handcuffed.

"If anything happens, *anything,* call me," Dane had said. "Trust me. You'll only be in for a few days." And I'd believed him.

No one was speaking. The agents were an enigma—one a man and one a boy-man. They could've been my brother, Jerry, or a man cheering for his son on the diamond ball field.

I jumped when the phone rang. The agent pressed the speaker button, the red light steady. *Stay calm.* I almost said it out loud.

"Ms. Myers," the voice over the phone drawled, drawing my name out, *Myyyers.* "I'm Agent Eric Elliot from the Eastern District of Michigan. Everyone is talkin' down here, down in Detroit. All your friends are talkin'. What do you think about that?"

Inside, I shook like a five-point earthquake.

"You don't have an option," he continued, "so why don't cha tell me what you know? We already know it all, anyway."

Silence.

"If you talk to me now, you'll only be helping yourself out of a very bad situation."

The room was shrinking. Again, I almost spoke—my mind desperate to do the right thing.

I almost believed him.

"I think I need an attorney" finally came out of my mouth.

The agents looked back at me, eyes blank. Instantly the phone call was disconnected, and I was taken from the room.

Here we go. Let the game begin, I thought, as if I knew what this meant.

I added more new "firsts" to my list: my first mug shot, and then my first fingerprinting. Over the next five years I learned that some institutions have a new electronic system for fingerprinting; the rest just do it the old-fashioned way with a stamp pad. This first time was the stamp.

The agent rolled my thumb. "No, relax your hand, honey." Index finger. Pinky finger.

"No, sweetie, we're not done yet." She asked me to place my

four fingers on the pad. "Like this, a little off to the side." The new position was awkward, and the stamp pad was messy. The black residue lingered on my fingers although I was given shop soap to wash it off—the same white slippery gel my father used to clean his hands after a day on the farm. The smell brought my dad close to me . . . and the inky fingerprints took me back to kindergarten.

Blue paint. Splat. I redipped my hand in the yellow and spread my fingers as wide as I could with my palm pressed carefully onto the white paper on the floor of the kindergarten classroom. Where the blue and yellow mixed, an odd muddy brown appeared. I stared back at my palm print, satisfied. J . . . E . . . N . . . N . . . Y. I carefully wrote my name below, dipping my little fingers in the paint jars sitting beside me. My mom hung the gift on the wall, displayed for years for everyone to see.

My prints no longer displayed my accomplishments and creativity; the innocence of my childhood years was forgotten and stained. In its place was a symbol, a sign of misuse and misfortune.

I was a criminal.

I was marked and tracked.

CHAPTER 1

HE'S SO CLEAN

The white linen cloth stretched wider than the sky between us. We were almost eye-to-eye except for the towering breadsticks. The strands of hair hanging from my twirled bun and the sundress that hid my legs felt unsophisticated to me now as I looked at Dane's tailored shirt and stylish glasses. My toes squirmed, playing invisible piano keys. The movement soothed me, but still I worried. *Was he bored?*

Dane and I didn't fit together. Dane was older—thirty-two years to my twenty-five—and he looked *clean*. It was a clean I didn't recognize. Maybe it was the same clean as the tablecloth or the stark whiteness of the napkin, so white it looked like it'd never been used, or washed. Or the way the pumpernickel bread and slender poppy-seed sticks came in their perfect white jar as if there was no other choice and they didn't belong anywhere else. I didn't fit the Oak Tree Restaurant high atop the fancy 500 Michigan building in Chicago. This I knew.

I'd arrived late and found him waiting at the top of the eight-story building with his friend Gianni. Why had he brought a friend? Instantly I felt alone and wished I had someone with me, too. I felt silly when Dane pulled out my chair and placed the white cloth napkin on my lap. Dane stayed standing until I sat. Courteous. I liked that. He was small like my dad, and I liked that, too.

I was on this date only because my friend Wendy—my roommate during my last year in college—had set it up. She was my favorite Pi Beta Phi sorority sister, and I trusted her.

Wendy lived in Arizona now, and for the last six months she had been dating one of Dane's best friends. Dane lived in Arizona, too, but he traveled and "had a lot of money," Wendy told me. When she said he was nice—"really, really nice,"—her words struck at the center of my vulnerability. She knew they would. My ugly breakups worried her. And I knew she didn't like Drew, the man I'd been seeing for the past two years.

The waiter appeared to fill my water glass and offer me a lime. I wasn't used to this. I was a girl who shopped at thrift stores and hung out at places funkier than this upscale restaurant. Dane seemed shy, and I was attracted by his quietness, another reminder of my father. It made him seem to be in control—disinterested—like my father could be, too.

After lunch, we stopped at J. Crew where my attention was drawn to the down winter coats. "What do you need?" Gianni asked.

Everything. But I didn't say it out loud.

Gianni looked like he had everything he needed. When Dane purchased a shirt, I stayed behind and pretended to be interested in the pink gloves.

Already I could see that picking up the latest expensive thing seemed natural to Dane and Gianni. Not so for me. I'd worked hard since my Ohio State graduation and move to Chicago. I worked a nine-to-five job, with dance rehearsals or concerts at night. I'd majored in dance, and now that I'd achieved a certain success in Chicago's modern dance world, I could almost say I was happy. At least my lack of money didn't bother me. It hadn't occurred to me to mind that I couldn't buy everything I wanted. I wasn't someone who could afford lunches at the Oak Tree Restaurant, but Dane had paid.

I was happy to leave the store—couldn't wait for the date to end. Later, back at my loft on Green Street, I called Wendy and told her I didn't want to see him again. "It was a disaster. He brought someone with him. He's not interested."

The next day Dane called and left a message on my phone, but I didn't call back. I couldn't imagine fitting this older man into my life. We didn't live in the same world. Besides, I felt guilty about starting anything with him when I hadn't broken up with Drew. True, I was looking for a reason to leave the relationship, but even so, Dane didn't seem right for me.

But some part of me couldn't dismiss him. Meeting Dane had left me feeling that I was supposed to be someone different, someone I didn't know yet.

Wendy was sure she'd set me up with a fantastic guy and seemed irritated that I'd let him slip away. "Jen, I told him you weren't flaky!"

Drew and I had just had another fight, which often happened after he'd been drinking. When I told him I was leaving, he yelled at me. "I SAID, you are not going anywhere!"

Had I made a mistake in not calling Dane?

It's too late, Jen.

I dialed Dane's number. He answered on the third ring, and I started to apologize. "Dane, it's Jen. Sorry I didn't call."

I could tell Dane was surprised by my call. His return flight to Phoenix was to leave in three hours. My heart beat quickly, like something was supposed to happen.

In my dancer's bodysuit, still damp with sweat from my rehearsal, I waited. No wings did I hear, no whispers from angels, and with his next words my life took a turn.

"Come with me to Phoenix," he said.

My breath caught in my throat, shocked. His invitation was bold.

So he'd brought someone with him on our first date, so he'd sat there not talking. So what? "What about the . . . details?"

"Don't worry. I'll take care of the ticket."

Usually, I heard everything going on outside my loft—stiletto heels, dogs, and drunks—but his words canceled the background noise, and in the silence, I felt excitement—and fear. Fear that, until now, I hadn't been living my life to its fullest. And underneath the fear was a subtle invitation, a summons. From the beginning, I was gripped by the power of someone who *belonged* at the Oak Tree Restaurant, of someone who bought airline tickets for someone he'd just met. I was gripped by the tantalizing power of money.

My heart filled in the silence, *a thump-thump, a thump-thump.* I looked around at the trash bags piled in my kitchen, clothing piled on the bed. Maybe I wasn't able to take care of myself. Dane's invitation sounded like, felt like, *care.*

And I felt lucky. Ladybug lucky.

"Mom, look at it!" I was six years old, delighted with the tiny red polka-dotted creature in my palm.

"It's a ladybug," she said, and I said the word to myself, liking the way the "L" trilled on my tongue. I said this word for the next week, over and over, sometimes out loud, but mostly to myself. Ladybug, ladybug, I see the ladybug. I found them all over that week, on my bedroom window, in my covers, on my knee while I ate my Cheerios. I liked the ladybug.

"It's good luck," my mom said when I found one on Wednesday and let it climb onto my finger. I carried it to her, then carefully shook my hand until it landed on the kitchen counter. I watched it climb the cabinet. By Saturday, the ladybugs were gone. Suddenly I didn't see them anymore. Where had they gone? Maybe they were there and I wasn't. All I knew was that I liked the way they made me special and lucky, like they were.

Ladybug lucky.

"It will be one thousand," the Northwest Airlines attendant said. Dane placed the ten one-hundred dollar bills on the ticket counter. Inside I shook. As the attendant counted the money, I held my head a little higher.

I'm with Dane.

I didn't really know who he was, what he was, but I said this to myself anyway. As I looked at Dane's pressed shirt and perfect black suitcase, I felt safe, and good, like I had been tucked in with my mom's good-night kiss.

I felt like everything was going to be okay.

Of course, I was wrong.

Dead wrong.

CHAPTER 2

I NEED YOU

My first weekend with Dane was all about "fancy." The fine dining and nice cars opened my eyes to a world I'd always wanted to enter but had never been invited into. My little-girl self had played in grain bins, licked ice cream from the DQ, and raced her brother through the pasture across from Rattlesnake Creek. She'd dreamed of the city and of "fancy," and my grown-girl self just couldn't back away. When our flight landed in Phoenix, the Arizona sky wrapped me in its red embrace and instantly I felt at home. Dane's friend Brad drove us from the airport, and we surprised my friend Wendy outside the mall where she worked. Like the expanse of the sky, Wendy's arms welcomed me to the West. Only hours ago we'd been speaking on the phone and now I was here with her—with Dane.

Every day I spent in Phoenix, I felt a growing "need" for him. His townhouse was impeccably clean. I watched the calculated manner in which he dressed, as if he knew what to expect from life. *I* never knew what to expect. I lived as if there were no plan, as if the training and discipline of my dancing life was the foundation, and on top of it I could be wild and free. Dane's life looked like a different kind of freedom—freedom from worry, freedom from want. When he offered his hand I took it, feeling safe, like I'd be okay.

In the morning I woke in Dane's king-sized bed. I read the paper while he made coffee. Later, we drove to the lake. Six of us were on the boat as the afternoon faded and the sun slashed the sky with magnificent red and orange. In this fairytale setting, my leotards and empty bank account fell farther and farther into the distance, until I could no longer see my life back home in Chicago. I steered the boat. The heat, hotter than hot, was divine and soothed me as Dane placed his hand on my back. I threw the throttle into high gear, laughing. Everything seemed possible with Dane beside me, his eyes twinkling. "I don't want you to go," he whispered. I didn't want to go, either.

In his bed, as he leaned in to kiss me, I saw a slim shadow of a man over my body. *Dane,* I said to myself. The name was new. *Dane,* I repeated. *Wonderful,* I reminded myself. *Dane is wonderful.* Polished, respectable—nice. Being with him was going to change how I saw myself. The truth was, it already had.

Before I met Dane, I was a woman who valued her education, an artist who treasured her creativity. In this new way of seeing, I was simply someone who wasn't quite making it. Dane's money loomed in my field of vision and overshadowed those deeper parts of myself. Already I was focused on a different dream, one of power and sophistication—and money.

"Jenny. You're so sweet," Wendy said.

She looked back at me from where she stood at the stove. We'd just returned from a late-night fraternity party. I could smell the macaroni cooking from the kitchen table. "Your mom's sweet, and your dad, he's so little," *she continued, laughing as she poured the cheese packet into the pan. I thought she was teasing, but I wasn't sure. I don't like "sweet," I thought to myself as I pulled my leather coat tighter around me. The black motorcycle coat wasn't "sweet." That's why I liked it.*

I thought of my Dad growing corn and beans, and children like me—sweet and stoic—with values city people didn't seem to have. "You're from Iowa, right?" they'd ask me later. "No, it's Ohio," I replied each time they made the mistake. But they were right: Iowa, Ohio—they all were the same to them. Life on a farm, in a family, in a place where people are "sweet" and are taught to be "nice." I felt exposed when my friends said words like "sweet" or "nice." Like the words were bad, and I was weak.

I need to toughen up, I thought to myself.

In bed with Dane, I wasn't sure who that Jenny was anymore, but I was getting an idea of who this other Jenny wanted to be. She was someone who'd never been to Ohio or Iowa. For her, sweetness wasn't an embarrassment but a tool to get what she wanted. The main thing she wanted now was to stay in this dream where money made beauty, made order, made fun.

During the next month my life turned around. Dane and I rented a loft in Chicago, where he'd visit part-time. At his request, I quit my job as a medical assistant so I could travel with him. And, as I'd hoped, spending time with Dane began to change me. At first, on the outside: the way I dressed, the place I lived. In my new environment, I thought I could be a new person. I wanted Dane to save me, to be my little-girl vision of the knight in shining armor like the silver, plastic statue my first boyfriend had given me when I was five. If I let him, Dane would take care of me and my life would be comfortable, even glamorous. I let go of the life I'd been living and simply created a new one. It happened so fast I barely had time to adjust.

In the two weeks since I'd gone with Dane to Phoenix, here was Dane, in Chicago, in my car. We'd enjoyed our dinner at Vivo, even though Drew had called—a call I hadn't answered. I hadn't really told Drew about Dane, and Dane knew I hadn't.

"Oh, God!" I shouted. In my rearview mirror, I saw Drew's Range Rover. He'd followed us from Vivo.

Is he stalking me?

"Jen, stop the car."

Dane was calm, and I did what he said. When I got out of the car, Drew was steaming, and the more we talked, the angrier he got.

"Jen, I love you."

I didn't respond.

"Get in the car, Jen."

I folded my arms and held my ground.

His eyes widened with surprise. I wasn't playing by our normal rules. Then his eyes narrowed, and he advanced toward me.

"Drew, it's over," I said. Only that.

He knew he'd lost control. Something had changed. He didn't know what or how or even why, but I wasn't about to explain. We both knew our relationship was finished.

As Drew walked away, he spit out a barrage of angry words—directed at me, except for one subtle remark, "Nice shoes, dude."

Dane stood beside my car and didn't reply. I looked down at Dane's shoes. They were expensive, those perfectly woven Italian slip-on shoes. Worlds away from Drew's Doc Martens—and worlds away from the old me. Dane's shoes suddenly seemed feminine, laughable. I was disconcerted by my pettiness and disloyalty. As I opened the door, this shame followed me into the car.

Dane and I drove to Chicago's waterfront. We parked my car—the area dark, hidden, and deserted. With only moonlight to guide us, we walked carefully, hand in hand to the lake and sat on the concrete edge.

As I looked up, the stars were bright. *I'm released from Drew.* I looked at Dane, satisfied. With him beside me, I was safe. I knew he was a good guy—no, a *great* guy. That was what Wendy and all her friends thought, too. Dane took care of his friends. No one asked about the cash that flowed endlessly from his wallet. I'd heard whispers of a trust fund.

"No, I'll pay," he always said. "Hey—sure, I'll take care of it." Dane told me he felt pressured to keep it up—the image, the giving. The image erased the old Dane, who'd been a nerdy teenager and then a bookworm who'd received his master's degree in accounting and computer science. Like I wanted to erase the farm girl, the good girl unlucky in love.

As we peered into the dark water, Dane must have felt safe, too. As though my breakup with Drew was a pledge of love. Something—maybe trust—led him to reveal a secret.

As we dangled our feet in Lake Michigan, he confessed, hesitantly, what I would never have suspected. His words pierced the silence, sharp, dangerous.

"I'm running a marijuana operation."

My left foot, which had been splashing in a methodic, lazy rhythm, suddenly stopped. *I could run. I should run.*

I could run far away and never see Dane again.

"I'm scared, Jen."

I believed him. My right foot began to gently rotate in the water.

He took a shallow breath. "I have three days."

I didn't know what to say. I watched the water circles vibrating, circles within circles, and they were beautiful.

"I owe half a million dollars. The Mexicans—they took someone's son last week. They're holding him hostage across the border; I have three days to get the money."

As the moon shone across the water, I took his hand and looked into his eyes. He needed money, and I couldn't help him. But he also needed comfort and support, and I had arms to hold him. His need was all it took.

I was hooked.

And I leapt, with no thought to the future.

CHAPTER 3

FARM GIRL DREAMS

The first four months of my relationship with Dane were a court-ship. A rushing, titillating journey, one that spun me around like the Tilt-A-Whirl I'd loved at the county fair. All our plans included each other. We traveled. A lot. Plane tickets, crisp shirts, and the smell of expensive cologne will always remind me of Dane. The fine wine, expensive dinners, and meetings with famous basketball players and ballet dancers led me to believe I'd won the "golden ticket." I was simply, with grandeur, "Dane's girlfriend."

I decided at twenty-five, it was my time to shine. Like the fire-flies I'd caught and put in a jar with holes poked in the top so they could breathe. As a child, I loved the way their lights shone like a lantern. I didn't know they would die in the prison my little-girl hands had made. Now my grown-up hands were constructing another prison, but I didn't see the parallel. As long as I kept mov-ing, I could ignore the glass walls that threatened to entrap me.

Even though Dane didn't talk about it, I suspected he wanted a serious relationship—one that included a wife and a child—a responsibility that I wasn't ready to handle. My impetuous leap into a relationship with Dane didn't answer my questions about who I was, how I fit in the world, and how I wanted to live my life. Instead I began to feel more and more frantic. My new relationship *should* have solved my problems. If it didn't, what was wrong with me?

In September, my close friend Shawn, artistic director of one of the companies I danced with, agreed to fly to Phoenix with me for a formal affair. She would attend with Dane's best friend, Rob, a blind date Dane and I had arranged long distance. She knew I wanted her to meet a great guy *just like I had.*

I'd never met Rob, but Dane said he was a good guy. Rob lived in Phoenix and worked as a pharmaceutical rep. Other than that, all I knew was they'd met at college in Tucson and had been friends ever since.

When Dane had to take care of some business—a last-minute shipment of marijuana that had successfully crossed the border—our plans to go to the event as a foursome disintegrated, and Shawn traveled to Phoenix alone. My not being there was no problem for her. She and Rob had fun, more fun than I wanted her to have, I thought, looking at pictures of the tall, good-looking guy in a tux with his arm around her waist. I didn't intuit the vital role Rob would play later in *my* life. All I knew was I wanted to meet Rob, too.

Soon, I would meet more people in Dane's life.

In October, he invited me to a black-tie event in Missouri—the unveiling of an Arabian filly expected to be the next champion horse. "It will be fun," he promised. And I would meet Mindy and Stan. I was curious about them. Stan had initiated Dane into the marijuana business. They'd been friends since Dane's college days in Tucson in the early '80s. Since then, both had been involved in some dubious financial schemes, and Dane had been desperate for money in 1991 when Stan presented the marijuana trafficking opportunity. Three years later, the marijuana operation had grown and now they were three: Stan, Dane, and Frankie. Stan lived in Tucson, and Frankie was in Detroit. But when Frankie's semi-trailer in Detroit was found and the marijuana impounded by the police earlier in the year—1994—Dane was asked to take over Frankie's job.

The loss had put the operation almost $500,000 in debt. With Dane's new responsibility, he began receiving a larger cut of the profit but was also accountable for the debt. He had confided some of this, but not all, the night we sat on the banks of Lake Michigan.

Stan had married Mindy. She was blond and my age—twenty-five—and with the money she and Stan collected from the marijuana, neither had to work. They lived on a ranch and invested in Arabian horses. Mindy loved her horses. And because Dane was tight with Stan, I decided I loved Mindy and Arabian horses, too.

Before we left for Missouri, Dane took me shopping for a dress. Although I'd lived in Chicago for years, the upscale stores on Oak Street were a mystery to me. When I walked into Barneys New York, everything fascinated me: the carpeted floors, hip displays, and unique textile designs. Only a few months before I'd been an observer as Dane and Gianni shopped at J. Crew. Now it was my turn. I still didn't have my own money, but I knew Dane would pay.

In the shoe section of Barneys, I held a boot to my nose and inhaled the leather, remembering Ohio and the halter I'd placed around the neck of my 4-H steer. Except these boots cost $600. When I tried on a blue dress, Dane shook his head. "That's not the one." I wanted him to like the way I looked. I giggled and peeked from behind the dressing room curtain so I could see him. He was still there.

He ain't going anywhere.

I felt alive as I stared at the high-end dresses hanging on wooden hangers: the yellows and blues, splashy tie-dyes and stripes, and the bare-shouldered black. Designer tags told me who the dresses were, who I would be. When Dane bought me the Jil Sander black wrap dress with matching jacket, and—"Sure, what the hell"—black pumps, I knew he cared. Like when my mom draped the table with a pink-and-white-checked cloth on my twelfth birthday. Like when my big brother pulled me in the red wagon when I was six. Like when my dad worked hard, tending the farm and livestock, to buy me school clothes, gymnastic lessons, steers, and even four years of college. I knew he loved me, because my mom told me he did. Now, when Dane bought me things—expensive things—I knew he cared, too. The high price tags told me his love was even bigger.

Four thousand dollars later, we exited the store with an outfit that would have taken two months' of my salary at my former full-time job. It wasn't that I'd wanted this kind of money before I met Dane. I'd never had luxuries like this, so I really hadn't thought about it. Now money grew everywhere around me. *What magic made it appear?*

My father always said it took hard work to win: "Daily long hard work."

It's not true, Dad, I thought, as Dane and I walked out of the store. The dress in the shopping bag was my proof. I hadn't worked to get the dress, Dane, or the loft.

Damn.

And, like Cinderella's sparkling gown and tiny glass slippers, I was afraid my new life, my luck, would just as suddenly disappear.

Dane and I arrived in Missouri the day of the filly's unveiling and met Mindy and Stan in the elevator of the hotel. Mindy looked sweet with her blond hair and freckles, and I wanted her to be my friend. But my attention was caught by the silver heart that dangled from the long strap of her leather purse. In our room, I mentioned it to Dane.

"It's a Brighton Bag," he told me. "Did you like it?"

"Yes."

"Don't worry; I'll get you one."

I knew he would. He always kept his promises, didn't he?

Dane then told me he'd be back "before you know it."

I hugged him good-bye and smiled, tightening my arms around him. "Where are you going?"

"To see Stan."

When Dane returned, he was carrying a shoebox, but I didn't say anything. I already knew not to ask. Later, he opened the box. The money was alluring, stacked up simple and clean. The bills had a scent. I learned to like this smell, to appreciate the worn bills. Later, I realized the softness of the used bills made them easier to count than when they were crisp and new.

I was curious about the money in the box, how it got there. Later I would see its journey: buyers on the street exchanged bills for a quarter bag of marijuana from a small-time drug dealer in Detroit who had, earlier, purchased one or two pounds of the Mexican weed from one of Frankie's boys. That pot was part of the thousands of pounds driven across the country in a truck and trailer, divided up, and sold by Frankie to his main distributors. The money traveled from Frankie's hands in Detroit to Stan's and finally to Dane's. Dane would take a cut of the money and give it to the Mexicans in Tucson, where the truck had been loaded with the marijuana. And the Mexicans would give the money to Tony, the big man who'd coordinated the marijuana shipment that crossed the border.

Sometimes Tony and Dane would fly to Mexico for meetings I was never privy to, and I'd feel left out.

Years later, I'd thank God I didn't go.

When Mindy, Stan, Dane, and I arrived at the event, white-jacketed men ushered us inside. Later, dinner was served outside under an umbrella of twinkling stars.

The moon was high and bright when we finally saw the filly. Outside, white-draped tables surrounded us. I felt "sparkly" and a little drunk as Dane held my hand. The spotlight clicked on and took the moon's overhead glow away. "She'll be a champion," I heard the man with a microphone say. I could feel the excitement around me. I didn't know much about this horse, but I was excited, too, to be sitting here in Missouri with Dane beside me. The spotlight roamed over the field until it settled on the filly and her jockey, pulling her burgundy-brown lead. It was a magical night. And, the one-year-old horse brought back memories of my farmgirl dreams.

The flaxen-colored horse my dad had bought me when I was a teenager wouldn't budge. I sat in the saddle, kicking its flanks, and pulling it by its lead.

"It just won't go," I told my dad.

Finally, one day the horse ran with me on her back. The pasture flew by blurry and fast. The wind whistled like a tuning fork, lovely and harmonic in my ear.

"I am the horse," I whispered, feeling its heavy-breathing flanks.

"I am the wind," I said, as I let go of one rein and held an arm over my head

I am free.

Not then, but one day, I would realize that freedom was all I really wanted—the freedom I'd felt when my yellow horse had run on that warm, Ohio spring day.

CHAPTER 4

THE SLEEPY

Traveling with Dane excited me more than living with him did. When he vacuumed with his new Shop-Vac, wearing Levi's, with a baseball cap tilted on his head, I wanted to run away. When he pounded a nail into the wall and caulked the area behind the sink, his methodical consistency—the quality that had made me feel so safe in Arizona—brought deadness into the room, into our relationship, and into me. The deadness was something I'd tried to outrun before.

I'd felt it as a child when I walked the aisles of the local greenhouse in Washington Court House, Ohio, with my mother. We always bought pink or red petunias. Although I liked the flowers, the greenhouse felt like a stifling bubble with its quiet, deserted aisles and humid air. I wanted to free the irises, daisies, and hanging green plants. "Let's go to the city," I'd tell the chrysanthemums. "Let's get out of this small town," I'd whisper to the lavender.

Riding in the family station wagon, that sleepy dull feeling would come again. The sun melted my mom's voice and the right blinker click-clacked as we turned into the bank's parking lot.

Click-clack, click-clack, it whispered hypnotically. It was only mid-morning, but my eyes closed with sudden weariness. I drifted in a tunnel where everything moved slowly. My legs, damp from the heat, didn't move. I was stuck to the leather seat and stuck in this Ohio small town.

Even then, I dreamed of bright city lights.

My mom saved a picture of me, at age eleven, standing in the water off the Lake Michigan shore on a family vacation. "Someday I am going to live in Chicago," I'd proclaimed to my family, even to the snail I'd picked up to examine. Walking the rocky shore, I was excited by the thought of my future—what was to come in my life. Dressed in my favorite blue bathing suit, the one with the rainbow stripe running from my left hip to my nubby, undeveloped chest, *I knew.* The city called me. It was in my childhood bones.

I laid the snail back down and I drew a line in the sand. Chicago promised excitement, success. The line was my future.

After summer, the excitement of sixth grade and a new tote bag overshadowed Chicago, burying the proclamation in my memory. But the promise never went away. Something was decided for me on that trip. And after college graduation, I moved to Chicago.

In November, I was beginning to recognize my discontent. In December, a reflexology appointment made my feelings even more obvious. The therapist pressed on spots I didn't know existed. Exhilaration sparked in my body. I giggled, but the therapist didn't let go of my foot. With his touch, I felt free from my life and my worries that I would never *have* enough . . . or *be* enough.

The freedom was like perfect back-handsprings, like the flow I felt when I danced on stage and everything moved in rhythm. The feeling stayed with me on the way home. When Dane and I returned to the loft that evening, the chandelier above the spiral stairs was lit, a welcoming beacon. Magic was in the air, spinning my stress in its whimsical web, transforming it into gold.

It was a cold, dark night—typical for Chicago at the end of the year. Although it was early, I was tired. My dusty corners—filled with unconscious parts that kept me from speaking and living true to my values—had been lighted and brushed clean.

Reflexology unlocks hidden parts of the self.

I could still feel the therapist's touch when I took off my shoes. On the couch, I continued to massage my feet, but soon I was restless. I walked over to the window that looked toward the El track and let out a sigh. The train cast a box of light across the floor, illuminating the truth I didn't want to see: Tonight I would tell Dane. I'd confess the discomfort I felt in our relationship. The reflexology appointment had uncovered what I'd tried to repress.

On the couch, I took the glass of wine Dane handed me, then looked away and stared at my fingers, stroking the roped, silver band on my wrist—the bracelet Dane had given me for my twenty-sixth birthday in October. But the bracelet's beauty had become a mirage, replaced by the magic of the reflexology appointment.

"It felt good," I said.

Dane nodded. "I've never had a foot massage."

I stayed silent as he twirled his glass. When the glass stopped moving, nothing else seemed to move either, not the train or the stars outside the window—not even my heart. A moment ago it had been beating with nervous anticipation about what I was going to say. For a moment, there was space. In the space was a precious stillness more beautiful than the bracelet.

Dane leaned close as if to whisper to me but instead touched his glass to mine. The bell-like sound of the glasses shattered the silence, tipping me off my emotional cliff. The unease I felt with Dane bubbled up like lava, and I overflowed. "We should break up," I told him. "I feel trapped."

He looked stunned. Confused.

My feelings ran over me like the train that passed our loft, and we argued until I ran out of words. Dane put his head in his hands, frustrated; and I climbed into bed.

When Dane turned off the light, our differences slept between us, unresolved. I froze when he touched my leg and slept with my back turned away the entire night.

In the morning, my feelings softened with the hug Dane gave me and with the bright sunlight shining through the windows. I was ashamed and wished I could take back my words from the night before. I blamed him, but I was the one confused. I'd uncovered something true about myself. I didn't want to have to consider Dane's feelings when I didn't feel like it. I didn't want to compromise. It wasn't personal. I'd feel the same about anyone. I knew this attitude would interfere with any long-term relationship.

My selfishness had made cracks in my relationship with Dane.

A different Jen had taken over. This Jen knew I couldn't afford to break up with Dane. This Jen was overwhelmed at the very thought of it. We had a Christmas party planned at our loft that very night. I was going to perform with Emergence Dance Theatre—the modern dance company I was in—and afterward there would be music with a live flamenco band. All of this was built on Dane and his money.

"Girlfriends and wives, they don't work," Mindy had told me at the horse show in October. I didn't understand it then, but she'd stated it as a fact. She knew. I'd already quit my job, and it was only a matter of time before I'd give up my aspirations, my life, for the money. And I needed to be available to travel, she'd said, to join Dane and his friends on their spontaneous weekend trips.

"Breaking-up" had vanished from my mind. Even though Dane and I had known each other for only four months, I realized I was afraid to be without him.

Because he loved me, didn't that mean I had to love him too?

CHAPTER 5

I SHOULD DRIVE

"Jen, let's go," Dane called from the bottom of the steps. Before I could answer, he sprinted up the steps and took the suitcase from my hands—one of the ways he took care of me that didn't feel confining. The Lincoln Town Car waited downstairs to take us to the airport for our flight to Columbus, Ohio.

Last night's party had gone well. With the stress of it over with, nothing stood in the way of my excitement to see my parents, to introduce Dane, and to travel to Hawaii where Dane was taking me in three days. I felt giddy when I thought of the new swimsuit in my suitcase, a one-piece with blue-green swirls, cut out on the sides. My anticipation of our trip to Maui, a place I'd never been, took precedence over my doubts about Dane, as if "temporary" made it easier for me to think, to live.

On the plane, Dane held my hand while I read a magazine. When I opened my peanuts, the nuts scattered on our seats and he scooped them up. When he ordered an orange juice, I ordered one, too. Mimicking Dane, following his lead, had become natural. He knew how to live the good life, so I relied on his judgment. It was easier that way. The rebellious voice inside had quieted. But for how long?

When the wheels touched the runway, I squeezed Dane's hand. "Everything is okay," my touch said. But inside, I was negotiating with my worry about our relationship. It followed me off the plane and into the Columbus airport. When I stepped into the red SUV rental, I tried to lock out the worry, but it rode with me on the drive to Washington Court House, the small town where I'd grown up.

The country homes, cows, and fields along Old Route 62 were new to Dane, who'd grown up in Los Angeles. The fields, planted in the fall with tall corn and beans, were empty except for the snow pillowed softly against torn, cut-off stalks. With the familiar crunch of the car's wheels on the gravel, I knew I was home.

Our suitcases trailed behind as Dane and I walked the brick path where I'd skinned my little-girl knees. My memories made pictures in my head of splashing in the rain puddles on top of my dad's grain wagon when I was six, and Jerry pulling me up the side of the white barn, the rope looped tight around my waist, when I was twelve.

When we reached my parents' driveway, we passed the cement bunny statue and the brick house we'd called the chinny-house. The plantation home was built in the nineteenth century, and the little brick houses used as smokehouses were common in rural Ohio, but I had my own story about ours. When I was a child I believed they *all* were called chinny-houses. I'd been horrified at eleven when my brother told me—and Dad confirmed—that Mom had raised chinchillas in ours until they were big enough to kill for their fur.

Kill the chinchillas?

My brother's laughter destroyed the chinny-house. It did not exist. It was a made-up word in my mom and dad's made-up world. Even though my mom had changed her mind about killing the cute squirrel-like creatures, I was still frightened, because I'd been fooled so easily for so many years. I wondered what else in my life was not what it appeared to be. Much later, I would think how much more devastating it was for my parents to find out the truth about me. It's always dangerous to smash people's reality, to knock them off their illusory foundations.

In my twenties I became a master at painting pictures of the separate parts of my life. Using a brush filled with half-lies, I chose which friends I let in on the truth of my criminal activity. If I'd honestly looked, I could have seen the "chinny-house" in my life, but I didn't. Not until I was arrested.

Until then my life felt *normal.*

When my mom opened the door for our Christmas visit, Dane's and my breakup conversation receded into the distance. Inside I knew something was wrong with my life, but I smiled when my mom said hello. I wanted to see my relatives who were coming for the holiday, to wake to presents under the tree, to smell roasting turkey.

I wanted everything to be okay.

The next morning, I woke to tingling hands and Dane's voice echoing through the heater grate on the floor of my second-story bedroom, the grate my cousins and I used to torpedo hors d'oeuvres down on to one another on past holidays. Like always, my mom was downstairs roasting the turkey. My pillow was soft and the aroma of turkey rose through the grate, but my hands were going numb and shaking them didn't help. I knew it was anxiety. I'd suffered it before, when I'd broken up with my boyfriend after college. But why was it back? Everything was okay, wasn't it?

When I walked into the kitchen, my mom stood by the roaster. She turned down my offer of help, and I reached for a bite of a hot buttery bun, a staple family treat. I was dressed in my mom's clothes, a Russ sweatshirt and gray sweatpants. I looked unattractive—especially with my new brown hair color—but today I didn't care.

The night before, my mom had mentioned my hair. "I like you better as a blond."

She'd taught me to care what other people thought, as if being pretty made me special—more desirable—something more than I would be if "pretty" was taken away. Fashion magazines had told me I could be beautiful with this new hair color, and I was anxious for my transformation. The colorist at the salon in Phoenix had frowned when I told her to change my blond hair to brown. When the stylist finished four hours later, I looked in the mirror: a girl with reddish-brown hair and shaggy bangs stared back. *Did I feel better?* Driving home in Dane's BMW, I couldn't shake the feeling that something still felt wrong. Hours later, I wanted to smash the mirror. I had not transformed. The change had *not* made me more beautiful. I hated my hair. I hated myself. I wanted my blond back. . . . I wanted *me* back.

This was only the beginning, the first of three more drastic hair changes to come. Yes, it was only hair, but I knew—and my mom sensed—that a crisis was brewing behind the mundane change.

I was not okay.

I didn't want to answer my mom when she asked where I was going. I didn't want her to see I was upset.

"I'm going for a run." I never "ran" and she knew it, but I resurrected my sixteen-year-old eye roll. She raised her eyebrows, but turned back to the roaster.

In the next room, my dad was talking shop with Dane about corn and beans and the farm downturn of the 1980s. I hugged Dane and was almost to the door when my dad said, "Here, wear this." He pulled his John Deere toboggan over my head. I looked ridiculous, but I wouldn't trade the knit hat for anything.

My dad had placed it on my head.

The screen door banged behind me, and I headed down the brick path, which turned to gravel, and then became the tar pavement of the road. The field's ragged corn stalks were forgotten until next spring when my Dad tilled them under with a plow. The fir tree where my brother and I had waited for the school bus was taller than I remembered.

I touched dad's hat, remembering when I was six, dressed in my favorite blue polka dot dress, swinging a tote bag with hearts. I'd looked sweet, until I pulled Dad's farm hat out of my tote bag and stuck it on my head. My brother had sighed and rolled his eyes. He was two years older, embarrassed by his sister in the silly hat.

Even then I had two sides: one, sweet as the blackberries that grew in our backyard; the other, wild as the vines that twined in a chaotic dance. Over time, I learned how hurtful the world could be to "sweet." But I also knew something not so nice was hidden underneath the sweetness, something loud, boisterous . . . wild . . . dangerous like the berries' secret thorns that poked and scratched. I was surprised the first time I was gouged and blood appeared.

I felt my own wildness as I ran. I wanted to roar, dive so deep into life I'd join the starfish that lived at the bottom of the ocean. I wanted to drive fast in a car, to skydive, to watch fireworks, and travel the world.

At the same time, I felt like I was at the mercy of life's velocity, that if I stopped, life would run me over.

When I came to the familiar blue grain bin, I was crying. I'd run away from my mother's concern a few minutes ago, and now I wanted her to tap me on the back and say those soothing words, "There, there, Jen. Everything's going to be okay."

For a moment I almost believed I would be okay. Then I looked up at the towering blue grain bin and felt trapped. I kicked the grain bin ladder and screamed, "I can't get out. Where's the key?"

But there was no one to hear me, and that's the way I wanted it, didn't I? I wanted to believe my life was leading somewhere like the long gravel lane that twisted between the fields. But I didn't know where. Dane was showing me the way, wasn't he? He offered me love and security, didn't he?

Then, a more dangerous reality emerged: I was relying on a man for money, and it was choking me. I thought the money would bring me the freedom to say, "Give me . . . I want . . . It's mine." That kind of *freedom* had been out of reach in my former life. But now, I'd lose everything if we couldn't be happy together.

That's when the idea germinated—the light went on in my head. Maybe trying to love Dane *wasn't* the only way to live the high life he did.

Maybe I should drive the marijuana myself.

CHAPTER 6

LADYBUG LUCKY

Tap, tap, tap. I tapped Dane's hiking boot with my own. We'd hiked to the wet side of Maui, and he lay beside me on his back on the black sand.

"I think I could be a good driver," I said.

He turned his head to look at me, turned back onto his stomach, and then looked away. "Okay."

That was it? The moment was simple, but inside I was shaking. His "okay" would change my life.

I took a picture of Dane when he rolled onto his back. His head was turned up to the sun, his legs in a V like he was making a snow angel in the sand. I hugged my knees.

Already, I felt lighter, less trapped.

My worries about being tied to Dane, about paid or unpaid bills, drifted away on that lazy afternoon.

He paused. "Gianni needs some product. Just a small amount, like a test."

I laughed and brushed off the sand from the crook of his arm. "When?"

He couldn't really answer. A departure date depended on the

weather, the drug's availability, whether the drugs made it across the border.

Time slowed then. Waves crashed against the rocks. Sand sifted through my hands. Tree's billowed more gracefully than they had before as sparkles danced across the ocean.

A light had entered my heart.

Was it hope?

I tried to hide. I was embarrassed by the Speedo Rob wore as he emerged from the water. Even so, I was attracted to Rob, Dane's best friend. He'd arrived on Maui a few days before New Year's Eve, a spontaneous decision after Dane invited him seven days into our vacation. Secretly, I'd wanted Rob to come. By then, the discontent I'd brought with me from Ohio had grown into full-blown restlessness.

Despite his promise I could drive the marijuana, I felt trapped by Dane again, and this created walls between us; the isolation snuck between our sheets. Every night I slept fetus-like, my back turned away. I wrapped my arms around my sides, their pressure reminding me I was alive. The fancy dinner at the plantation house had promised romance, but it wasn't fulfilled. I didn't understand the ocean's whisper that I'd find the beauty I sought *inside* myself . . . not with a man.

The aching grew. I'd changed my brown hair back to blond with a box of color from the drug store, rediscovering the "pretty" my mom always prided me for. But nothing filled the emptiness inside. In Maui, I felt lost, but it was a "lost" that felt better than being alone.

I remembered the dark void of *alone*. I'd had the realization when I was ten. "Why am I here?" I'd asked the sky, my back pressed against the white barn.

Days later, I asked my mom what happened when we died. "*If* there is life after death, then how come I don't remember it?"

She had no answer.

"And if I don't remember, then what happens when we die?"
Silence.

Within her silence, I became silent, too. I was desperate to understand my sadness. Disturbed, I sat on the floor and carefully drew a red line down the middle of the blank paper with my crayon.

My mom knew everything.

If she didn't know, then who did?

I'd looked at the box of crayons beside me and, for a moment, the unease I'd felt from the weight of the unanswered question faded. That is, until I focused on one particular crayon.

Maize.

I never knew what to do with this muddy color positioned half-way between Magic Mint and Midnight Blue. I was annoyed with this color's lack of place in my life, annoyed with questions that didn't have answers.

Maize never found its proper place in my childhood, and my question never found an answer . . . then. Instead, the question became my little-girl quest. I'd ask everyone I knew and those whom I'd just met.

Years later, I'd begin a formal spiritual quest that brought me answers—and more questions. Life would become bold, full—the red line I'd drawn as a child now exciting. The burnt-yellow color in my adult box of crayons less muddy. The unfamiliarity didn't scare me.

I could finally color with Maize.

Rob's arrival changed everything. My restlessness disappeared, and it had nothing to do with my existential searching. Rob was here in real time—tall, lanky, and intriguing. Before Maui, I'd only met this man in pictures, but I already wanted him to like me. He'd climbed into our jeep at the airport, his head inches from the roll bar. I'd felt safe with his arm around my back when he'd hoisted me into the jeep's front seat. I hadn't forgotten the photograph of him in a black tux, his arm around my friend Shawn's waist. Now he was here with me, and his arm was around *my* back.

Rob made Maui fun, our threesome exciting—sexy on New Year's Eve at the hotel's soiree—daring back at the condo: Rob's hand on my leg, his lips almost touching mine. The bond Dane and Rob shared was a safe net I fell into. With Dane's attention focused on someone else besides me, I could relax.

Rob had a secret. He was involved in the marijuana business, too. He drove the marijuana across the country with Dane, and flew back west with the illegal money. Before Rob arrived, Dane told me he'd had been involved for several years. "He'd be upset if he knew you knew."

"Why?"

"We don't tell girlfriends, only wives."

"Why?"

"Because girlfriends leave."

I'm not leaving.

Did I say this out loud?

I knew what leaving meant. My first love, Tommy, had left—moved away—when I was six. In his place he'd given me a gift. The silver-colored plastic knight I kept on my bedroom mantle. I didn't want to leave anyone, *ever,* and I definitely didn't want anyone to leave me. Breaking up was hard for me to do. And, when I did do it, I didn't do it well, either slipping in the back door with my break-up sword or lunging suddenly, with a violent, swift, and unconscious thrust.

I knew I couldn't leave Dane, but why? Did I *need* Dane's love?

Yes. No. I don't know.

The answer loomed large, more seductive than love.

Dane was key to the money and power I craved.

I'd lined up my justifications for trafficking like dominos, already threatening to fall: Rob and Dane were professional, nice . . . mature. Aside from occasional recreational use with my friends, I didn't like marijuana much. I'd never seen Dane or Rob smoke it. But people *did* use it, so someone was going to distribute it. Shouldn't that someone be me?

The last justification, one of pride, almost snuck by me. My secret knowledge about the business. Most people don't know anyone connected with hundreds and thousands of pounds of weed that magically turned into *hundreds, thousands, and millions of dollars.*

My justifications were sails billowing in a sudden gust of wind, propelling and directing my life. Soon, I would trust other people to keep me safe. I didn't know the risk I was taking. Later, when I was deeply involved in the drug trafficking, I didn't think about the grittiness of the illegal business anymore. Instead, I found normalcy in the routines that Dane and I created. I learned that, with "pretty"—pretty hair, pretty clothes, pretty house—my fears would dissolve. Dane and I were good at living in our own Disneyland. An easier place than real life.

A place where angels built castles and diamonds lay on top of the sand.

New Year's Day was lazy. The three of us found a deserted beach beyond a grove of palm trees. Rob and I stretched out on our towels beside each other. He faced the trees next to the road, and I faced the ocean. Dane was in the distance, his head bobbing in the waves—a dark speck lost to the violence of the sea.

I wanted to feel closer to Rob—to tell him I knew his secret. I felt powerful when I spoke, but, even then, I knew the power was false. I was as weak as a schoolgirl. Usually, I could keep a secret, but I craved the intimacy of sharing this knowledge with Rob.

"I heard you're going on a trip."

Rob stared at me. He frowned, his face twisted like he had something in his eye. He shook his head.

"You know . . . the marijuana." I stopped, uncomfortable with Rob's lack of response.

I rushed to complete my words. "Dane told me."

Immediately, I wished I hadn't said anything.

Rob wouldn't look at me. My hand touched his towel, and my fingertips inched toward his head, wanting to brush across his hair. Though we were only inches away, he avoided me. Then, with his towel in his hands, he got up and walked away.

His silence hit my heart like a hammer. I couldn't stand being left. I'd feared abandonment since the day my dad had told my brother and me that mom was sick. Her kidney had failed, and from then on I worried that she'd die.

Rob's sudden and silent departure shamed me. And the casual way that I had mentioned his secret scared me. I'd been naïve. I hadn't respected the *business,* the business I was poised to enter.

He left the island suddenly, that same day. He didn't tell Dane why, just retrieved his suitcase from the condo and took a taxi to the airport.

"He's pissed," Dane said.

Ashamed, I had to tell Dane why.

Rob's anger toward Dane for telling me about the marijuana was short-lived; he knew, like I did, that Dane held the purse strings. But Rob still wasn't talking to me two months later. He turned his back when I flew into the Phoenix airport to join Dane at his townhouse. I said hello, but Rob didn't respond. When I finished unpacking and came out of Dane's bedroom, Rob was gone.

Rob didn't want me involved in the business. "He won't drive with you," Dane said. Not now, not ever. I begged to drive anyway, so Dane set ground rules: Rob wouldn't know when I drove. I wouldn't know when Rob drove. I had destroyed the threesome that Rob, Dane, and I created so briefly on Maui. My fantasy of driving the marijuana with Rob died. Eventually—three years later—it would reappear.

Instead, Dane and I became an expert driving team.

It wasn't a large load—only 200 pounds—barely worth the trip, Dane had said. But it was a test to see how I'd handle the stress. We drove through Moab's four corners where Utah, Colorado, New Mexico, and Arizona come together. The red rocks took my breath away. The cozy inn and Mexican café added to the magic, creating further distance between me and the reality of what was in the trunk of our rental car. When Dane unzipped the duffel bags, I'd gasped. The bundles, wrapped in tan contact paper, lay innocently inside. I felt a tingle of excitement. The bricks represented freedom and a new lifestyle. I had a shopping list ready in my head. For the first time in my life, I was doing something *really* wrong.

So, why did it feel so right?

We weren't supposed to stop. Any deviation from the plan—any mistake—increased the risk of getting caught. Even so, when I'd screamed with excitement at the large red rock shaped like a doughnut, Dane had stopped the car. Up close, the red rock was terrifyingly beautiful, like the marijuana in the car.

For years I kept the picture Dane took of me that day—arms stretched over my head—standing in the center of that rock. I look like I'm flying. The picture represented promise, possibility, freedom, choice—a time when I chose a radically different direction—the first time I committed a crime.

When we arrived in Chicago—our final destination—the plan was that Gianni would take the product. This first trip would have been a total success if Dane hadn't rear-ended a car on Wolcott Street. We'd arrived in Chicago on day four, and it was snowing. The ice was slippery. The snow, blinding.

"It's not good, Jen," Dane said, after the driver took his name. "You don't want to make mistakes."

But this is Dane. He'll come up with something.

When Dane got out to talk with the other driver, I stayed in the car, listening to an operatic song bellow through the rental car's speakers. Lazily, I turned the heat up and leaned back into my seat. Even with the marijuana in the trunk, foolishly, I felt safe.

When Dane is around, everything is under control.

I watched Dane outside in his leather coat, the one lined with rabbit fur, the one I liked to wear. It had a feminine look, the way the puffed fur hugged his neck. I took a breath and closed my eyes until the opera singer's final crescendo. By then, Dane was writing something down, the other driver pointing at the damage we'd done to his car.

Everything will work out just fine.

My life always worked out. And so did Dane's.

Dane gave the man cash for the damage to his car—and all was well. No police report, no inspection of our rental car with its dangerous cargo.

Now, we were ladybug lucky times two.

CHAPTER 7

HOUSE OF MIRRORS

U-Hauls, trucks, and trailers rocked side-to-side, whipped by sudden gusts of wind. My trained hands kept the wheel steady. With three successful trips behind me in the past six months, I was a pro. Hours were a slow-burning candle, melting away time. In a few hours, it would be dark—too dark to drive. But I knew we'd make it to Amarillo, Texas—our calculated destination. Bright lights and big billboards would mark the end of another day's successful drive, the last leg—four hours. I held our vehicle straight beside the yellow dashed line, but my mind jumped like a Texas jackrabbit recalling our mini-adventures as we committed our mini-crimes. We'd make the Eight-Mile exit in Detroit—our drop-off location—on the fourth day. There, the thousand pounds of Mexican weed hidden in the back would be unloaded.

I followed a trucker, speeding when he sped, keeping our trip on track. Interstate I-70, a main artery that runs through the middle of the United States, had become a part of me. State lines bled one into the other. Gas stations recognizable, exits less mysterious. Oklahoma City turned into Tulsa, where the police wore cowboy hats and drove big trucks with hidden lights. Cows stood in fields, drinking water or standing still, looking like cutouts of make-believe cows. Herds ambled in Texas fields behind Oklahoma fences eating Missouri grass.

"They're not moving," I said.

Dane was driving now, and he turned his head toward me. "What?"

"The cows, they're still not moving."

"And?"

"They weren't moving in Oklahoma, either."

He slid another glance toward me, but I continued. "*Over* three hours ago."

I kept watching the cows, all doing the same damn thing. *Those stupid cows. When they do move, all they do is follow each other around, meandering as if they had nothing better to do.*

I was depressed with the cows' lack of purpose.

I was depressed with my own.

I stared out the truck's window, wanting to shake off the deadness I felt inside. When we got to Missouri and passed a big white cross almost three stories high, I felt guilt, burdened with the weight of the secrets in my life—burdened one minute, excited the next.

Drug trafficking had its kicks. *The marijuana is stacked in the hockey bags right behind us. Nobody knows. But we could be caught.* And seeing the money. Well, that *really* knocked my socks off.

It was a thrill, a risk, like spinning around the high bar in fifth grade.

"Eight, nine, ten, eleven . . ." Little-girl voices counted as I spun, one leg bent at the knee, wrapped around the single metal bar. I had to do twenty like my best friend, Stephanie. My stomach dropped. My calloused hands loosened their grip, just enough so I could spin faster, just enough so I wouldn't fall. I was a spinning machine. The buzzing around me grew, climbed into my ears and tingled my toes. I felt so good I thought I'd explode . . . fall apart.

I could fall. . . . That was part of the excitement.

I first saw uncounted marijuana money in a hotel near Detroit's airport—a place I'd never been before.

The door opened when I knocked. I didn't recognize Frankie's men. My eyes widened. The room looked like a huge piñata had broken inside, spilling out dollar bills of all denominations. Usually I saw the money stacked, organized in bundles of one thousands, neatly separated with rubber bands, given to me in a bag or a box.

This was different. And for the first time I was scared. I was in a room—alone—with a shitload of illegal money with two men I didn't know. They looked like Detroit to me—big-nosed, dark-haired, burly.

"Well, you're here, so start counting," said one man.

The last thing I wanted to do.

Counting wasn't my job, but we were running out of time. My flight left in five hours. Dane would be waiting in Phoenix for me—and the illegal money. I sat down with the two men and started to count.

Worn twenties were the easiest.

"We count 'em in groups of fives," the other man said.

One, two, three, four, five. One, two, three, four, five. One . . . oops . . . two, three, four, five. Four, two, three, four, five, or was that six?

Jesus.

A man dumped another pile of money onto the table from a crumbled brown bag. The newly opened bag let loose heavier danker smells that traced its trip from Detroit's anonymous brick-front houses with their brown shag carpets and oak wood furniture, where Lebanese grandmothers cooked *shish kafta* behind closed doors and Arab-American men drove Jeep Cherokees, picked up brown bags of money at diners on corners and slung the bags onto back seats.

My face flushed.

My head was a pressure cooker as I counted. I knew driving was dangerous, the marijuana stashed right behind my head. But I was in control then.

Not in control here, not in this room.

I waited for cops, but they never came. No one opened the door.

Counting the money had taken forever. In real time, it was four hours before the money was finally counted and packed: $95,000 or so hidden beneath the zipper lining of my suitcase and inside my make-up case. Five bundles were in my purse, two in my wallet, three in my coat pocket, and six stuffed inside my suitcase in my socks.

After I checked off the items—stereo system, designer watch, leather coat—on my shopping list, I didn't know what to do with the illegal money. I was just happy I could pay my bills. Before Dane, I'd never wanted lots of money, hadn't thought about it. So, Dane taught me to shop. I followed his path through fancy salons, day spas, fine restaurants, high-end wine shops, and designer clothing stores for Gucci boots and Bally coats. I collected expensive make-up, facial creams, stacks of CDs, and bed sheets with thread counts of 500 and beyond.

Then a childhood dream surfaced. I could now afford my own dance rehearsal space where I could produce my own show. So, I found a commercial space in Chicago's produce district, signed a year's lease, and funneled money into its renovations, giving no thought to a return on my investment. With Dane's help, I organized a dance concert in Tempe, Arizona. For the next six months—between the marijuana trips that financed the project—my dancers, my friends, and I prepared for the modern dance show.

In the third piece, Dane took center stage. His back was to the audience, arms crossed. I ran. I leaped. I clung to Dane's body, but—as choreographed—he dropped me, and I fell to the floor.

Exit, stage left, his cue said. The audience laughed as he walked away. The lights faded, the curtain came down.

Was the dance a premonition, a glimpse of what was to come in my real life?

After the show, I threw my dance bags in the trunk of Dane's BMW—the maroon convertible I liked to drive. Being with Dane was perfect . . . sometimes. His love was safe. He protected me, especially when I drove the marijuana. He'd told me what to do if anything "bad" happened on the road.

I knew about "bad." Bad things happened in states like Nevada. Dane never liked to talk about it, but I'd heard rumors. Someone we knew had gotten caught.

I didn't want to get caught.

Dane explained what to do if "bad" happened. "Just call Joseph. Don't worry. You'd only be in for a few days."

In jail, he meant. But he didn't say the word.

Dane gave me Joseph-the-attorney's number. I kept it in my wallet for years. Joseph was a top-notch attorney in Los Angeles, a bigwig, Dane's close friend. I'd find out later how little he *really* knew, how little any of us knew.

I was a good girl. Good girls didn't traffic drugs.

But I did.

Was I still a good girl?

Dane had attended boarding school and was generous with his friends. So he must be a good boy.

But he trafficked drugs.

We were smart, too. Dane was smart. Joseph was smart. I was smart. But we didn't know all the rules.

Why take this risk?

We weren't starving, homeless, unloved. So why do it? Were we bored, discontented with our lives? Or, did we feel trapped, powerless, and this was one way to gain control.

Maybe we wanted to feel special, to feel *something.* Was the thrill of our illegal activity the only way we could feel alive?

Even now, when I look inside to find the right answer, there is none. Nothing about our "crime" was so earth-shattering or grand that it warranted—or eradicated—the risk.

Six years later, I met Joseph—a meeting that lasted the four days it took for us to drive marijuana across the country together.

Joseph be nimble, Joseph come back, Joseph jumped over his lawyer back.

I wished I could take back my drive with Joseph. Those four days cost him his law license and five years of his life.

I wish I'd heard that soft, still voice inside, that clear conscience that *must* have been there . . . somewhere. But it was lost among big lights—blinding, tempting lights—and big Texan billboards. I wish we *both* had listened and heard.

I became used to Dane's love, accustomed to hockey bags stacked in the back of the green van. The loads of marijuana— and the vehicles we drove—grew bigger, like the burden of Dane's love. Sometimes I despised the green van as much as I despised the control I'd given to Dane. But new clothes, still with tags, hung in my closet, and designer shopping bags lined my closet floor like trophies, tempting me. My friends had always commented on my good taste; now I could finally buy beautiful things.

I'd looped a noose around my neck that only I could remove.

Only *I* could say when I'd had enough.

I looked at the clothes, reminding myself again that they symbolized freedom.

After eight months, the rush of the money and traveling became exhausting. In a moment of fatigue and desperation, I called Drew. My old boyfriend was familiar. He liked sports and watched movies. Maybe he lacked direction in his life, but so did I.

When Dane found out about Drew, he was hurt. Pain elevated

his voice to the familiar high-pitched shriek he reached when he was upset.

"How could you?"

Tears streamed down my face as I ran barefoot after Dane across the grass. I didn't cry out of pain. My tears were of fear—fear that he would leave. How could I be without Dane? *How could I be without the money?*

After my rendezvous with Drew, Dane moved out of our Chicago loft, and Shawn moved in. Drew faded away, leaving the abandoned puppy he'd found at a gas station.

Although Dane wasn't around, I continued to mimic his lifestyle.

I can live the good life, too, I thought to myself, *just like Dane.*

I didn't realize, then, that Dane made hundreds of thousands of dollars more than I made—more than I'd ever have. All I knew was I had money, and Dane wanted to see me, which meant I'd become indispensable. The only way he could see me *now* was to let me drive the marijuana. My supply of money wouldn't be ending anytime soon.

Still, I felt prickles of discomfort.

Deep inside, I knew I had no control over my greed. In only six months, I'd orchestrated my life into a new pattern—a pattern that relied on the money. I paid high rent, bought designer clothes, traveled, made expensive choices. The freedom of having access to large amounts of cash now felt like a *need* to have that money stacked in shoeboxes under my bed.

Poof.

My mind tried to wrap itself around my new life that had emerged like a misshapen butterfly from my cocoon. Sometimes I felt vulnerable, a little awkward, like the pipe cleaner and paper butterfly on the bookmark I'd made when I was seven. Little-girl hands gluing sparkles onto paper, innocent expressions of my little-girl heart.

Even then, I'd yearned for freedom, for flight.

Now, my wings stretched uncomfortably to cover two separate worlds: one where I was supposed to be honest, responsible, and work hard for my money and one where money comes fast and easy.

There's dog pee on the floor. Again I'd walked into the loft and almost slipped on the smelly puddle. It wasn't the first time dog urine had dripped through the cracks in my floor onto my landlord's architectural plans below. It wasn't the first time my landlord had yelled at me for having a dog.

Shit. I didn't have time to be responsible. I was traveling. A lot. Driving marijuana across the country or flying money back west . . . rehearsing, dancing. In July—only one month away —I would travel to Avignon, France, to perform in a festival with Joeluine, my dance partner, and Sher, her dance teacher. I would have to leave Stacia behind. And she cried when she was left alone.

"Cries very LOUD," my landlord complained.

I never asked if I could have a dog when Drew dumped her on me. I just took her. I was used to doing what I wanted and justifying it later. From the outside, my life looked good. I was busy performing and choreographing. My peers in dance looked up to me, and I was asked to teach classes.

Still, repressed feelings were bubbling inside. Deep down, I knew I didn't want to face the choices I was making—choices that created the chaos swirling around me. Like my dog. I passed this responsibility onto Shawn, who didn't mind. She was living in the loft, rent-free. She'd care for Stacia while I was gone.

I *chose* when to be responsible, acting as though "responsible" was part-time.

My excuses gathered speed.

I flipped from one moment to the next as quickly as I'd spun around the metal high bar in fifth grade. As quickly as I'd shifted my life, I morphed beyond twisted butterfly into a dragon, a snake-shredder geisha, a circus act.

My life, a house of mirrors.

By the third day of a drive, I would be exhausted from the stress: stay off the yellow line, don't speed, look to your left and always use your turn signal.

Always watch your back.

The rules—and the trip—always began with a phone call from Dane, in code: "We're going on a trip." And I'd purchase a round-trip ticket from Chicago to Phoenix, knowing I wouldn't use the return.

Never purchase a one-way ticket. "It looks suspicious," Dane explained. "The people at the airport will clock it."

He taught me never, ever, to fit the profile of a drug-trafficker, a mule.

I shopped at J. Crew, Ann Taylor, choosing the clothes with care. To look conservative. Demure. *Boring.*

Dane's disapproving eyes would tell me when I'd made a mistake. Then he'd send me back to the dressing room. Feeling like a failure, I'd try again.

Lately, I'd gotten the attire right—khaki pants, blouse, sweater tied around my neck—and become used to more rules of the road: Know your story—why you're on the road, and where you're going. Pack light and for all seasons. Don't carry too much cash in your wallet. Never transport cash *and* drugs. Pack the illegal money next to odd-shaped objects. Don't rent a U-Haul with Arizona or New Mexico plates. Never *ever* purchase a ticket to Tucson; fly into Phoenix at all times.

Brush your teeth before you go to bed. Don't slouch in your chair. Eat your fruit, say thank you. And never, ever take something that's not yours.

I always wanted to do it right.

Whatever I did.

I was good at following rules . . . even while breaking others.

CHAPTER 8

THE CHARISMA OF JOE

Sometimes we meet a person who impacts our lives to such a degree that we are forced to grow. I've met two: Dane in 1994 and Joeluine a few months before.

When I first saw her, Joeluine sat straddled on the floor, hugging one leg as she stretched. Her hair was wrapped in a bun, her warm-up pants pulled up to her chest. *She's so tiny* was my first thought. But when she lifted her head, it was her eyes . . . *oh* . . . so large, almond-shaped, beautiful. They captured me. I felt sparks, like the fireflies that once lighted my childhood jar.

I'd felt threatened at first because Joeluine had been offered a starring role, even though she wasn't even a member of Shawn's Coyle & Company. But when I saw her dance, I understood. She left me breathless. She looked like an angel, no sign of the darkness beneath her wings. Although she wasn't perfect in form, her passion was raw. I was driven to dance, too, but not like this. Everyone—including me—was attracted by Joe's charisma.

Joeluine was a chameleon. Onstage she'd run, grab, twist the fabric of her costume dramatically in agony and drop to the floor.

Offstage she appeared innocent, tiny in boyish clothes or sexy in short mini-skirts that barely hid white cotton briefs. A pale-faced cherub in red lipstick and Doc Martins, she shot her arrows at us and they hurt.

We were at a club near Shawn's loft the night I took over the job of watching out for Joeluine. "I can't find her anywhere. She's gone," Shawn said.

"What do you mean *gone?*" I yelled over the loud music.

"Just gone. . . . This isn't the first time, Jen. I've had it."

Then Shawn walked away.

I couldn't leave. I looked in the bathroom and in all the dark corners of the club.

Joeluine wasn't there. I hated to do it, but I gave up the search.

The next morning Shawn opened the front door and there was Joe, pale, tired, silent.

Where had she gone?

Joeluine never told us where she'd been, and we never asked.

The summer before I met Dane, Joeluine moved into my Green Street loft, part-time. She was still dancing with the Kalamazoo, Michigan, company, but Emergence Dance Theatre in Chicago—where we both danced—was taking most of her time. She was tired of making the four-hour train trip from Kalamazoo to Chicago. The loft was a natural move.

At first I was excited to have Joeluine close. But after a few months, she seemed increasingly uneasy, lonely. I saw disappointment in her eyes, and I didn't understand. She couldn't hide the depression that kept her writing in her journals late at night. I worried about her isolation. She no longer went to clubs, and she isolated herself in her room.

When I found her urine-soaked sheets stuffed into the bottom of the hamper, my worry shifted to her health.

Joeluine pretended nothing was wrong. "I was drunk," she said. But I knew it wasn't true. I'd seen the prescription drugs, and she'd shown me the scars on her stomach from cancer surgery.

"Half my stomach's gone," she'd told me. "See?"

The scar was long, running around her body from front to back. Thin, lightly protruding.

"Can I touch it?"

"Yes." Her voice was a whisper.

Gently, my fingers jumped the scar's track. I held my breath as a childhood fear took hold. *Could her sickness enter me?*

I knew sickness, had seen disease.

I couldn't hug my mom—too many needles in her arm, too much apparatus in the way. I was only nine, and the blood in the kidney dialysis unit scared me. Bright red, the tubes of blood arced in circles in the churning machine—like a pinwheel or a spinning magic mirror. Like Romper Room on TV when Miss Barbara looks through the magic mirror and says "I see Tammy and Laura and Stephanie . . ." When I kept the TV pictures in my mind, I felt better about looking at my mom's blood in the machine. But the worries would return. If Mom's blood stopped spinning, would she die?

After meeting Dane, I used my money—just like he did— to try to bribe my friends to do what I wanted. Money was power.

"Please stay," I'd say to Joeluine.

"I can't, Jen. I need to go home."

The train to Kalamazoo left in an hour. But I didn't want her to leave, didn't want to be alone. Sometimes she needed me. Sometimes I needed her.

"If you stay, I can give you some money. You know, for food, the train." I was begging . . . bribing.

Joeluine always needed a buck. But she stayed silent.

"We can order pepperoni pizza."

Please. Please stay.

Even as I tried to draw her closer, the danger inside Joeluine scared me. Her health ebbed and flowed. On nights we went out, her danger slithered between us, sexy and daring, as she danced at a trendy Chicago club. She'd down vodka drink after drink, wave to me, and disappear into a corner with a man we didn't know. I'd feel angry first and then concerned. The next morning, somehow, she'd find her way back to my Green Street loft.

Although Joe and I both wanted to be loved by everyone, Joeluine's increasing needs dictated our relationship. In the fall when I met Dane, he became the balance I yearned for. I took care of Joeluine, and Dane took care of me. We were a perfectly running taking-care-of-each-other machine.

"I thought I'd be okay."

Joeluine sat on Dane's couch in Phoenix, crying. She looked so small in her red cotton dress. Last night's mascara dripped down her face, and she wiped at her tears with the Kleenex Dane had placed in her hand.

She'd drunk too much sake and stayed out too late with too many men. When she tried to board a flight back to Chicago the next morning, she was turned away because she'd seemed ill, or medicated, which she was.

On the couch back at Dane's condo, she hugged her body tight and whispered, "How could this happen? I mean, *Dane* was there."

Another burst of tears.

Dane put his arm around Joeluine's back, just as he did with me.

Her voice was a child's whisper. "When Dane's here everything's supposed to be okay, but it *wasn't* okay."

Dane consoled Joeluine. "*Mmmm.* I know." His voice was a father's whisper, "You're here now. Don't worry."

Then, he merely held her tighter.

Ten years later—my first night in prison—I would know that feeling when the guard locked the door and everything was *not* okay.

If only I'd listened more closely to Joeluine's words or the whispers of the trees of my childhood.

Come home . . . come home . . . come home. Their limbs sway with the wind, their roots dig into the earth . . . and somehow reach my heart. As a child, I'd seen them as a line of soldiers protecting me, their pine cones offering comfort, love. I should have understood their message. They were telling me to grow up, to come home . . . to myself.

I couldn't save Joeluine, and Dane couldn't save either one of us. Not then. Not later. We could only save ourselves. But, Joeluine and I weren't grown up. And neither was Dane.

No, we weren't grown up at all.

The summer of 1995, Joeluine and I traveled to France with Sher, the youthful fifty-year-old director of the Ballet Theatre of Kalamazoo. We had been selected to perform in a dance festival in Avignon—at least that's what Joeluine had said. When we arrived, we were shocked to find the location under a bridge, lit only by bonfires. Undisciplined French teenagers milled around, frightening us. The festival was too fringy, even for Joe. We had expected something nicer, more refined.

We immediately left for Marseille, a port town on the coast, and arrived there at midnight.

Three days later, we were still in Marseille.

"What now?" Joeluine asked.

I grabbed the guidebook. "Let's open it and see where my finger lands."

Sher agreed, and Joeluine giggled.

"There."

My finger landed on Cassis. One small paragraph described the coastal town. We arrived to find an idyllic storybook town, perfectly situated by the sea. The inn owned by a French family was a blessing, Sher said, as we sunned by the pool on yellow-striped chairs.

Every morning Sher walked to the church on the hill, while Joeluine and I slept, tired from the previous night's escapades. We'd met two French men. One owned a boat. They dined us, wined us, and one took me to bed.

Neither of us understood the French language and this separated us from the men and from each other. Something dark brewed between us. I felt Joeluine competing with me in indirect ways, flirting with the man who liked me, ignoring me as if I wasn't there. The anger behind her silence was palpable, and, lately, had been directed at me.

Was she jealous? If so, of what?

All I knew was that I loved her—her red lipstick, her fire. Her darkness mirrored back my own. But her crimes were only of the heart.

Although we were close girlfriends, I also wanted to mother this little lost girl. But how could I, when I needed to mother myself?

Sadly, I didn't know how to do either.

CHAPTER 9

SPLIT IN TWO

Sher and I left Joeluine behind in Cassis. Or did she leave us? She looked sullen as she waved good-bye from the back of a big yellow Jeep, en route to Paris. Did she already regret her decision? The men we'd met in Cassis had invited us both, but I'd declined. My eyes rolled. I couldn't believe Joeluine had decided to stay, again trading our friendship for a man. Maybe she couldn't believe that I would leave *her,* trading our friendship for my rigid plans. But I never knew her feelings, only mine. In that moment, I was finished with France and with Joeluine.

The ten-hour drive to Geneva, Switzerland, was uncomfortable in my tiny Fiat rental car. When we finally arrived, I dropped Sher at the station for the train to Bosnia, as planned. Alone in a Swiss hotel, my frustration with Joeluine grew. I felt she had abandoned me. The next day was no better: I couldn't read the Swiss instructions on the money machine or the road signs to Paris, and I cursed them all. Joeluine couldn't understand Swiss either, but she was *supposed* to be here, so I cursed her. I cursed my life. When I finally arrived in Chicago, I cursed the hot sticky heat that greeted me.

Exhausted when I reached the loft, I slept in my clothes with my dog Stacia's head next to mine. Both Stacia and Shawn seemed happy I was home.

Still tired from the drive and the overseas flight, I wasn't thrilled to get Dane's call at nine in the morning. Still, I had no choice but to go. I needed the money. I'd spent $6,000 for three weeks in France. I repacked my bags and booked my flight to Phoenix, buying a round-trip ticket like I'd been taught.

Dane picked me up at the Phoenix airport, this time in his new silver Toyota Land Cruiser—a luxurious ride. We drove to the Tucson mall that had a guitar shop, sat in the SUV, and waited for the man who'd take our truck and, hours later, bring it back loaded with marijuana. I knew he'd drive a pick-up. Maybe white or red or gray—a Chevy, Dodge Ram, or Ford. Dane had met most of the smugglers involved in the drug trade. Still, it was a challenge even for him to recognize the right man in the right truck.

"How about that one?" I asked, pointing to a dusty Dodge that had just pulled in.

"No. I don't think so."

We waited, anxiously looking around. After twenty minutes, a white Ford drove up, and Dane finally said, "Ah . . . yes. That's him."

When Dane got out of his SUV, a tiny olive-skinned man with a mustache walked toward us. These drug smugglers always sauntered confidently. Short men wearing cowboy hats, mirrored aviator glasses, and hemmed Levi's jeans.

Dane met him halfway across the parking lot. I stayed in the truck.

I was a newcomer, not trusted to talk to the men from Mexico, not privy to their names. But it wasn't all about trust. Dane wanted to protect me. The less I knew the better. When Dane came back, I exited the SUV.

We waited for hours—sometimes up to four—for the vehicle to be loaded. The guitar shop became familiar, the latte at the coffee shop, routine. Time was suspended. No one could know where we were, so we made no calls. We hid what we were doing, where we were going, who we really were. As our lies thickened, the waiting worsened, at least for me. The trip—the next four days—was always an odd adventure, a mirage lost in time.

Dane never told me how he felt about the business, and, as far as I knew, never told anyone he was involved in the drug trade. I did, though Dane told me not to tell. I chose which friends I told, never realizing the danger.

The location of the drugs and the time and place of the pick-up were supposed to be secrets. Secrets I didn't keep. I believed that secrets kept hearts locked. I didn't want secrets to get in the way of intimacy with those I loved.

Why couldn't I see?

In the end, all it took was *one* person to rat us out.

Näively, I trusted my friends not to turn me into the cops.

Foolishly, they trusted me, never thinking that just by knowing my drug running details they could get arrested, too.

By late afternoon, the man brought Dane's SUV back, the hockey bags loaded with marijuana. Dane and I would spend the night in the themed rooms of the Little America Hotel in Flagstaff, Arizona.

At 6 a.m., I opened my eyes to the wake-up call and to French Provincial, which looked nothing like I'd seen in France. I felt even more lost in this room, where brassy baroque clashed with log cabin décor like my good-girl image clashed with my drug-runner self.

When I drove the marijuana, parts of me temporarily ceased to exist: the child who'd sewn a tote bag and skirt in 4-H in the '70s, the student who wore oxfords and penny loafers in the '80s, and the college graduate with the wholesome Mary Tyler Moore look in the early '90s.

In 1995, I'd split in two. The duplicity was intense and dramatic—two identities—my new life filled with risk and danger, a life way more exciting than the early '90s when I was a modern dancer, working in a medical office to scrape by.

I didn't realize the trauma caused by that split. The inner wounds that never scab over without some tending, some mothering. Until then, they just keep bleeding.

Today it was my job, as it often was, to bring Dane's Toyota Land Cruiser to the men to be loaded with the marijuana. I flew into Phoenix and drove the SUV, empty of drugs, to Tucson. I hid the keys under a wheel and stayed the night at a fancy resort on Ina Road.

Ina Road became my friend.

"Ina." I felt good saying this word. "Ina-Ina-Ina." The word slid off my tongue like the *clack-clack* of a castanet and the *stomp-stomp* of high-heeled shoes in a Spanish tango.

Ina was luxury. Ina was mysterious. Ina was money.

Outside on the hotel room's *casita,* I would wait for hours for Dane's call telling me he'd finished inspecting the marijuana that was to be packed into our truck. Ina Road was where the stash house was located. I didn't know exactly where, but that's what Dane had said.

For the first few years, I didn't see where the marijuana was stored once it had successfully crossed the Mexican border into Tucson. I didn't see our final drop-off destination in Detroit either. But, I knew the road names. They were important. Used in guarded phone conversations as markers, codes, and hidden keys.

In Detroit it was Eight-Mile.

Eight-Mile was an exit off I-94, a freeway that ran through downtown Detroit near the final marijuana drop-off somewhere, I didn't know where.

I'd wait while Dane and the men-I-never-saw unloaded the marijuana from the truck, left at a diner or corner café.

Ina seduced me with the dry heat, room service, and palm-tree-lined resort drive of Tucson.

Eight-Mile repulsed me. I didn't trust Eight-Mile, and I didn't trust Detroit.

Detroit's dreary streets and gray skies unearthed everything about myself I was trying to repress—my crime and my love of the money. In this tough, industrial city, I could no longer deny I was doing something illegal . . . and profitable. Once the drugs were safe, stored in one of Frankie's secret locations, I got my cut—$20,000.

The elegance of the Ritz Carlton in Dearborn—a high-class subdivision and thirty-minute drive from the Metro Airport—rocked me back to sleep. Only after I'd left the last three days and the empty vehicle behind in the hotel parking lot, only after I'd walked through tall doors held open by men with top hats, could I relax. By then, I was tired, anxious for a drink, and for solitude. Not the solitude of the road, of the three-day journey before, but a relaxed calm where I could let my guard down.

If it wasn't the Ritz-Carlton, it was the Hyatt—only a few blocks away—with the rotating bar on the top. I'd stay at this hotel after a mystery man brought a mystery bag—the money I was supposed to take back to Phoenix. Until then, I was a prisoner in my luxurious room, waiting four and five hours for the knock.

Finally, the man would arrive, his eyes dark and blank. We'd exchange a few brief words, pretending we had something to say, ignoring the greed that drove the meeting. Our protective walls of distrust stood tall and invisible between us.

"There's one hundred and ten thou'," the man would say, and drop the bag on my bed.

I don't count it. I don't care.

I inclined my head in a nod to him, prepared to do as I was told—the part of the job I hated the most. I would hide the money in my suitcase, and fly to Phoenix.

Afterward, I went to the rotating bar on the fifth floor. Detroit lights at night were tantalizing, almost beautiful. Usually the city felt cold and depressing but at night, in this rotating bar, I could pretend I was anywhere. I felt peaceful. I spent hours sitting on the red leather stool, drinking two or three decadent Kir Royals. I passed the time writing on napkins, the stack beside me on the bar growing.

I wrote poetry:

> *I am waiting,*
> *slowly waiting,*
> *a child in the rain.*
> *And time seems to stop*
> *on your breath again . . .*

I wrote lists.

Lists of how I'd spend the money: trips to Europe, clothes, and later, seminars. The first list would calculate the "debt" I'd run up since the last time I sat on that stool. Or rather, the money I'd already spent that I felt I *needed* to replace in the shoeboxes in my closet.

When I look back at those times, I remember that ten or more trips a year was not unusual. The money left my hands as quickly as the trips flew by. Since I spent the money in my head before I had it in my hands, I felt like it was already gone. And since it was already *gone*, I believed I had no choice but to keep trafficking the marijuana.

I saw no release. No escape.

I had no idea how fragile my life was becoming. I'd built a glass house. And a glass house eventually breaks.

In my twenties, I fantasized about the woman I'd become in my thirties—a woman in her power. But, this power was false—and dangerous. I wasn't in physical danger, I told myself. No one would kill me—stab or shoot me on the street—or even arrest me.

Foolishly, I never contemplated that.

The risk I took was unconscious, unseen. I was risking my inspiration, vision, dreams.

Keep it real. Keep it simple. Keep reaching for the stars, whispered the trees of my childhood. Instead of growing upward toward the stars, I was stuck on a Ferris wheel going round and round with my eyes shut . . . suspended in time.

Blind to the little girl inside who needed me. Blind to the stars.

Dane's anger over my hook-up with Drew had softened by the time I returned from France. But it had taken its toll. His trust in me was shaken. Still, he'd asked me to drive. Not with him, but with Doreen, the mother of his friend and business partner Stan. Seventy-five years old and jolly, she'd smiled from inside the truck and offered me *baklava.*

Dane had introduced us in Tucson and said good-bye in Phoenix, hockey bags of weed hidden in the back of his Toyota Land Cruiser. I took off for the first time without Dane. Doreen was a good cover and she understood her son's business, but she couldn't drive. Without Dane, I felt unprotected and burdened with responsibility. The three days felt like years, fear and worry a party in my head.

By the time we reached Detroit, I had a stress hang-over.

Within a few months—the fall of 1995—Dane was willing to drive with me again. His one condition: I couldn't see Drew.

He knew that Drew was a threat, that I'd loved him. "*Anyone* but him," he said.

And then came Stefan. He knew Drew, but they'd had a falling out. Stefan looked like a model with his thick black hair, white teeth, and square jaw. He lived in the fancy Chicago Twin Towers, high above the water.

The attraction between Stefan and me was instant, but love crept up on me. By then it was too late, Stefan had become my best friend.

He helped me move out of the Ohio Street loft when Dane said he was tired of paying half of the rent while not even living there.

Though he didn't say it, I knew Dane was tired of feeling tied to me as well. I moved into a four-story walk-up with Kelly, a dancer, and another friend Bud.

The move to the artist's funky old loft in Wicker Park created more distance between Dane and me. But I called Dane every other day to make sure he knew he was still at the top of my list. To keep my finger on the trigger of my life—the money and my lifestyle—I needed him.

The move had changed nothing. Money was still stacked in shoeboxes under my bed; my bills were still paid at currency exchanges all across town in groups under $2,000; and my bank account stayed under a thousand. I used my credit card but still believed the illegal money was invisible to the IRS.

A new year—1996—was just around the corner. This would be the year I drove the most trips—close to twenty—the year the noose tightened around my neck.

Something had to give.

On our trips, I was Dane's "girl." Neither of us was in a committed relationship, but Dane knew I liked Stefan. We didn't talk about him. I'd sit in the passenger seat with my collection of crayons, journals, and other toys I brought to entertain myself. On the road, Dane and I developed a flow. He'd drive four or five hours, and then we'd switch.

"Bathroom, Jen?"

I nodded my head, and he took the next exit.

I knew the drill: empty coffee cups, water bottles, and snack packets from the vehicle, so it wouldn't appear we'd been driving a long distance. Go to the bathroom to pee, the snack counter for fresh drinks, and the gift shop for anything fun I could find to distract me from boredom on the road. If we were lucky, there would be a Subway—the healthiest choice for something fresh to eat. Dane took care of other things: pumping gas, washing windows, and buying bottled water.

I was always constipated on the road. All that sitting, all that bad food, all that worry as Dane reorganized the decoy clothes, boxes, and other items that hid the drugs. But I thought we were safe because of his attention to detail. Dane was calm, calculated. He opened the car door for me during the day and unpacked our luggage at night. He took care of me on the road.

In bed, at night, I took care of him, too.

Valentine's Day, 1996, we stopped in Indianapolis.

"Let's celebrate," Dane said.

We parked the green van in the garage of a fancy downtown hotel. While I shopped, Dane checked with the concierge for a restaurant recommendation. The hotel was conveniently connected to a mall. I wanted something special to wear and found black boot-cut stretch pants with a zipper down the back.

For our special night out, the concierge said we should go to a hidden gem—a place only locals knew. We did, but since it was twenty minutes from the downtown, we had to drive. And so we broke the fourth rule, an important one: drive the vehicle with the marijuana *only* from point A to point B, never anywhere else.

Like my mother's rule—"Never take your brother's car, unless you ask"—that I broke when I was sixteen.

Now Dane and I had broken our own rule: We drove the van to dinner with 800 pounds of marijuana behind us.

"Another glass of wine, please," I said. As the waiter walked away, Dane looked at me and smiled. Across the table, I held his hand. Over my second glass of wine, I giggled.

Were we joyous with each other . . . the money . . . the tantalizing excitement of committing a crime?

"Happy Valentine's Day," I said, and smiled back.

The restaurant was homegrown—just like the marijuana we drove—and family-owned, friendly. Red leather seats, Parmesan cheese and red pepper flakes in glass jars with screw tops. The Italian joint *was* special. And that's how I felt when we walked outside after paying our bill.

Special.

Until I saw cops cars lining the drive.

Our van was surrounded by cop cars. Ten cars parked, dark, and empty.

Why? When?

Should we run or should we walk slowly, with caution, to our van?

That we were naïve and caught up in our romantic evening only made the situation scarier. The fifth rule, and a hard one for me as a woman: no emotions on the road. Break down anytime you want, but *not* with the marijuana. Keep it together.

I was good. I was a pro. I was a marijuana-trafficking ho.

"Let's take it slow," Dane said.

We walked—children walking toward our punishment, our hands caught in the cookie jar.

Horror and fear consumed me. Like they did that snowy Ohio night when I was sixteen.

I heard the thump and then the scream of the deer we'd hit and the scream of my friend Karen in the back seat. A symphony of pain. I felt sick. My three friends were with me, and we couldn't tell anyone. Rebellious, we'd snuck out of the house. Now I was praying like I had as a five-year-old, praying for God to keep me safe.

The deer had bled. The deer was dead. But nothing bad had happened to me . . . to us. We wiped down the car, said nothing. When we snuck back into the house, we were safe. My parents were still asleep.

Nothing happened this time either. No red or blue spinning lights. The dark night stayed dark.

Silently, I thanked God again.

"Give me a high-five," Dane said.

Inside the van, he slapped my palm.

"Oh . . . my . . . God," I whispered. I looked at him, eyes wide. Then I broke down in giggles, giggles close to a cry.

Special. I felt as special as the night. Sort of loved and wrecked at the same time. I know Dane felt that way, too. Close to invincible, above the law.

That night solidified my belief that we would never get caught; that I was in control of my destiny—and my crime.

CHAPTER 10

SHATTERED BALLERINA

"Go to the rock," I told Joeluine. "When you're there . . ." I scratched my head. "Hmmm . . . slowly climb to the top." This was our last tech rehearsal for *Slick Rock*, an operatic concert about a hiker who'd been bitten by a snake. I was changing the choreography at the last minute before the show.

I paced, deep in thought.

Joeluine and I had been rehearsing the show since last summer—even before France. During the last eight months, we'd performed *Slick Rock* numerous times. This performance at Western University in Kalamazoo was the last run of our last show. The black box theater—literally a bare square room—was ice cold.

My feet touched the black Marley floor and my hands supported my choreographed fall, as I rolled toward the cube at center stage that Joeluine and I called "the rock."

"Once you're there, stand up . . . stare at the audience. . . . No, that's not right. . . . Stare at *me*. Now roll your head in your hands."

She stood, glaring, hands on her hips. "Then what?"

"I don't know. . . . Try *something*."

Quickly her arms shot straight up. Her body arched. Then, gracefully, she fell on the rock.

God, she was good.

I walked offstage, satisfied, and pulled warm-up pants over my knit leg warmers. Jim, a music professor at the University of Wisconsin in Madison had created the show, and he looked satisfied too—with our performance and with Kelly. Two weeks ago, we'd asked my roommate to join our show. I was happy they were here, especially since Joeluine was so silent on this important last night of the show.

Lately, her silence was as cold as the vinyl floor.

Joeluine skated toward me on the hems of her sweatpants, her toes as hidden as her heart. "Yuk." Her voice hit me like a slap, and she dropped a swatch of long blond hair on the floor beside me. Moments ago, the miniature horsetail had been glued to my head like a hundred other extensions. They were eighteen inches long—a thousand dollars' worth of real hair—and flowed behind me when I walked.

Maybe I was the only one who liked the extensions. Stefan made fun of them, saying I had a "big fluff of hair." They had begun falling out—landing in odd places—but I needed long hair to feel sexy. Money no longer did the trick, nor did Stefan's casual love. Shopping for expensive new clothes with my new money was sexy, but the new clothes were a temporary fix that failed me after one wearing. Then I felt worse.

Joe said she had nightmares that my hair extensions chased her. "They're gross." She made a face. "I mean *really*, Jen."

Tonight, though, I was happy to get any reaction from Joeluine. We usually chatted while we stretched. Not tonight. Joeluine stayed quiet, removed. Still, I didn't have time to be concerned. My mom and dad were driving 300 miles from Ohio to Michigan to see me dance. This wasn't unusual. My parents had attended my events for years: watching girls in V-neck leotards tumbling, cheerleaders in short skirts jumping, girls in prairie skirts with parasols twirling.

I always felt stronger, supported, when I saw Mom and Dad in their seats.

I barely remembered that Dane would be there, driving from Detroit after meeting with one of the dealers. He was a shadow, a quick thought—the tail end of an extension. *Except when I needed him.* When I did, I'd stick to him like glue.

And it wasn't just the money. If Dane was in balance, so was I.

As the lights came up, the audience first heard a cello, then a piano and a high male voice. Then Joe and I danced. After the third piece, I ran offstage. Kelly stood in the wings as I caught my breath. The cello played—Joeluine's cue for her solo—but she did not appear.

"Kelly!" I whispered, frantic "Where is she?"

Nobody knew.

When I checked the bathroom, I heard Joeluine sobbing in the stall.

"Joeluine. You're on stage!"

"I don't feel good," she squeaked from behind the door.

I'm not going to let her get away with this, again. Not this time. Not this show. No way.

"Well, you're on, so get out there!" I'd learned to ignore pain at twelve, when I'd cut my foot on a piece of glass and my gymnastics coach made me practice anyway—even when I cried, even when I fell.

Toughen up, Jen, that's the way. But Joeluine wasn't buying it.

I ran back to the stage, knocking against four lights hanging from a metal branch—our "tree."

Joeluine's not coming.

I grabbed Kelly's arm, tight. "Get out there, now!"

God. I sound just like my old coach.

Kelly looked stunned, confused.

I pushed her on the stage and called instructions in a low firm voice as she rolled away from me on the floor. "Go to the rock. . . . Get on it. . . . Act tormented."

"But, what do I do?" She mouthed at the top of one roll.

"Do anything. . . . When you see me jump, run in a circle. Spiral offstage right." I prayed the audience couldn't hear, wouldn't know.

Jesus. I was pissed, even when Kelly told me Joeluine was crumpled against the trashcan crying. "Jen, she puked."

No, I thought to myself, *I'm not falling for it. Not this time. I'm not stupid, not me.*

I wasn't any tougher on Joeluine than I was on myself. With every dance performance, I was competing with my childhood successes in gymnastics, Girl Scouts, academics. Did I even have a goal now? I felt like an adult failure. Marijuana and money had taken precedence even over dance. Part of me wanted to reach out to Joe, to comfort her, but how could I? That part of myself was hidden, lost beneath deceit and bundles of cash.

I'd be a fool to give up the good life, a voice inside my head would say. With my new money, I could travel anywhere, experience worlds I'd never seen. I was the ballerina doll in my childhood jewelry box, spinning around and around. . . . I didn't know how to make me stop.

In my darkest moments, I saw that nothing was mine anymore. I belonged to Dane and the trips. Later, Dane would tell the DEA that I'd *begged* to make the trips.

It was true. I was a whore for the money.

We all were.

Two months later, Joeluine and I danced in Kalamazoo together again. She had forgiven me—for what I don't know—and we were friends again. "Please stay," she said, looking at me from the doorway of the theater. She batted her eyelashes, but I was tired after my guest performance with the Ballet Theatre of Kalamazoo. I wanted to sleep in my Chicago bed.

God, our roles are reversed. I used to beg her to stay in Chicago with me.

"I can't. I need to drive home. Joe, it's a three-hour drive." *I won't* is what I didn't say, but her eyes looked sad. She knew what I really meant.

"I made the guacamole for *you*." Her words trailed off. She knew it was my favorite, just as I knew pepperoni pizza was hers.

"I can't, Joe."

Those were our last words to each other—ever.

The guacamole had been for the cast party after Sher's production where Joe was a principal dancer. The house had been packed, but now the crowd was thinning as we stood in the lobby in our black dresses. I hugged and kissed Joe. I think she knew I loved her. I felt selfish for leaving, but it didn't stop me.

Standing at the exit—my left arm heavy with overflowing bags, my blue costume draped over my right—I looked back one last time at Joe. She was as exhausted as I was, but she gestured to the man in front of her, her hand stretched long and eloquent. He stared, hypnotized. She'd drawn him in—a natural response from anyone who saw her.

We were all in love with Joe.

Not a pin-drop of God's secrets was given away that night. Everything seemed in perfect order.

I was relieved when the wind slammed the heavy metal door behind me—ending the day.

Outside, my face felt tingly from the wind, the cold. After a solid performance, I felt alive, feeling for a moment that I was happiest when I danced. As if the universe existed especially for me.

As I walked in the darkness toward my car, one yellow streetlight clicked on and off and on again, the bright light glowing in the night like Joe's friendship.

I reviewed the night's performance—my perfect and not-so-perfect moves—as I drove home. Tonight I'd felt a flow on stage. My thoughts shifted back to the yellow glow emitted by the streetlight—

and the dreamy memories of the imaginary yolk from the egg game we played when I was a child.

A-tap-tap. Little-girl knuckles rap lightly on my head, cracking imaginary eggs, creating goose pimples.

Tonight, I felt warm, fuzzy like that. My thoughts shifted back to the click of the malfunctioning light—to the stage where I held Joe, my feet scraping against black Marley. The light clicked again. *Click.* In contentment, I drove.

Sunday I rested, my energy expended from the performance, the drive. Monday, Dane called. "Jen, the marijuana's no good. It's Mexican-bad. Like so bad they couldn't sell it." I had to fly to Detroit, right away. The green van was waiting, parked at the Hyatt Hotel.

"Johnny will meet you."

I pulled the covers over my head.

"It's a mess, Jen," Dane continued. "We're sending it back."

I hid under the covers. *Addict, addict, addict,* I thought to myself, *addicted to the money, not the drug.* But I couldn't say no. I needed the money, because I'd spent the money, and even if I hadn't spent it, I wanted it. I told him I'd make it to Phoenix in three, maybe four days.

Wrapped in the security of my sheets, I counted slowly to myself.

Three more minutes, then I'd call the airline.

I dreaded the travel, the energy drain—packing, unpacking, tensing, unwinding—grinding it out on the road. Anxiety from the road swept over me. Outside the loft the train rumbled past, then screeched to a stop.

One minute, then I'd pack.

I pictured the train doors sliding open, people exiting, the doors sliding closed. The minutes ticked past, my life going by just like the train.

In an hour, I was in a taxi headed for Midway Airport to catch my plane to Detroit.

The van was already packed when I picked it up. The vehicle and I moved at an even pace, the night silent, the yellow line down the middle of the road soothing as I left the city behind. It was late—maybe seven o'clock—when I pulled out of the Hyatt parking lot. Looking at the bags with an experienced eye, I guessed I was carrying about 700 pounds. As the sky darkened, and the weight of driving alone grew heavier, I tucked my worry behind the illusion that I would be okay.

I'll make out just fine, I told myself every day.

An hour and a half into the drive, the call came.

"It's Joe," Sher whispered, "an aneurism." She paused, waiting for my answer. "Jen, did you hear me?"

I'm here.

"At work . . . she fell . . . Jen?"

I'm here.

Finally I found my voice. "I took care of her, didn't I?"

"I know." Sher spoke softly, like a mother. "Come . . . okay?"

"I'm here, Joe. I'm coming," I whispered to myself.

Blinding headlights. A truck passed. Orchestrations of unseen forces were already sending me to Kalamazoo.

I was only an hour away.

The road was icy, the air cold as it blew in the window I'd cracked to let the cigarette smoke escape. I usually didn't smoke in the green van—another rule—but I was stressed and in shock. I lit up before I realized what I was doing.

Joe is in a coma.

The windshield wipers swished back and forth, back and forth, accompaniment to the pelting rain.

Joe is in a coma.

I pictured her delicate face against the pillow in the hospital bed, her arms spiked by IV needles attached to tubes.

I had to stay calm. The marijuana was stacked in hockey bags in the back.

Inside my head, I was screaming.

The parking garage was dark when I arrived in Kalamazoo. I knew I shouldn't leave the load alone.

Joe is in a coma.

Tangled in her back-and-forth, hot-and-cold attitude toward me, I tried to blame her. *The collapse is her choice, the coma her preference.*

I checked the locked van doors, shaking the handles one more time before leaving. Everything was in vain—the money, the lies.

Joe, my dearest friend, is slipping away from me.

I felt her breath against the back of my neck as I walked through the garage. On stage, we were one—simple and pure. Offstage, our friendship was flawed.

In the hospital's fourth floor hallway, Sher pulled me into her arms. Her students—my prodigies—were crumpled in confusion and pain over chairs, across the floor.

Joe lay in the bed—hair spread like a dark halo on the pillow, eyes closed in unnatural sleep, nose ring shimmering beside the plastic breathing tube. Her parents and brother clustered in her room, in the hall. I felt misplaced. An outsider. As if our friendship existed only as a memory. The girl lying motionless, expressionless, in the hospital bed couldn't be Joe. The change was so shocking that *my* Joe seemed like a dream.

They pulled the plug that night, the same day she went into a coma.

Afterward, I drove home to Chicago with the marijuana in the van. My feelings zoomed from confusion to torment to shame— even to my own safety—as though Joe were watching me from Above. I imagined her large French hat—the one Dane bought for her in Chicago that she never wore. I pictured guacamole shoved down the drain at the end of the cast party I didn't attend.

Selfish. Why hadn't I stayed when she asked?

One, two, three lights bled into a brilliant celestial galaxy as Chicago came into view, almost erasing the smell of death. When I parked outside the loft, Kelly met me. I cried and held her tight.

Before Joe's death, I—we—felt invincible. One night we had sped down Lake Avenue in my red Toyota sports car, T-top's off, Joe sitting on Kelly's lap, laughing. The wind wild as we sped through the intersections, ignoring stop signs—five of them.

Nothing bad happened. No crash. No wailing siren.

"Fun!" we all said when I finally stopped. Joe lit my cigarette. And Dinosaur Jr. screamed from my stereo: "So what else is new? Won't you give me some?"

We were unbreakable.

But now, Joe was shattered.

Gone.

And so was I.

Two hours later, I stood in front of the bathroom mirror in the loft, my fake ponytail swung behind me as I lined my eyes with bright blue shadow. We went to Vivo for dinner, then later to Danny's bar. My mourning bubbled, festered, and burst into recklessness. I'd driven us there in the van filled with the drugs. Kelly knew what was inside the hockey bags.

"Jen, be careful."

Joeluine is dead. I don't care about the drugs.

My anger and rebellion roared. All my past hurts rolled into this one huge loss.

Under the dirty neon walls of Danny's, I mourned. I drank my wine and watched the pink light wash onto the Formica table—speckled brown meets candy pink—dirtying the pink like mud . . . like the danger inside Joe . . . like the danger I refused to see inside me.

It's late. In one of the back rooms at Danny's, I hit on a girl. Really, I'm all over her. I nuzzle her neck and caress her thigh. I'm aggressive in my pain. As I whisper promises in her ear, Kelly pulls me away.

"Jen, it's time to go home."

It was way after midnight, close to two in the morning. I was drunk, laughing, looking back at the girl on the couch.

She was pretty . . . dark . . . ethnic.

But she wasn't Joe.

The already shaky foundation of my world threatened to crumble under my grief. Months—nearly a year later—I finally recognized the enveloping pain of Joe's death had cracked open a door for me, an opportunity for transformation, a second chance.

I could unfold like a real butterfly.

CHAPTER 11

LOST

Seven days after Joeluine's funeral, I was trapped in Mexico with people I wanted to escape.

Raw with grief, I hadn't wanted to go.

Dane had persuaded me. "It'll be fun, Jen. Come on." He'd told me who was coming, and I imagined the drug-talk—the superficial banter.

I need deeper waters.

"It's exactly what you need . . . the sun, the ocean."

I need healing.

"Are you there, Jen?"

I could be alone in Mexico.

I still paused.

Trusting Dane, I'd said yes.

At first, the beauty of the resort hacienda had eased my grief. The ocean matched my restless spirit and then calmed me as I watched the waves go in and out.

After two days, I felt empty . . . cold. No butterfly feelings.

By then it was too late. I was a thousand miles from home—and a thousand miles from Joeluine. Outside, it was hot—80 degrees and climbing—but I couldn't shake the cold inside my heart.

Inside, the big living room was empty, except for Johnny and the cocaine he snorted off the top of the marble dining table.

Outside by the hotel swimming pool in my bikini, the white towel fell away from the top of my lounge chair and hot vinyl strips burned into my bare back. The pain was sudden, surprising, like the hot jolt that branded my heart every time I thought, *Joeluine is dead.*

On this trip, I couldn't splash in the pool like Mindy did, laughing with a drink in her hand, nor could I dance at the bar with wiggling, gyrating hips between pool tables, to 2Pac's *California Love.* I felt alone as I sat on the slated wooden bench in the Mexican bar.

Dane sat down and clicked his Tecate bottle against mine.

Still alone.

Last year, I'd wanted Mindy to be my friend. Not now. In place of her former sweetness was a crash woman with a gigantic ego and—just recently—bigger breasts. She'd shown me her new chest in the restaurant's bathroom before dessert, exposing C-cup breasts—almost perfect—except for the three-inch gap between them.

"They'll settle . . . you know . . . closer together."

She blanketed her disappointment with a laugh, and then guided my hand to touch one breast. The distance between us faded with my touch, but her eyes mocked me when she looked up. I dropped my hand. She dropped her shirt and, with a flip of her hair, turned back to the mirror and smacked her gum. The moment of closeness was gone—vanished.

Like I wished the Mexico trip would vanish.

Like Joeluine had vanished—forever. I yearned for her—my ballerina girl—to magically reappear.

When I returned from Mexico, I kept picturing Joeluine in the coffin, her made-up face and pink tutu, the worn ballet shoes tucked under her arm.

Now, Joeluine was buried in the ground.

I can't eat. Can't sleep.

The next week, Kelly and I drove with Jim to Big Bend, Texas, for a ten-day photo shoot. Joeluine was supposed to be with us. For the first eight hours of our trip, gusts of wind rocked the camper back and forth. After a week of taking medication with labels warning me to avoid alcohol, I drank a sip of champagne from the bottle Jim uncorked as he drove.

I threw up, first into the thin paper bag Kelly held, and six hours later, into a paper cup.

Was I purging? Sick with grief?

In the desert, Kelly and I climbed over rocks and crawled into canyons as Jim took pictures. Silk scarves rippled behind us in the wind. Jim's music bellowed from his box above. Tinkling piano keys and haunting flutes echoed off canyon walls, mirroring our grief.

One night, the mushrooms from Jim's plastic baggie brightened the sky's fading red and orange as Kelly and I walked arm in arm and naked as nymphs between desert trees. Sparkles came alive, and we laughed as we hunted fairies.

Another night we left Jim behind playing guitar in a local bar, and mourned, crying between beers and cigarettes.

At night, the camper was hot.

Droplets of sweat outlined my body as hours were laid to bed, empty beer bottles discarded, words slurred.

Inside the camper, we traded stories about Joeluine.

Outside, stars popped like kernels, appearing one by one in the desert night sky. Our stories and our memories grew as bold as the stars. Jim had known Joeluine first, so I latched onto him, like he could bring me closer to her.

I felt guilty I couldn't save Joeluine. Guilty, I couldn't save myself.

When Kelly and I returned to Chicago fourteen days later I was thin—ten pounds lighter—my body tan, my hair extensions tangled.

"Too tan, Jen . . . too thin," Stefan said.

He drove us to the G-Man's house. "It'll be fun," he promised. I should have known. Dane had promised the Mexico trip would be fun, too.

Like a magician, Stefan tilted the liquid drug into my mouth.

But it wasn't fun, or, if it was, I didn't remember it. I lost eight hours and woke to a tangle of arms and legs, and a man I didn't know.

I wanted to be taken care of—especially in my grief. Dane hadn't protected me from Mindy in Mexico. Now, Stefan had let me down, too.

Late dinners, late nights, too many drinks. With a wave of my hand and my cigarette, I'd wish away my tears—laugh away my pain. My mother was concerned when she came to visit. My legs looked "stick-thin" in my mini-skirt, she said, and my health, "not good."

"A-rat-tat-tat-tat . . . TAT-TAT-TAT-TAT-TAT . . ."

The jackhammer screamed below, belting off-tune. Chicago in July was hot—sticky hot—even hotter high in the loft with no air-conditioning. Yet, I burrowed further under my sheets.

Outside, the train screeched as it stopped. I couldn't escape the shrill pounding noise that climbed up through my toes, into my ears—surrounding me.

Had my grief unleashed, come to life?

It had been two months since Joeluine died. I had to get out of my life—out of the traps I'd made. Out of this mess.

Wake up, Jen.

The jackhammer kept pounding the sidewalk.

Wake up, Jen.

The train's wheels grated across my heart and came to a stop. People opened the door.

Open your heart. There's more to life. There's more . . .

My head pounded from too many drinks, not enough food, not enough sleep. I rolled over and a pink vibrator fell onto the floor.

Kelly had bought the toy for me the previous week, but I'd been too embarrassed to use it.

Jesus. Depressing.

I didn't even have a man. Wasn't there something more than the deadness I felt in my so-called *life.*

I was frustrated, caught in a vicious cycle of grief. Enraged that I didn't have a lover. Enraged that Joeluine was dead.

The noise outside mocked me.

The sparkles I felt when I was happy were gone. Buried, along with Joeluine and my dancing career. Dance felt like death to me now. I still had the trips, the money. But I was a mess.

Something needs to change.

I made a vow to take care of myself, to be gentle, stop the violence that raged inside my heart. I had to move on from my pain. I had to nurture my spirit, something I hadn't done for years. I made the first change I could think of. I moved out.

But first there was Italy . . . France . . . and my rendezvous with Dane in Milan.

In Florence, Dane and I found the outside cinema. We ate at tables under the stars, surrounded by stone walls. He held my arm—the balance I needed—as I walked over worn cobblestones in my high heels.

And we traveled.

The Tuscan villa's mystique wasn't enough to re-kindle the love between us—or to turn me on. In the villa above the hills on the outskirts of Portofino, Dane took my picture in my favorite pale blue sweater set.

That night, wearing my vintage pink nightgown, I crawled into bed with Dane, spooning after one quick, soft good-night kiss.

In France I had my first bite of liver pâté. And then I found

Chipsters—my favorite Ohio chip. I squealed with delight when I found them at the corner French market—small red boxes lined up on the shelf of my childhood dreams.

I bought twenty boxes and two duffle bags to carry them home. At the airport, I watched the airline attendant casually throw them onto the conveyor belt. The man didn't realize they contained childhood dreams—memories of twelve-year-olds in leotards dangling over heaters after gymnastics practice, of iced tea, sharp cheddar cheese—and Chipsters.

I watched anxiously as the bags disappeared.

After the chips disappeared from Ohio stores, I'd searched for them like I searched for my childhood dreams.

Where had they gone, and why?

Now I knew. The chips had been transported to France.

But where are my dreams?

When I returned from France, I gobbled the Chipsters. They lasted only a few days. My fleeting hopes of recapturing my childhood traits—drive, ambition, and creativity—disappeared with the last chip.

With a flick of my wrist, I threw away the last box and made a face at the hallway mirror, sticking out my tongue, taunting my deceit—my lies.

I wished I could turn time around and see a different girl standing in front of the mirror—the "oh so sweet good old girl" my mom wanted, the girl I'd tried to be . . . before.

But, the good girl didn't exist anymore.

"You're not the Jenny *I* know," my mom would say, and sometimes she'd cry.

So, where did I go?

I wanted to tell her what I was doing, where I was going, but then I'd have to stop the drug trips.

My mind spun.

Then, I won't have the money, and if I don't have the money, I'll have to find a job, and what will I do? How will I live? How can I make this kind of money? What will happen to me?

Freaked out. No way out. Yet, the song in my head continued to play like an old country ballad, *I'm a lookin' for this good girl again.*

The move to Burton's Place was the change I yearned for. The apartment was a perfect home base for the deeper change I sought. Burton Place was magical—a mansion from the roaring twenties where famous writers and artists had thrown wild parties. Now it was separated into units.

The stained glass window of No. 1 spanned the length of the living room where Kelly and I lived. At night, the yellow glow of a gothic chandelier kissed me good night, mothering me as I slept.

I prayed that I'd be okay—that my life would work out just fine.

Joeluine's death had ripped the lid off my life and, instead of seizing the opportunity for change, I'd dived straight into self-destructive behavior. But that stage was over. I felt more balanced now, remembering my little-girl question, "Mom, what happens when we die?"

I knew something was going to change. I could feel it. Smell it. Feel it in the tingles in my toes.

But, what was I searching for?

Still, the drug trips stayed on track and my shoebox of money was full until—depleted by my travels—I was down to only two bundles . . . a few thousand.

The fall of 1996 had been all about travel: Mexico, Texas, France, and Italy.

In October, I bought a motorcycle jacket to wear on a Palm Springs dirt-bike trip Dane promised me for my birthday. Yet, when Kelly and I stepped out of the limo at the airport, she led me to terminal number two—the international terminal.

Dane jumped from behind a large column, surprising me with

three tickets to London. That's the moment I really did believe he loved me. No one had ever surprised me, not like this.

Dane knew I'd want Kelly along. The trip to Italy and France had confirmed that we— Dane and I—couldn't make it alone. I loved Dane, but was I *in* love? He seemed to believe I'd come around—that I'd fall back into his arms.

Arriving in England jet lagged, the three of us fell into a deep sleep. I woke, revived, more alive than I'd felt in months. Like we'd been "kissed by an angel," Kelly and I agreed. We felt Joeluine— our *angel*—had been in the room.

Later, Dane took us to dinner and to a private club, but he left early. Kelly and I met two men. Both were young—one eighteen— and when they invited us to their flat, we went with them.

After cocktails and banter with the not-so-proper English men— too late at night or too early in the morning—I stumbled, drunk, in my long black dress and tumbled down twenty carpeted steps. Unhurt, I staggered to my feet, as Kelly looked on, stunned. I'd broken one Prada shoe heel and waved it in my hand with a laughing battle cry. With the other hand, I waved a maniacal good-bye to the men, chopping the air with frantic motions. I was still giggling (even *I* was amazed at my fall) when Kelly pushed me—no, pulled me—into the taxi. The taxi man drove us back to the hotel, back to where I was safe again . . . in Dane's arms.

Later, Kelly showed me the picture she took in the back of the taxi—a crazy lady with dripping mascara and red lipstick, hair in disarray, who had tumbled down, down, down.

I was still out of control. The move to Burton Place hadn't done the trick.

I made more changes.

In London, I chopped off my long blond hair.

I began to read spiritual self-help healing books, and I continued taking the acting classes I'd begun with Stefan the year before.

I began to notice serendipitous events. After reading *The Art-*

ist's Way by Julia Cameron, I'd created my vision board—a collage with a lion, a woman kneeling in prayer, and a waterfall I'd cut-out from *Travel + Leisure Magazine.* I tacked it above my desk. It was a reminder of my devotion. When Stefan had invited me to Tahiti and handed me the travel brochure, I'd gasped.

My waterfall was on the brochure—*exactly* the same.

Was this a sign my life was finally on track?

In Tahiti with Stefan a few weeks later, tattoo artist and surfer Runi tattooed a bracelet design around my arm. For days, Stefan and I had searched Moorea for Runi—a man that only locals knew—and found his small hut at the edge of a cliff, on private acreage, up a private road.

When we returned to Chicago, I had another synchronistic event. Runi stared at me from the cover of a photography-surfer book enclosed inside the pages of *Elle* magazine.

Again, I questioned my life, longing for *something* I couldn't touch, or see. Something I'd always known was there.

Was that *something* at the wheel of my life? . . . *But what? Who?*

CHAPTER 12

THE UNFOLDING

The trees and their secrets were postponed. Again.

I'd flown to Phoenix—to Dane—and another marijuana trip across the country.

This time a U-Haul trailer attached behind Dane's Suburban held the drugs. While Dane drove through Texas, I wrote a poem for Stefan, who'd slipped on the ice and broken his leg. In Oklahoma, I slept with pillows against the truck's window. In Missouri, I drew pictures with crayons.

My employment hauling marijuana had become routine, simply a job—a job I was good at. Making a living off the illegal money felt normal. I almost felt safe, relaxed—too relaxed—since I was supposed to stay on the lookout for cops when Dane drove. Our cover as newlyweds moving to Chicago was almost a reality. We knew each other's habits, favorite exits, and special snacks. Dane and I were smooth, a perfect drug-trafficking machine.

As I drove, I secretly pined for Stefan, thinking back to the nights we'd shared. My so-called love life unnerved me, but I couldn't afford to be distracted on the road. Potential trouble was right behind me—the marijuana. When we passed a cop, I'd be jacked-up—wired—when I thought of the bales we were hauling. Still, I grew hypnotized again as we passed stretches of open road, lethargic as we drove through snow.

On this trip, we listened to a thriller, *Kiss The Girls,* on cassette tape—one of the ways Dane and I liked to pass the nine-hour days. I was driving and briefly took my eyes off the road to look at Dane. He was picking his nose, which irritated me. I did feel like we were married. Not to each other but to the marijuana and all it represented. *Without the money, I'll fall apart,* I thought, my stomach rumbling as though the falling apart had begun.

I can't imagine Dane—or the marijuana—not being in my life.

I knew what to expect on our cross-country trips. At night we shared a room, and sometimes a bed. Cuddled, sometimes touched. When I drove with the drugs, I didn't feel sexy. By day two, signs of stress appeared—irritability, constipation, depression. Still—since neither of us was in a relationship—I slept with Dane when we were on the road.

He was solidity in my life. And he wasn't going anywhere, was he? I couldn't see an end to our marijuana drives. And Stefan wasn't going anywhere either, not with his broken leg. I wanted to keep everyone—and everything—in its proper place in my life.

Don't rock my foundation.

Stefan was dark, handsome, creative. Dane was stable, consistent, safe—interesting, with his olive skin, slightly long nose, and pretty eyes. Odd to feel safer with a kingpin in a marijuana drugring than an entrepreneur with *legal* businesses, but I did.

Which reality should I trust?

As I suspected, off and on, possibly *I* was the one breaking apart.

My routine had finally shifted since Joeluine's death. I rarely went out. I was on a sabbatical from drinking and was in bed by eight o'clock. Although I lived with Kelly, I felt alone, but not lonely, as I read my spiritual books.

More change was coming.

I could feel it.

Stefan called me, exhilarated, on the third day of my drive. I was tired, impatient, barely able to deal with his excitement. On the pay phone inside the truck stop—Exit 35—his voice rose to a fevered pitch. "Jen, I understand *everything* now."

"Understand what?"

"You know, how it works."

I knew he meant the world. *The parts we couldn't see.* Stefan was searching, just as I was.

"Ireadthebookyougaveme," Stefan continued, words running into one another.

Bored and immobile in his cast, Stefan had begged for something to read. I'd handed him *Adventures Beyond the Body,* which had been collecting dust on my bedside shelf. I'd found the book at the store next to Whole Foods. The book jacket had given me pause, reminding me of my spiritual experiences from childhood.

The feelings I still had.

Would I ever have read it?

Dane and I dropped the marijuana in Detroit. I flew to Chicago and dropped my share—$21,000—into a shoebox under my bed. The next day I borrowed the book back from Stefan and read it in one sitting.

After I read it, I was on fire like he was. My childhood question—What happens when we die?—had been answered.

A light went on.

Instantly my life filled with color, as if I'd been living in black and white before. I connected to the author's description of out-of-body experiences, where he explored a multi-dimensional universe. I believed what he described as the true nature of the universe. Although I hadn't read much about quantum physics, I knew what I felt in my heart. I had questioned what happened when we died. Now, I felt limitless—like the world was filled with possibility.

I was hungry, voracious for more.

Fuck.

I had a date tonight with a man from my acting class, and I didn't know what to wear.

I'm not drinking. I don't know how to be, what to do tonight.

My date and I walked to the diner a few blocks away. I was bored, anxious for the evening to be over. When he left me at the apartment, all I wanted to do was burrow into my bed—alone—and read books more fulfilling than Sam's peck on my cheek. He'd been my attempt to get my mind off Stefan.

A few weeks earlier, Stefan had told me he didn't think we should sleep together any more. I felt rejected, annoyed. He didn't want a personal relationship, but he wanted my help. Stefan's neediness had grown since he'd broken his leg. In the beginning, I'd been happy to stock his refrigerator with snacks and bring him books. But now he was calling several times a day to complain or to ask me to bring him art supplies and take-out. His demands were wearing me down. Still, I believed there was a reason Stefan was in my life.

After the book incident—and after the Christmas holidays—Stefan and I planned a trip to Virginia to explore out-of-body experiences at the Monroe Institute. I was excited to go and felt safe—my men secure—when I went to sleep that night. Although I couldn't have Stefan the way I wanted him, I knew our friendship was solid. Behind closed eyelids, I thought of Dane, too. Although he was somewhere in Phoenix without me he saw the same stars I saw. I knew he loved me best.

With this last thought, I fell asleep.

After Virginia, my inner life took off. At the Monroe Institute, I met Bill, who introduced me to Kurt—an energy and bodywork healer in Chicago—who introduced me to Susan—who helped people uncover their life purpose and reconnect to their "soul's calling," according to Kurt.

And she did.

Susan was the next catalyst in my life.

I met her first in a Chicago high-rise off Michigan Avenue. I remember what we wore because of the contrast. The chains of my Prada purse straps clinked as I walked through the corridor in my brown Mui Mui Mary Jane shoes. My hair—pixie short and bleached-blond white—made me appear thinner and taller than my five feet four inches.

Susan was tiny—less than five feet, less than 100 pounds—and dressed in a black crinkle flowing skirt and silky maroon top. Her first words were blunt. "How long have you had an eating disorder?"

My mouth dropped open in shock.

I don't.

I hadn't gained back the fifteen pounds I'd lost after Joeluine's death. I liked myself thin—around 110 pounds—though Stefan had said, "Too thin, Jen . . . too tan." I swallowed, a slow gulp, as I remembered my flat breasts and narrow hips in seventh grade. I hadn't liked being thin back then. I'd covered my skinniness with extra layers of sweatpants hidden beneath my jeans, tucked into my socks.

I wanted to look like Tammy, round with hips and large breasts. Tammy was lucky. All of the boys in school thought she was sexy. Even Gary, who French-kissed me in the gym stairway.

I stared back at Susan.

I'd never sat with a therapist before.

"I just *can't* eat." I couldn't, not since Joe's death. It was a year before I got my appetite back.

At the kitchen bar I told Susan I had a secret.

She asked me to tell.

I giggled with nervousness, and my face turned red. For the first time—I guess because I was confessing to a therapist—I was really ashamed of my role in the marijuana business.

I *knew* it was wrong.

"I can't tell."

She swirled her stool around. "Say it to my back."

So, I told her.

For the first time, I'd told my secret to a professional—not a close friend or someone involved in the drug trade. But I felt relieved. Not judged.

As a therapist, Susan was bound to confidentiality.

She became my mentor—introducing me to Osho's mystical principles that could be applied to daily life. Eventually she became a friend.

During the next year, I had more deep sessions with Susan. Her questions about my core values prompted me to ask myself why I continued to drive the marijuana, but they didn't stop me.

The very next month I flew to Phoenix. Which was normal for me, except for the bag I checked.

The airport's hallways stretched forever, and the ride down the escalator to baggage claim was endless.

That's the feeling when you have $100,000 cash in your bag.

Awful scenarios filled my head:

Would the suitcase appear on the baggage carousel with all the others?

Would someone grab me before I'd grabbed the bag?

Was someone watching to see who would claim it?

I saw the bag . . . *thank God* . . . and grabbed it off the conveyer. My body relaxed—finally.

I used Dane's hide-away key to let myself into his deserted townhouse, where I fell onto his bed, lost in a dark cocoon for eight hours.

A steady breeze from the ceiling fan cooled me from the May

heat, its blades whooshing as they rotated. The cool air blew memories of childhood into my dreams—memories of shivering under nylon sheets snuggled next to my friend Stephanie when we were eleven. I sank into the bed's big pillows and into my past. I'd been a worrier, even back then, and I'd been comforted when we scratched each other's backs before falling asleep.

I wanted comfort again. Safety.

Instead, I woke swaddled in cotton sheets, bright light streaming in the window. From the bed, I could see my suitcase with its neatly packed clothes. The vacuum-packed bundles of cash—a new procedure Dane had come up with to hide the bills' smell—were hidden underneath. Dane wasn't home yet, so he hadn't yet claimed or counted the money.

I rolled over, my back to the suitcase. I wanted a reprieve from thinking about the cash. I concentrated on the soothing, distracting sound of the fan. When I turned over again, I looked beyond my suitcase to Dane's cologne. I was tempted to stroke the clear glass bottles perfectly arranged on the bathroom shelves.

Dane will be home soon. Then, we'll count the money.

Dane always smelled good, but the extravagance of the bottles depressed me. I over-shopped, too; easy money was easy to spend. A ray of light from the window touched the first bottle on the shelf, exposing its transparency and mine.

I am guilty.

When light scattered, patterns of diamonds lit the bottle's insides. I saw swirls of bouncing light, like the rainbows and diamonds I saw when Mom held a prism to the light. She had used the prism to help me understand the math formulas, calculations, and logic that were important to her as a math teacher.

The illuminated bottle took me back to my mom's world, where logic and honesty were important, where a suitcase of money and hundred-dollar cologne didn't belong.

I want to live in a world where people are honest, don't I?

I want to be honest, don't I?

In the comfort of Dane's bed, the money lost its grip. My greed dripped away as quickly as ice cream on the Dairy Queen cones my dad used to buy me in the summertime. For a moment—in my memories of those innocent days—I felt space. I could breathe.

Then Dane came home.

One kiss. One hug.

"Where's the money, Jen?"

Dane piled the thousand-dollar bundles onto my lap on the bed. I scissored open the vacuum-sealed packages and placed the cash beside Dane for him to count.

He threw three of the packages on the bed. *One-one thousand . . . two-one thousand . . . three—*

"For you."

I leaned over and kissed him.

That's it. I'm done, I thought to myself.

Yet, my part was never finished.

Dane gave me money, and I gave him love. We didn't talk about the crime, yet it was always between us, sometimes seducing, sometimes taunting—but always present.

The crime taunts like a bobblehead doll, picking up secrets with every dip. With an erect spine it judges—folded hands in a prayer, a nun, a Buddha in a shrine. Other times, it's like a seductress with beckoning palms—tassels rotating, swinging as the strip-tease dancer descends quickly down her pole.

Dane was consistent. Reliable.

Me? I was a storm at twilight—an evening dark before its time.

And, yes . . . we were committing a crime.

"Hey, take another." Dane threw a bundle of cash on the bed.

"What's this for?"

"Expenses."

I'd earned one thousand for flying the money, then another thousand for reimbursements—the plane ticket, the taxi. I flopped onto my back and fanned myself with hundred-dollar bills. Sometimes I forgot what my life was like before I met Dane.

The ceiling fan continued its hum. *Whoosh . . . whoosh . . . whoosh.* With the money, I felt loved.

Yes, Jesus loves me, floated through my mind, a sweet childhood church memory that soothed my worries like butterscotch.

But my words were, "Yes, *Dane* loves me."

I could hear pieces of conversation as Dane talked on the phone in the other room to Tony or one of the Mexican suppliers. When he hung up, he told me the load had been delayed. "It's not happening."

I looked at him, surprised. I could feel my eyes narrow almost to a squint. I'd made my plans for the week, built a stack of lies for why I would be away from Chicago.

"When?"

I wanted to ask why, but that wasn't appropriate. Dane didn't know either. Maybe someone got caught crossing the border.

"I have no idea. You know how it goes."

And I did.

Instantly I had a gap of time in my life.

I took off: free from my "job" and Chicago, free to continue my spiritual quest.

Alone, I flew to San Francisco where I rented a car and drove to Santa Cruz and the redwoods. In an outdoor amphitheater among the trees, I danced—spinning in warm sweats layered under my white gauze dress, twirling with Susan's mentor and two other women.

That night on the phone, Susan told me about Mt. Shasta. "It's a special place, but not an easy place. The mountain tends to uncover what you try to hide."

"I want to go."

That night, I dreamt I was in a classroom waiting with anticipation, an I-think-I'm-going to-explode feeling. Stefan was there, too, but distracted, playing with toys on a shelf.

The dream told me *they* were coming.

I'm going home. They're coming to take me home.

Dane's call on my cell was the opposite, an interruption, but kind of a blessing, too.

"It's here, Jen."

The marijuana had crossed the border. And I needed that money. I'd already spent the $3,000 on my two weeks in Northern California. The money was helping me now, I told myself. I wasn't squandering it on meaningless luxuries. I knew where I needed to go, what I needed to do, what I had to understand.

The first three months of 1997, I took stacks of cash out of my shoebox over and over again.

First was the Gabriel Roth dance seminar in Chicago, then the Kripalu Institute in Massachusetts. I had Rolfing sessions with Joseph the shaman, acupuncture treatments, colonics, floating tank sessions, Holotropic Breathwork, and a vitamin program.

I felt that I was cleansing inside and out.

Yet, nothing cleansed the marijuana out of my life. Not a nudge, not an inch. Not a bit. In my mind, the money bought me freedom to explore important parts of myself that I was beginning to cherish once again. In childhood, I had offered thanks to God for my parents, my dog, my brother, and the new green carpet in my room. Now I prayed, *God, thank you for bringing the marijuana into my life so I can travel my inner and outer worlds.*

Why did I think my crime (a high-risk adventure) and my spiritual search (an honest, authentic quest) could exist side by side?

Dane called on a cold, dark, dreary day in March. "Jen, someone got caught."

"What do you mean 'caught?'"

I froze, scarcely breathing. My impulse was to close up, lock the house down, and move away from this part of my life. But, I couldn't give up the money, even in my fear.

Dane didn't have the details. "All I know is . . . the police took the money."

I swallowed hard.

Kelly stood in front of me, eyes big, mouthing "What? . . . What's happening? What!"

My friend felt my tension, knew I was talking to Dane.

"If you have *anything* in your house, get rid of it," Dane commanded.

I had the cash—close to $25,000—plus $30,000 profit from the sale of three ten-pound bales of marijuana. Someone I knew had sold it to someone else in Chicago. *That* money wasn't mine.

My heart thumped.

I squeaked out my next words. "What about the extra money?"

"Just keep it."

And, just like that, I hit the jackpot.

The night felt ominous, but promising, too. I was scared, but I'd been handed a gift—cash.

"There's nothing you can do, Jen," Dane told me. "Lay low for a while."

I didn't see the marijuana trips ending. I mean, someone had lost a shitload of money, and he would have to be paid back. Dane's and Tony's cuts had been taken but, worst of all, the Mexican suppliers had lost money. And, they *never* forgave a debt.

Dane always rolled his eyes about this fact of the business, as if he didn't have a choice. "Always behind the eight ball," he'd complain, "always in debt."

Just keep it.

And so, I did.

The next week I traded in my eight-year-old Toyota for a sporty two-year-old BMW.

Someone gets busted, and I buy a car. Is my life really on track?

For three months, I got no calls about the business, none at all. I counted and re-counted the money under my bed. I had lots of bundles left. In June, I planned to swim with wild dolphins in Key West.

After one week in Key West—on the last day—I finally got my swim. A swim I'll never forget.

Looking up, I see the sky. Underwater in my snorkel and flippers, I see the dolphin, and the dolphin sees me. So big, I am almost scared. I'm slow, not very good with those flippers, but the dolphin slows down, looking back to make sure I'm there. Like he wants to swim side-by-side.

For a moment we did.

The dolphin seemed to look into my soul, and I felt a sudden burst of profound joy . . . joy that reverberated for days.

I was still in the middle of snorkels, didgeridoos, and bonding with my New Zealand friend Sarah when Dane called. I was to fly from Miami to Phoenix where Dane would be waiting with the loaded vehicle. This time we'd drive "somewhere different," but he couldn't tell me where.

Then, in person, Dane told me: New York.

New York?

"Your eyes are *so* blue," said Matt.

Maybe my bright orange shirt made my eyes look more blue— or my tan. Or maybe he saw the openness that I felt inside. Even after the four-day drive from Phoenix to New York, the feeling of the dolphins stayed with me.

Matt was the *new* New York contact.

I thought the same about his eyes: so blue, so open, looking directly at me just like the dolphin—as if he, too, could see into my soul. Actually, he was sort of yummy: handsome and fit with dark curly hair. He wore navy basketball shorts and white high-top tennis shoes. The drug-deal talk made Matt seem even sexier.

That night Matt, his Thai girlfriend, Dane, and I went to see *Cats* on Broadway in Manhattan. Matt had bought the tickets. He dined us, wined us, because he wanted Dane's business.

If only he had known.

Back then, we were naïve, flirting and having fun. Dane had told me Matt liked his pot. He didn't have much money. I could tell by the quality of the blue pinstriped suit he'd worn to the show.

Five years later, I saw Matt again. This time he was dressed in an expensive, tailored dark suit; had a Porsche; and a big house in Jersey. Neither of us acknowledged each other—*Did he even recognize me?*—but I thought, *Matt has really done well.* He and Dane and other people I didn't even know had made a shitload of money off their deals.

And I drove some of those loads.

Looking back, I'm sad.

Matt's pinstriped suit had been cheap and unfashionable in the summer of 1997. He had not yet become a wealthy man, but back then he'd had a chance at real life.

Now, the small-time stoner boy from Jersey was locked up. Not for fourteen months . . . five years . . . or even ten. He was locked up for over twenty—maybe twenty-five years—first in a medium security federal prison and then, if he was good, in a prison camp.

CHAPTER 13

DESTINY?

I was leaving the Sedona restaurant when the girl-with-the-dark-hair touched my shoulder. I'd seen her at meditation the night before when she'd spun in a solitary circle, eyes closed, white robe swirling around her feet.

Now her eyes were open, looking into mine. "You *have* to go to India . . . you'll *looove* it!" The word *love* spun off her tongue, fluid like the way she had danced. "The commune is beautiful. I go there every year."

The seven-day retreat in Sedona, Arizona, had been difficult. I listened to the teachings of Osho and did exercises that focused a magnifying glass on my life. In a basement filled with toys, I picked the Barbie and the tiger plush-toy to represent the parts of myself that kept me spinning in life, kept me stuck—the perfect good girl and my competitiveness.

Sitting near the back, I'd felt invisible until the female guru pointed me out, took my hand, and told me I was brave. I felt shy, but special. Acknowledged, like the times I'd been singled out for my performances as a child.

On the seventh and last day, I hiked to an open clearing of trees.

In the center, someone had placed rocks in a large double circle that spiraled—two circles within circles. I sat in the center and thought about my life. I hadn't danced for over a year and only once since Joe had died. My passion for dance had been redirected into my spiritual search.

A goldfinch landed beside me and flew away when I reached out my hand. The clouds seemed to swallow the bird as it climbed higher. Inside, I felt lighter after the retreat, *strong*. Like any moment I could slip into feathers of a deeper happiness than I'd ever felt before, and fly away with the finch.

The magic of Sedona brought alive the peace I felt inside. I leaned my head back and let out a warrior's cry. Although I could no longer see the finch in the sky, I felt free, too.

One week later, I was back driving the drugs.

Doreen's head jerked sideways. The tape of my guru's soothing words about creation, evolution, and freedom had lulled Stan's mother to sleep. I didn't care. The first four hours of our trip, she'd talked nonstop about growing up in Detroit.

The second day she'd deflated, a dead weight in the passenger's seat. Sometimes she slept; sometimes she ate, opening foil-wrapped packages of Lebanese home-cooked food. I gave up trying to engage her and instead dove into a quiet, automatic rhythm where I became one with the road.

The bright sun tracked heat along the truck's inside door. I felt joy, especially as I listened to the tape. *Midmorning in Missouri is beautiful,* I thought dreamily. Suddenly—at a velocity as fast as a rain cloud covers the sun—everything changed.

Red and blue lights flashed in my rearview mirror.

The heat . . . the guru's voice the girl-with-the-dark-hair. I felt dizzy, confused.

As the lights spun, my chest tightened. Quick palpitations tore through my body. In between, Dane's words came back to me: "Stay with the flow of traffic."

I'd been speeding. The guru's voice had taken me somewhere else—way off track.

This is not good. No, not good at all. The cop directed me to the side of the road. When I pulled onto the gravel shoulder, Doreen woke up.

Usually the marijuana was stacked farther away from us, enclosed in a U-Haul trailer or truck. This trip, the marijuana was *inside* the SUV. The back seats had been pulled down to make room for stacks of red and green hockey bags behind our heads. Strips of lemon-scented carpet freshener were layered like lasagna noodles between plastic wrap and contact paper wrapped around the bales. Still, a musky-sweet order permeated the truck.

Dane had warned me of mistakes like this. I couldn't make this one go away.

The cop swaggered toward the truck. His tan highway patrol uniform scared me more than the blue of a local cop.

I pasted on my cheerleader smile.

My good-girl past has prepared me for this moment.

Doreen was good cover, too. She belonged in a kitchen making *falafel* and giving big grandma hugs. Not in a car with drugs. When the cop took my license, Doreen started chatting non-stop: children, recipes, scenery. She wouldn't stop, even when I glared.

Was she distracting the cop? Was her nervous talking a dead give-away? I didn't know.

The cop looked behind my head, sort of checking things out.

He's looking right at it . . . 700 pounds of pot.

Only a thin layer of clothes, a laundry basket, a basketball and five cardboard boxes lay between us and disaster.

"I clocked you going eighty."

Jesus.

I was paralyzed, numb.

I wish I could say my life flashed by, that I had an epiphany. Instead, I just wanted to get away with my crime, to escape detection.

We did.

I stared at the ticket the officer handed me and then, in the side mirror, at his dark chocolate boots walking away.

Did he see my hands shake?

The officer's final words "slow down, be safe" reverberated in my head for days. In one way, I felt more invincible than ever. In another, I felt watched. The two feelings fought inside me as I drove on with Doreen and the pot.

After the speeding incident in November, Dane and I barely talked.

"There's nothing happening, Jen," he would say.

I didn't believe him.

Doreen had sworn she'd never tell, but I knew she'd ratted me out. Otherwise, Dane would call. Otherwise, I'd be driving.

There was nothing I could do. So, I hunkered down, went inside myself, and thought more about my life.

In October, I'd moved into another apartment up the stairs, while Kelly moved across the courtyard. We both were ready for a change, but we still wanted to live at Burton's Place—close to each other, but not too close.

The new apartment with its high ceiling and towering stained glass window became my new home, my church.

I prayed. Cried. Listened to mournful music and danced on the mosaic steps that led to my bedroom. Something had shifted.

I wanted to give to others, to those who needed help, but I didn't know how . . . or where.

When my friend told me about the church that housed the homeless, I decided to volunteer. I slept overnight in the upstairs chapel, while fifty homeless men and women crashed on the floor downstairs. In the morning I gave each person a cup of Orangeade and a doughnut.

After the second time, I stopped going. I couldn't stand my guilt. *I spend so much money without thinking.*

In the morning, I'd cross the courtyard to Kelly's front door with my mug of coffee. I'd meet Brian from Unit No. 4 for lunch in the courtyard where we'd sit on wood-slatted chairs. Then we'd gather with friends on the upstairs deck for afternoon drinks.

At night, I lit candles and burned incense between deep, questioning conversations with new friends: Lane, who was introduced to me by Susan; or James, whom I casually dated.

Stefan and I had drifted apart. We'd begun our journey together, and the last year had been a glorious ride. Now, I was searching for something different, a place I had to go alone. When Stefan hugged me, I no longer felt safe. Although he talked freely about giving and feeling more love, he felt cold, totally self-absorbed. I didn't understand his obsession with a woman who channeled new age information.

Lane was just the opposite. He was lively with a big wide smile. We shared drinks at the Cocteau Twins concert, talked long into the night, and ran barefoot in the rain. Lane could see me the way I *wanted* to be seen. I could see in his eyes that he liked what he saw.

I thrived on our friendship. I thrived on one-on-one connections, deep conversations. I wanted to know how and what other people thought and felt. I wanted to *listen.*

Lane went outward and James went inward. I could *feel* James—especially his pain. James was pale and his walk was sort of a sulk, as though he carried a burden no one could see—as though he knew something *I* didn't.

I wanted to know.

James had a secret. He showed me the tapes hidden under his bed, an electric synthesizer pushed to the side in the spare room.

He composed music.

This time James brought a CD.

"You'll like it," he said, and handed it to me to play.

I'd already opened the wine. Another bottle waited on the counter, just in case.

When Australian singer, musician, composer Lisa Gerrard wailed on the CD, I turned the volume up and James closed his eyes half-way. In between wine and cigarettes we talked and traded stories about our dreams, disappointments, and fears. Candle wax dripped and ashtrays overflowed like bad dreams and dirty laundry. We could trust each other with the good and the bad, the clean and the dirty.

We shared experiences we had had, scary ones we couldn't explain. Like my vivid, kaleidoscope dreams. Like whispers I'd heard since childhood in the space between awake and asleep. About my dreams of creating art, directing multiperformance events, opening a boutique. Talk, not action. *I did none of those things. What if I should fail?*

Safer not to try. I didn't know it then, but James was my mirror—my partner in pain, my shadow side, the money addict, the victim who walked through life with unfulfilled desires and dreams.

It would be another year before I'd find the tools to do the real inner work, tackle my hurt, and move through my fleeting emotions.

In the meantime, I want to feel.

Ceci, a Cuban friend who owned a Pilates studio, knew I was investigating. She thought I needed to find the right man. So, she introduced me to Bruce, a recovering alcoholic who had earned his wealth through pure hard work.

Ceci was right. Bruce was a prize.

But my life had shifted. I wasn't ready for a committed relation-ship or for any relationship beyond casual. Bruce was looking for a wife, and I had nothing to give. My focus was on myself. Strangely, this didn't bother Bruce. He just kept on giving. He brought over cases of bottled water; took me to The Palms, a fancy Chicago steak house; and secured twelfth row seats at the Chicago Bulls' game where I could almost reach out and touch Michael Jordon.

Without my lucrative cross-country trips, I was running out of money fast. Bruce didn't ask questions about my money or why I didn't work. After three years of easy marijuana money, it didn't occur to me to get another job. I was caught in a mirage and still believed Dane would call, that a trip would happen soon. Most important, Bruce gave me space to talk about my adventures and where I wanted to go.

I knew where I wanted to go: India. "You have to go," the girl-with-the-dark-hair had said.

When I looked in my shoebox, I could see cardboard between the stacks of cash. Only $8,000 remained. I could pay my rent and eat out for a couple of months, if I was careful. And I wasn't.

Would I be okay?

Sure I would. My life would work out, just like it always had when I was little.

I stood defiant with hands on my hips, staring at my mom. She wanted me to call the doctor, but I didn't like to talk to people I didn't know, even if I did need a checkup.

"Jen, you should make the call yourself. You're thirteen years old."

I pleaded with my eyes. Was she really going to make me? She loved me, and I knew that meant I didn't have to take responsibility for myself. Mom was always there. She'd make the call. She'd take care of me.

Somehow, everything always worked out.

Okay, I was a *little* worried. It had been three months since Dane called.

And I *had* to go to India. The girl-with-the-long-dark-hair had said so. I didn't know when, or if, such a trip would happen. I didn't have enough money to pay rent, much less buy airline tickets. When Bruce offered to pay for my ticket, with no strings attached, I made plans. Bruce had been a member of AA for years. He understood my desire to work on myself. I'd fly into Bombay, hop a commuter plane to the city of Pune, and stay at the commune for six weeks.

My parents weren't thrilled about India or the commune. They didn't understand why I would pack half my bags with maroon-colored clothes—the only color worn inside the commune—and fly alone to a country they'd only seen on TV. Still, they were supportive and trusting, even as their usual unanswered question lingered between us: "How do you have the money?"

For years, I'd maneuvered around that question. They knew Dane supported me, that I assisted him with his business ventures, but I invented the details: the printing shop, the laundry mat chains, the medical supply company. Last year, I'd told them I had a part-time waitressing job.

How can I ever come clean?

My mom and I talked on the phone almost every other day, and I wanted to please my dad.

How could I shatter their picture of me?

To them, India was shattering enough.

One month later, I flew to India with a promise to call my mom at each stop along the way.

First impressions in India were of the senses. Dust penetrated my nostrils. My lips were cracked, dehydrated from the fifteen-hour flight. People were everywhere in the Bombay airport, rushing, shoving to get out the door. Chaos. A sea of fog covered the doorway to the outside. Gas fumes stung my eyes.

When I found my way through the cloud, arms reached out for coins. People swarmed, clanked, and banged. Buses honked. I was frightened. I had no one to greet me in this very foreign land.

Then, I saw the taxi. At last, something familiar. The driver wove through the chaos of Bombay's streets blasting Madonna's "Holiday" through the speakers, a tape the taxi driver had chosen on my American behalf. "All American girls like Madonna."

He was right. I did feel more at home.

In Pune, the man in the rickshaw called me "blonde" and then tried to charge me triple the agreed-upon fare for the mile-long ride to the commune. Nearby, I rented a scooter and a flat with marble floors. I drove the chaotic dirt roads, beeping like the taxi drivers had taught me on my way to the commune. I avoided cows and trucks stacked with furniture and buses filled with people.

Every morning at 5:30 a.m., I went to the commune for a one-hour meditation. I returned at 10 a.m. to take the free meditations offered, the private bodywork or counseling sessions, and to sign up for seminars and intensives, one of them a seven-day dance and movement therapy workshop. The commune was filled with people from all over the world—the US, Europe, Holland, and India. I loved the diversity.

I swam in the commune pool in my maroon two-piece bathing suit, modest compared to my usual bikini. Met a man. Rode his motorcycle. Felt abandoned when he left so quickly after I told him I was there to meditate. Eventually I realized that some men—and women—considered the commune a kind of Club Med where they could connect with each other.

I didn't care what they thought.

This trip was not about a man.

In India, I had a date with God.

I managed to call my parents from the corner, when the phone was available. I guess it wasn't often enough. When I returned, my mother often told the story of how I "went off to India and just never called."

To my parents, going to India was a sign something was wrong, that I was lost, directionless.

To me, India was the opposite, a torpedo pointing the way home.

After two weeks, I saw the girl-with-the-dark-hair. Her eyes widened in disbelief. "You came!" And we hugged. I told her I was interviewing for the group, Path of Love, which had a waiting list.

"I can't imagine how you'll get in."

I felt crestfallen.

Only seasoned *sanyassins,* people who'd been devotees for a long time, were chosen. I was determined to be accepted. I knew the group was my next step. I felt electric. Like I was walking in a different world, and something, or someone beyond me, was leading the way.

The third day, I was called for a second interview. On the fourth day, my name was posted. It was a dramatic moment. I had tingles up and down my arms.

I got in.

Rumors swirled about the group. No one knew what was involved. Once in, I found the seven-day process arduous, intense—electrifying. The process—to which we were sworn to secrecy—included tactics to confront the ego and the parts of ourselves that kept us from living to our fullest potential. Active five-to-eight-hour meditations fueled the fire that had rekindled a year ago when I'd read *Adventures Beyond the Body.*

I'd felt this fire inside since I was eleven, but I hadn't understood—then. Years later, my partner, Tim, would teach me to fuel the blazing, roaring fire inside me.

This fire was powerful, beyond measure.

On the last day of the group—not in meditation, but during lunch—the mystical moment of healing came.

Once our seven days of silence was broken, the idle chatter began again. I felt unnerved. "I *really* don't want to talk," I said to the woman next to me.

She placed her hand in mine. "Then don't."

I went silent and felt space . . . nothingness. For the first time, I allowed myself to relax, to not care what other people thought . . . to *be* myself. For once, I was *not* the smiling cheerleader.

Then, it happened.

My mind unlocked. A movie screen appeared, like a theater in my head. Even if I'd tried, I knew I couldn't have stopped the multi-colored pictures that flipped, one after the other, in my mind's eyes. With my head dropped to my chest and my eyes closed, heat rushed through my body. I saw Dane's face, as he opened the car door for me, as he took a bag from my hands, as he showered me with gifts.

Why this? Why Dane?

Then the message became clear as the pictures in my mind showed all the scenarios, all the different times, all the different ways Dane had shown his love for me and I had taken his love for granted.

In the pictures, I felt Dane's feelings seeping into my bones. What I saw about myself made me sick. I couldn't stop crying. Alone that night, I cried some more. I'd been shown something about myself that rocked my foundation. I felt a new pain—an awareness of my selfishness, my judgments. The unloving places inside.

How I hurt others.

The next day I felt pummeled, exhausted.

Open.

I respected what I'd found. I'd never felt more in touch with myself. I'd never felt more free. On the last day, to declare my devotion to my inner spiritual growth, and to Osho's teachings, I applied for a Sanskrit name.

There was no turning back.

The night I received my *mandala* was thrilling, a one-of-a-kind ritual. I sat among the other fifteen men and women who would be receiving new names and mandalas as twenty other participants from Path of Love watched from the sidelines. A woman in a white robe hung the sacred emblem—a disk with Osho's picture attached to wooden beads—from my neck. Then she gave me a paper with my new name and whispered the name "Apurva" in my ear as music played.

I was joyful—no, ecstatic—a big rush that blew the lid off the other part of my life: the money, the shopping, the men, and my greed. The experience blew the lid off my winning at gymnastics, academics, dance when I was nine . . . thirteen . . . eighteen.

In that moment, the world felt much bigger than *me*.

Afterward, my friends stacked garlands of gardenias around my neck until they reached from shoulders to chin.

I reached toward Rafia—the leader of the Path of Love—and he took my arm.

Linked together, traditional flowers high around my neck, we passed laughing people. Light bounced off the marble from the twinkle lights overhead.

I pretended it was starlight. I looked up and counted the *stars* that shone overhead. *One, two, three . . . and, there's the big dipper.*

I'm seven, looking up at the sky from our front porch. "Keep looking, and it will appear," Mom says. All of a sudden, I see the ladle. Mom calls it the big dipper. As I look, I see the smaller one close by. The stars seem to move closer to Earth, so close I can reach up and touch them with my fingers. In touch with the stars, I feel much bigger than I am, like the world is an extra-special place, and I am an extra-special little girl.

On that night in India, the world—and I—were special once again, and like a long-lost friend, the magic I'd felt as a child, reappeared.

Returning home, I asked everyone to call me Apurva. I invited my friends to sit in a circle, to be honest, and to share how they really felt.

Just like in India.

"It'll be good for our friendship—for *ourselves.* Let's start by holding hands."

I shared my feelings with Kelly, Brian, and Lane. Kelly looked stunned when I told her I loved her but that sometimes she didn't listen when I talked. Brain and Lane looked around, clearly uncomfortable. They didn't understand, and they definitely didn't want their feelings out there in front of everyone.

Finally, Brian spoke "I have to leave."

Then Kelly stood up.

One by one, they gave their excuses and left the circle.

It didn't matter. They were willing to try, so I loved them all the more.

Brunch with Bruce didn't go well either. He felt confronted— almost offended—by my new views. When I talked about wanting to break with my attachments to the material world, he misunderstood, thinking I was judging *his* material success.

Possibly I was naïve when I talked about the teachings, but I had to start somewhere. My friends clearly expected me to be the same person as before.

But I wasn't.

Within two months, I knew I had to move. I was finished with Chicago. I needed to explore, to *really* take off. My old life no longer fit. I applied at the Indian embassy and received a seven-year visa for India. I beamed when the attendant stamped my passport.

By now, Dane had called me to drive a small load from Chicago to Detroit. It wasn't much money but gave me enough—about $5,000—to make it through the next few months.

Before my April departure date, I went sailing. The director of a trance dance institution had invited two of us to the Bahamas, me and Audrey, a free-floating artist from the dance seminar. For the occasion, I changed my hair from short blond to long braid-extensions with two smaller blue braids on the left. I flew to the Bahamas, found my friends, and boarded a forty-foot sailboat headed for the Exumas.

With open sails and open waters, we snorkeled in the nude and drew with pastels on deck. Paddling in the jimmy skiff with Audrey, we explored deserted islands, drifts of sand, unique rocks. On one island lived a boy: just one house, just one boy. For two days he took Audrey and me out to his house for grilled fish, on his boat to a secret lookout. For two days I fantasized I could make a new life.

Romanticizing again.

I fell in love with that boy—or did I fall in love with the clear turquoise water and white sand? I *think* he told me he was nineteen. I returned to Chicago, still thinking about him.

Should I forget India and go to the boy in the Exumas?

I called him, and this time I *think* he told me he was sixteen. I was twenty-nine. Time for me to go deeper than what could be an unhealthy relationship.

I would go to India.

In May I sold my BMW to Dane, and with that $7,000 in my pocket—the only money I had—I waved good-bye to my parents and to Kelly, Lane, Brian, and Stefan. I'd parted with Bruce before I'd gone sailing. He knew he'd lost me to India, and he didn't understand.

First stop was Cologne, Germany. I'd promised to volunteer as staff for Path of Love, a repeat of the retreat I'd attended in India. I stayed in a flat with a German businessman I'd met at the commune in India. The second week, after he'd crawled into the bed where I was sleeping to "cuddle," I moved into a room above the spiritual center where Rafia had temporary quarters.

After six weeks, I was tired of the harsh cold of Cologne, but my feelings for Rafia remained warm and affectionate.

"What are you going to do in India?" he asked.

I shrugged.

"It's passé, Jen. India's not like it was in the seventies."

Where is he going with this?

"There's nothing new there that you can't find in the States."

I'm listening.

"You should go to San Diego."

"Why?"

Seriously, California?

"It's where the group came from."

That was new information. Now, I was *really* listening.

In actuality, I hadn't had time to fall in love with India. I'd fallen in love with this group and the process that confronted the ego. After the sharing and meditations, I'd feel open, elated, more loving.

I talked with Rafia about my views of life after death, and when I used the words "going home," he said the words reminded him of the San Diego teachings. He was not involved with the California community but was the leader of another group that had branched off from San Diego. He explained how I could contact the San Diego group from Cologne.

And that's exactly what I did.

The woman on the phone told me I had to do the seven-day intensive first.

"I'm in," I told her. "I'm coming."

I'm home, I told the trees of my childhood.

I faxed my application, got a one-way ticket to Chicago, flew to Phoenix where I met Dane, and drove a load of marijuana across the country. Then, as planned, Dane paid me to drive the white Suburban from Detroit to Ohio, where I saw my parents and my brother. From there, I drove my belongings—including a half a million dollars stashed in the back—to Southern California. Dane had moved from Phoenix to a new house by the sea. The car I'd sold to Dane was in his garage, waiting for me. Like God had known all along— even before I'd figured it out—that San Diego was my destination.

Everything seemed primed for my move.

The month was August, the year 1998. A time for radical inner and outer change.

Other changes had taken place in the months I'd been out of the trafficking loop. There was a new setup called Speed Racer. Now Dane's people were transporting up to 7,000-pound loads camouflaged as a racecar and equipment.

The minute I arrived in San Diego, I was pulled right back in. It wasn't Dane's fault. I just couldn't resist.

I counted the remaining money in my pocket: $4,000.

On this next trip, I'd make thirty.

Thirty thousand dollars in four days.

Some things in my life had changed, but not this.

CHAPTER 14

SPEED RACER

I was startled when Rob walked through the front door of Dane's La Jolla home. He didn't even knock. I hadn't seen Rob since Maui—four years ago—when I'd mentioned his marijuana involvement and he'd left, angry that I knew. Today was only my second day in Southern California, and I'd barely adjusted to the ocean's waves and Dane's redwood deck. Now Rob was here. *Should I act angry? Standoffish? Or pretend like nothing had happened?*

He smiled, so I said nothing, just reached out my arms when he walked toward me. I didn't hesitate, grateful that his anger had finally cooled. My memory of the 1995 Maui trip was still fresh, and Rob's touch still felt good.

That morning I'd begun to unpack. Dane had taken the money out of the Suburban, but my belongings were still inside. I didn't have a home, but at least I had a car to drive—the BMW I'd sold to Dane.

"Actually, Jen, you can just have it back."

He said if we towed it behind the truck on one of our trips, I wouldn't have to reimburse him the $7,000 he'd paid me for it two months before.

I agreed.

He also invited me to stay in his guest room until I found a place to live.

Dane's move to La Jolla was recent, and I hadn't seen his new home before. I knew the San Diego area from previous visits with Dane—one in 1994 when I'd met his parents. They lived in the oceanfront condo they'd owned since Dane was a child. I remembered the visit well because I'd liked Dane's father, a retired—still respected—diagnostic physician from Los Angeles. I'd seen Dane's likeness in both his gentle father and his nervous, chatting mother. And I'd wondered if Dane was *the one.*

But, now it was 1998.

I was a different person this time. I felt far away from Dane's focus on the material aspects of life—the focus I'd shared until Joeluine died and I was thrown into a spiritual search. Now I saw the drug money mainly as the means to finance that search.

Dane didn't say anything, but I knew he felt the gap between us.

For whatever reason—no matter the history between us—I felt that the gods had chosen for me to be closer in proximity to Dane, closer than I'd been for years, living in his house. After the images of him that had appeared when I meditated in India, I wanted to appreciate Dane. I wanted us to heal.

This was my chance. This is the way I saw my life now, looking inward, then outward, for divine signs and signals of where I should be, what I should do.

I felt comfortable about our next trip, even anticipated it, when Dane told me Rob—after all these years—was actually willing to drive with me. I prepared for the trip, packed traveling clothes, bought my ticket, and flew to Phoenix with Dane and Rob.

When we drove to the resort on Ina Road, I saw how drastically the setup had changed. Rob and I would drive one white Dodge Ram pickup, a dually with four large wheels on the back that would pull the large trailer. A matching pickup would precede us as a lookout.

I was overwhelmed.

The setup was bigger, with more people, including some I didn't know. Originally made to haul a race car, the trailer now would tow large loads of marijuana—from 5,000 to 9,000 pounds—across the country. Our final drop-off location: the Poconos.

I'd driven the marijuana to New York only twice, both times with Dane, and not since 1997. The last time we went to Amityville— which I knew only through the '80s movie, *The Amityville Horror.* We'd met Patrick—a loud New Yorker—and his wife, Rona, who had a cockney accent and said she was from London. We'd leaned against the Formica countertop as Dane and Patrick unloaded the marijuana into the garage.

Though I hadn't been to New York since, Rob had—regularly— for almost a year, on trips Dane had told me weren't happening.

This time, Rob let slip the numerous marijuana trips he'd taken to New York.

It was confirmed: Dane hadn't wanted me to drive.

Maybe it was the speeding incident or maybe Dane didn't like the change in our relationship. I didn't know, and I didn't ask. He'd asked me this time, and I wanted the money. This wasn't a battle worth fighting. I was grateful just to drive.

In the hotel room on Ina Road, Dane handed me the blue polo shirt I'd wear for the next three days. "Speed Racer" was stitched onto the front. Khaki pants or shorts would complete our attire. Rob and the other two men would wear them, too.

That night in the hotel dining room, I sat at the candle-lit table anticipating the money I'd make, nervous as I looked across the table at two men from Detroit I didn't know. They were Johnny's wife's nephews, and I didn't have any say about it. To me, they seemed young—too young.

Were they even twenty-five?

They acted like teenagers, awkward and shy. Rob and I called them "the boys."

The name stuck.

I could picture them in the future, destined to become the Detroit men I knew with protruding stomachs, balding pates, and long noses. One of the boys was stick thin, the other, muscular and good-looking. Too good-looking, I'd think later, as I kissed him in the hotel at the end of one of our trips. I pushed the fish around my plate as the men planned the trip.

"They'll drive in the front truck," Dane said.

Everyone nodded in unspoken agreement.

When Dane pointed, the boy with the dark hair seemed to expand with pride. His feeling of importance was contagious and soon encircled the table.

Drug talk. Banter. Male testosterone.

I felt important, too. Driving across the country with an illegal load of drugs alongside the men and "the boys," outwitting the law, making all that money. The excitement caressed my thigh better than any man could. I was drawn in, attracted to the wild feeling of it all. I couldn't turn it down. Maybe it *was* an addiction.

Where are my spiritual yearnings now?

Sidelined maybe, but the money *did* pay for my search.

That night in our hotel room, I rummaged through Dane's leather toiletry bag. Once I found the face-scrub, I washed my face. Dane brushed his teeth with his bright green toothbrush from Costco.

I turned the television volume down, and Dane climbed into bed.

He wore boxers, his usual.

I wore my blue nightgown, a favorite, painted with dancing ballerinas holding umbrellas. I'd worn it on other drug trips.

I felt safe in this familiar routine.

"The trailer's been loaded."

I stared at the white trailer, imagining what was inside that I couldn't see. Sometimes I never saw the marijuana.

Today in Tucson's dry heat, I wore shorts, a ponytail, snappy clean tennis shoes, bobby sox, and a ribbon in my hair.

I laughed when Dane handed me the yellow walkie-talkie.

What a boy thing, I thought to myself. "What's this for?"

My laughter died when Dane glared. He was serious. "The boys will have one, too. They'll radio to tell you and Rob what's ahead."

The boys in the front truck would watch for trouble—cops, roadblocks, closed roads, or checkpoints. With Dane's help, they'd make our hotel reservations, pay for the rooms, and get the keys. Dane and the boys would have everything set up so Rob and I could concentrate on our job—towing gigantic loads of marijuana from Tucson to New York.

We all knew the boys could face real physical danger: if a cop started to pull us over, they would create an accident—fast—no matter what it took.

I thought it was ridiculous—all this story. All this drama.

"You don't understand," Dane told me.

I probably didn't. Sure, bigger loads meant bigger risk and bigger money, but I skipped to the truck with a pink ribbon in my hair, even more naïve than "the boys."

Dane jerked his head with a snap to alleviate the pain from an old injury. The motion was familiar, like his tailored pants and crocodile belt. His behavior and his clothes were symbols of comfort, like eating Cheerios in the morning when I was ten.

Like the relief I felt when the marijuana is taken away safely at the end of the trip.

The front truck matched ours, white with tan stripes on the side. When I looked at the two trucks side by side, I felt safe, too.

The four of us were a team.

But, there was more protection. The list kept growing.

Dane would follow us in a rental car, protecting us from behind. A Mexican couple I'd never met would drive an hour ahead of us on the lookout for traffic jams and cops hiding in bushes. I pictured the woman-I-didn't-know and her husband-who-needed-the-money in my head. Why were they doing this? How much were they getting paid?

Later, I wondered if it was worth the price—their pictures on a federal hot sheet.

Once on the road, I always felt safe. I mean *really* safe, especially with Dane behind us.

What could happen to us?

I hadn't learned my lesson yet, the lesson I should have learned alongside Joeluine that morning in Phoenix. That time she was so hung-over that she was turned away at the airport. "When Dane's here everything's supposed to be okay," she had said. But, it wasn't okay.

At first, I was intimidated by the big truck, the trailer we towed, the strange new long setup. But once I put my hands on the steering wheel, I was in control. I felt just as important as I had during dinner.

This big-deal setup changed the way we were viewed by the public. We didn't blend in any more. Drivers in cars gawked when we pulled into the gas stations. Gas station attendants with stained teeth, Mohawks, or hair-sprayed flips asked questions in slow Texas, Oklahoma, or Missouri drawls.

"Whatcha got in that there trailer? . . . A car? . . . A real racecar?"

Their eyes would become large, hungry.

Like, we were *somebody* and, by talking to us, they were special.

I felt special, too.

"Yeah," we'd tell them. "A race car."

We felt even more special, more invincible, as days passed and we continued to fool everyone and transport our load of 7,000 pounds of marijuana across nine states.

By now, Frankie's brother, Johnny, had taken over the Detroit job. Frankie had gone to prison when the pot and money were confiscated in 1994. Now released, he'd "turned Christian," Dane had said with a smirk. "No way does he want to be involved." Sure, Frankie had gone to prison, but nobody—including Dane—ever admitted that it could happen to any of us. The list of protective measures just grew a little longer.

During Speed Racer, Johnny would coordinate the marijuana's drop-off. In the darkness of night, Rob would pull off at a rest stop a few exits before the Detroit Metro Airport. A U-Haul would appear behind us, and Johnny—and men I didn't know—would unload half the boxes.

Our last stop: the Poconos, Pennsylvania.

In the Poconos, once again I saw Matt and the New York-cockney couple. The ex-Londoner showed she was in charge of her house by inviting me to sit on her velvety blue couch, our feet resting on shag carpet. The frilly matching drapes and fussy figurines were like her chatter about secrets, recipes, and craft tips. I was silent, trying to dry my sweaty hands on my pant legs.

Both of us pretended the waiting was normal. We were *girlfriends* having lunch while *the boys* unloaded box after box of drugs into an underground cellar in the back.

I didn't like this house, and I didn't like sitting here chatting like silly wives like it was normal to have two tons of marijuana around.

This is way too much, way too obvious, way too dangerous.

There was a house next door. Not right next door, but one and a half lots over—close enough. They *could* see. Someone *could* know. All it took was a phone call. It had happened to Frankie.

I chose to believe it wouldn't happen to us.

By the time the trailer was unloaded, it was late—sometimes 5 p.m. Someone had to drive the empty trailer back to Detroit—usually me. I'd make it to Detroit by 3 a.m. and rent a room near the airport, anxious to take the first flight back to San Diego, anxious to get back home. If I was lucky, Rob and I would arrive at the Poconos early in the day and unload by noon. Then, Rob would accompany me back. We'd arrive in Detroit by 8 p.m., in time to catch the red-eye back to San Diego, where we'd both arrive home exhausted—a mess of fatigue and hidden stress.

Once home, fatigue crept into my bones. I had no more stamina.

The following days I'd take rock salt baths, buy new lip gloss, take Pilates class. But nothing erased the grittiness inside. That's when the voices of the star-struck people of the Lone Star State, the Sooner State, the Show-Me State echoed in my head.

"Where ya been, Jen? Whatcha got in that there trailer."

Back home, the trailer called *my life* hauled two and a half tons of guilt. I'd looked down on the poor people who'd gaped at our "race car" trailer, but I was poorer than they. Poor in spirit. To redeem myself, I ran straight into God's arms and into a communal way of living. Back on track, doing the right thing.

Ecstatic meditation.

Shaking off the layers of my ego that blinded me.

But the joker inside wouldn't let me go. He pointed his finger, keeping me bound to the desire for more money, to the acts that the Feds would call "a crime."

Despite the move, my prayers, meditation and cleansing, I didn't confront my desire for money or my continuing drives across the country. When I was with my new spiritual community, this part of my life stayed safely tucked inside, a safe place, like the pocket of my craft apron where I'd stowed secrets when I was nine.

My stay in the room-off-the garden at Dane's house by the ocean in La Jolla lasted only a few months. Once I'd made enough money and completed the San Diego community's seven-day seminar, I lounged around, writing in my journal. I relaxed with the clinking of ice cubes in my tea, thinking about the dolphins, thinking about India—but *what about my life?*

Dane was getting exasperated. "Jen, what *are* you going to do?"

I was embarrassed.

What he didn't say was *when are you going to find your own place to live?*

We both knew I couldn't stay here forever. We weren't lovers. We were business partners, and I was on a different personal path.

Dane's words, though gentle, reminded me of my mother's when she'd wanted me to call the doctor. The words forced me to take action. The next day, I called the community center and asked for more work.

They needed volunteers.

The next two weeks, I helped the management team prepare for the monthly intensive seminar. I was asked to join the management team, to staff the seminar and assist Ian—the manager of the intensive—and his team of three. In Germany, Rafia had told me to find Ian, "a special man."

But first there was Dane.

And Dane had met Aaron.

Rob and Dane had rented a limo for the evening. I heard them come in late, about one in the morning. Then feminine giggling and high heels clicking on the brick walkway. From inside the guestroom, I squeezed my eyes to stop the tears. I pulled the blanket over my head and rolled over. I stifled my tears, crying into the cotton fabric.

Dane isn't mine. I'm not his. I have no right.

I'd discarded Dane years ago. Though distant, we'd held the relationship rope taut between us. Now he'd let go.

The pain surprised me. Did I love Dane? I was surprised by the intensity of my feelings of loss. He'd been my lover . . . my *father* . . . my security.

Now he wasn't.

He'd wanted me; needed me; loved me best.

Now, he didn't.

He'd been the source of those beautiful boxes of cash.

He still was.

The next morning, like every other morning before, I slipped through Dane's front door to his bedroom to cuddle with him. This time the bedroom door was locked. I went back to the guest room. An hour later, I returned.

This time Dane's bedroom door was open, and I walked in. Everything looked the same—except for the pair of Chanel black wedge heels in the corner.

Small. Expensive.

Not mine.

I felt unraveled.

The next day—first day of the seminar—we meditated before the participants came in.

Then I stood, dressed in black slacks and a black lace shirt, facing the wall. The pop music pounded, and I began to dance manically, screaming, shaking out my hands, pounding . . . pounding . . . stomping my feet. I was shaking Dane out of me in the Miracle of Love cathartic meditation.

I was afraid. And, this time, it wasn't about the money. I was losing a piece of me. I was losing Dane.

CHAPTER 15

COME HOME

The first time I met Aaron was by accident. I'd walked into the main house to make coffee and there she was, curled up on Dane's couch just like *I* had been only a month ago when Rob had walked in.

Seeing Aaron surprised me and took me off center. My anger sparked. She looked comfortable on the couch, youthful with the ponytail layered on top of her head, even though she was 38—eight years older than I was. Blond highlighted hair spilled over a hidden band, and arced high. I thought of the Arabian horses prancing proudly around the ring, their tails held high, at shows Dane and I had attended four years before.

Red-framed glasses perched atop Aaron's round cheeks and swallowed her face. The glasses were large and nerdish, but they increased Aaron's cuteness . . . and my jealousy.

Do the glasses mean she's smarter than me?

With one leg underneath the other, Aaron looked like she belonged on Dane's couch. Now *I* was the outsider.

As Aaron flipped through *Condé Nast* magaine, I tried to sneak past her to the kitchen. I wanted to disappear, but she looked up and saw me. First a pause, then, "Hi . . . I'm Aaron."

Her smile was disarming, and my anger disintegrated like tiny particles of sand.

The words she'd spoken were simple—only three words—but in my jealousy, I imagined she'd said her name more softly and delicately than I would have said mine.

Did she know me, the girl staying in Dane's house?

What had Dane told her, if anything at all? I wanted to know.

Her strong hand grip staked her claim on Dane and his house. Just seeing her, I felt taken aback. Yet, I felt no jealousy from Aaron.

Could she feel mine? Wasn't I still beautiful, cute, bubbly enough to be a threat?

I felt envy, guilt, and darkness. I'd been replaced.

The next week, I moved out of Dane's house into a North County home near the coast, an affluent part of San Diego County. The two couples and single woman who lived in the '80s-style house participated in the community, like I did. We would practice the teachings together. Moving to this house showed the community I was making a deeper commitment, plus with Aaron around, I'd felt uncomfortable staying with Dane.

The house was a forty-minute drive from the community center, but I didn't mind. I had the downstairs bedroom to myself and two palms in the back. The trees towered fifty feet above us. At night, the wind, swirling between their fronds, whistled a tune I recognized from the Ohio firs of my childhood. Their music carried me down to the ocean, swept me under the waves, and returned me to myself.

I liked this house, and I liked my life volunteering every day at the center. Focused on the spiritual, I had no reason to spend my money, except for basics like rent and food.

I treated volunteering like a job. A job I wanted. My motivation was fueled by my desire to be closer to God—to be closer to myself.

The community's teachings focused on finding "inner freedom."
What does this mean? I asked myself.

Part of me knew. Since India, I'd had glimpses—moments of unlimited space inside of myself—where time slowed down. Then, I could really breathe. Then, I really felt alive. I knew there was more for me to understand and to experience.

I pursued this path with all my passion, like I had my dancing, my gymnastics.

For the first time in four years, I had a routine, a focus. I hadn't had something to look forward to—a purpose—since I had left dance. I staffed seminars and confronted my own shadow and ego-driven behaviors as I helped other people unveil their dark places. This time I was serving a higher purpose.

At the end of each three-hour meditation, my tension would melt. My thoughts would slow to rest, and I'd feel a sense of home—a particular sense of wholeness I'd never felt before.

The inner rules that had stifled and stopped me had been hidden until now. I began to pull out those old judgments and complaints as though I was pulling the white synthetic stuffing from the gingerbread dolls my mother and I made at Christmastime.

And like the Christmas days of my childhood, when the chain of gingerbread dolls were hung above the mantle, I was content. Everything was in its proper place.

Neat. Perfect. Until self-judgment swept me away. I'd feel better if I were perfect, *wouldn't I?*

When imperfections appeared, I felt like I was exploding, along with my perfect childhood gingerbread chain—button eyes popping, gingham apron splitting apart, white cotton stuffing exposed.

I wasn't perfect, and I didn't like those darker parts I saw inside. But underneath the tears and pain the sparkles danced—ten million of them—creating ten million opportunities for how I could live my life. Through practice, meditation, and study, the world was opening up to me. Not on the outside like when I'd first met Dane and begun living the high life, but inside, where it mattered.

My darling, everything you want is inside, intoned my inner divine voice.

"Come home" was not a phrase only in my childhood dreams and memories, but one used by my new guru at the community, whom I'd not yet met.

This time I followed rules. They weren't "have-to" rules, but guidance—the structure the guru set up for the community to follow, though the rules were always changing.

At first I relished those rules that were like a revolving door where I had to stay on my toes and dash through at the peak moment. I had to scramble out of the box I was in and demolish habits I'd formed. To prove to myself that I was serious, I took part in an experiment set up by the guru. We were to "let go" of our attachments to choice and personal preference.

I gave up my collection of designer clothes.

I took them to the community "store," where I tried on other clothes left by other participants. My excitement flipped over into frustration, tears falling when I couldn't find anything I liked. In one moment, all my clothes were gone. I left with an armful, "just enough," nothing more, nothing less.

But it looks like less.

I wanted to believe letting go of my clothes centered me, gave me balance.

But, it wasn't fair. Thousands of dollars of clothes carefully chosen and bought—five years of fine-tuning as I bought clothes I'd never dreamed I could afford: the blue $1,000 Paul Smith fur coat, the red $600 Prada sandals, the long $900 silk skirt by Dries Van Noten.

Few people in the community could shop like this, and it showed in the quality of their clothes. I couldn't help noticing this. Was I judging?

I wanted to want to let go of the clothes, *didn't I?*

Even when I was a child, my family had joked that I was a "princess" because of my eye for style and my appreciation for nice things. With the successful farming business he had built, my father provided us with everything we needed and gave us a solid upper middle-class life, but we didn't have money to throw around—not like Dane, and not like I had now.

With my new experience of money and expensive clothes, had I become a snob? After so much hard work in the community trying to uncover my desires and to reach beneath them, I couldn't ignore this painful new knowledge of myself. But, in the back of my mind, I also knew I could always buy more—so long as I had the marijuana money.

Community rules forbade us from "shopping." Wanting to be a "good disciple," to push myself, to grow—I followed the rules—those revolving rules. Usually, I rotated three pairs of pants and tops: the black Capri pants and coral sweater set, the black velour pants and tank top, the Capri jeans and blue T-shirt. My options had drastically shrunk.

The first day after my un-shopping I walked into the office wearing my favorite item, a red polka dot vintage dress. Ian looked up, then quickly looked away.

I felt shunned.

But Ian's look had nothing to do with me. The dress had belonged to his girlfriend. "She wore it only last week." Ian's voice was sharp. But he was a good disciple and tried to keep his feelings to himself.

At least I had good taste like his girlfriend did.

Two women I liked had chosen some of *my* clothes. But where were the rest? I knew the guru dressed nicely. Maybe the nicest clothes were sent to her or to someone on her team. I never saw them again.

Maybe my lesson was not to take everything personally, but I did.

When I was arrested, I missed my clothes like an old lover. Images of lost clothes like childhood flash cards: the gold velvet pants I wore out to dinner with Kelly in Chicago, the Cargo tank dress I layered in 1997 on New Year's Eve, the military pea coat that kept me warm as I stood beside Stefan and the small chopper plane in Virginia. *Every day another article of lost clothing comes painfully to mind. Something missing, something wrong.*

I'd said "none" when the prison therapist asked what items remained of those I'd purchased with illegal money. But I wanted to say, *I worked hard for those clothes.* It wasn't the *right* answer, and I still felt like a good girl who had to say the right thing. My words could affect what she thought of me, maybe the length of my sentence.

She may have thought *easy money—free money—funny money was easy to waste.* But I missed those damn clothes. *Fuck letting go of attachments.*

I hadn't fully appreciated the quality of those eight damned good years, when I shopped at whim in fancy, exclusive boutiques.

Was *that* a crime?

My clothes saga at the community was far from over.

"Jen, I think you need new clothes," Georgia told me. She was the guru's sister and CEO of the community.

I looked at her with open-mouthed surprise. "I gave away my clothes. Aren't we supposed to?"

She'd been away, living with the guru in Hawaii, but surely she knows.

"But look at what you're wearing!"

I looked down at my black stretch-pants and white tank. *Dull, lackluster, cheap.*

"Trust me, you need new clothes."

So, against what I'd been told—the rules given to the community—we went to shopping. I left Marshall's with three sundresses and two skirts, a total of less than $100. The price I usually paid for one Splendid tank top.

Georgia was the CEO. She knew what was okay and what wasn't, didn't she? But why had she told me not to tell? And why was *she* wearing a perfectly coordinated blue outfit, stylish on her voluptuous figure.

In this "chinny-house" moment, I saw that the guru, the management, and the followers did not always follow the same rules.

But who was I to criticize? Despite my best intentions, I still didn't face my other life, that life where I made boxfuls of money driving truckloads of marijuana from Tucson to New York.

Despite the intensity of the ensuing year with the community, I found time to drive *Mary Jane.*

During the past year, I'd participated in four seminars and staffed twelve others as a member of the management team. Now it was time for the annual Christmas party. We worked nonstop to prepare, putting systems and setups in place, planning and decorating and taking 4 a.m. group phone calls. The fire in my belly burned. We were preparing for the guru's arrival in San Diego after a year's seclusion.

I'm so excited. She's coming.

The feeling was similar to the one I'd had in my dream when I was told *they* were coming to take me home.

This was no dream. The guru was real, and she was coming.

By now, I was growing closer to Ian, the manager of the monthly intensives. The first time I'd met him, his back had been to mine. He'd looked up briefly to say hello, but I'd been too shy to say anything and just nodded. Ian was darkly handsome—as handsome as his girlfriend was sexy and beautiful. I'd worked closely with Ian on the management team for a year, and we'd developed a flow—Ian, the team, and myself. The routine of event-planning, logistics, and paperwork planted seeds between us that would sprout years later into a vital relationship.

We had some moments of connection but would eventually part ways, live on different continents and, a year later, find our way back to each other.

Enveloped in inner work and community business, my interest in the marijuana driving diminished. For the first time, I told Dane I couldn't go. "I'll be in the middle of the seminar."

He seemed startled. I'd never said no to a trip before and this was a Speed Racer trip worth $30,000.

"The seminar is important to me."

Dane chuckled. He couldn't believe I was giving up the cash . . . for this.

He didn't understand.

By now, a lot of people in my life didn't, not even Stefan, who was on his own journey. He'd moved to Key West and was slowly fading out of my life.

Dane called a month later. This time he offered to pay more. He "needed me." He had "no one else to turn to."

Nobody wanted to make $30,000?

A ton of pot? Sure. . . . Right behind me for four days. No problem.

Although it was only a week before the party, and I was one of two people in charge of the decorations, I finally said yes.

I wanted the money and knew, eventually, I'd *need* the money.

I still didn't have a job.

Maybe it was the large load Rob and I towed behind us in the white car trailer or the snowstorms we encountered in Colorado, Missouri, Illinois, and Pennsylvania or maybe my new life with the spiritual community. Whatever it was, this trip was even more exhausting than before. It felt disorganized, out of control—a mess.

Then came the snow.

Snow created a choice. Usually we'd be told in advance if a storm was coming—nobody wanted us stuck in the snow with a truckload of drugs. Dane tracked the weather and Rob called Dane: Should we drive through Colorado? Would our truck make it over the Colorado pass? Or should we detour and veer off into New Mexico? Would the trailer climb Colorado's steep mountain with the large load we towed behind, even without the snow?

Dane decided the truck wouldn't make it. The load was too big, over a ton.

The snow had begun in Joplin, Missouri. Flakes fell from the top of the St. Louis Arch, down the flying red "J" truck stop sign in Illinois, and blanketed the car tracks ahead of us in Ohio. In Pennsylvania we hit a snowstorm.

My eyes were tired. Visibility at night was worse with the high beams, and the snow had slowed me down. The roads were white, icy, slippery, and I felt like the big trailer was tied onto my back.

Stay focused, Jen. Gotta keep that trailer straight. Can't let the trailer pull the truck off track with its weight. Speed limit's now fifty-five in Illinois. Ohio. Don't get too close to the trucker coming on the right. Watch for the little car in front—the one that's slowing and speeding up. Careful not to tailgate.

Cold. Fried. Ready to go home—to my community.

Dane had flown to New York for drug business and was driving to the Poconos to meet us. Someone in charge—like Dane—needed to be there when the drugs were unloaded, to take responsibility for the promised marijuana, to make sure the quality was the same—the same bales the guy-who-picked-out the marijuana a week ago had claimed. Still, I was surprised to see Dane when Rob and I arrived.

Dane gave me a big smile and a peck on the cheek.

The marijuana had arrived safely. Dane grinned. Usually, I smiled, too, but this time Rob and I were exhausted. All that driving, all that snow.

"How was it?" Dane asked me, but turned to look at Rob.

The drug run is always about the men, and I'm just the girl—a sideshow act.

"The snow was blinding," Rob said.

"Slippery," I added, acting as though I hadn't been ignored.

"Well, good job, guys," Dane said, and slapped Rob on the back. He looked at me, "Dinner?"

I hesitated, but Rob said yes. I didn't want to go. I was too damn tired and looked forward to a glass of wine with Rob, alone.

Though Aaron and Dane had only been together for a year, I'd heard they were engaged. Later Dane confirmed it.

Dane isn't mine.

I'm not his.

But Dane planned the trips, took the lead. I knew Rob was taking some of the pressure off by helping Dane more, but did Rob really have any say about the business?

Who did?

Was it the Mexican men who grew the marijuana, sold it, and smuggled it across the border have control? Or was Tony, the man on the US side, really in command? Or did Dane and Johnny coordinate it all?

Maybe no one was in control.

Was it the money? Was it the drugs? Maybe it was both.

Drugs and money, they go hand-in-hand, said Uncle Sam.

Just like green eggs and ham, said Sam I am.

The updated childhood tune rang in my ears, but I couldn't be a child around the loads of marijuana.

Dane reserved Rob and me a room in the Poconos for the night. He slapped down the key—"Number 7" on a gold heart.

"Want another drink, Jen?" He ignored my answer and signaled the waiter.

Still taking care of me. Never mind what I really want.

"No, I'm fine."

Dane's "Come on, stay" was subtle and familiar, but I held my ground.

"I'm tired."

Rob chimed in. "Me, too."

Dane looked down at the tabletop. I could tell he was hurt that I—we—didn't want to stay with him.

I had to give Dane up—to let go. And, slowly, I was.

When Rob and I pulled into the hotel driveway, it was dark. Snowflakes danced in front of the headlights like the ballerinas on my blue nightgown. My mind drifted to the beauty of a first snow in Ohio—my brother, Jerry, taking the lead as we drove snowmobiles, stopping to lick icicles we pulled from trees.

I wanted to disappear as these flakes disappeared into darkness. I wanted to travel back to a simpler less frenetic time.

Rob pulled my arm, jerking me back to the present, a place I didn't want to be.

"Jen, come on. Let's get the bags."

When I opened the door to our room, I gasped. Dane had said it was a suite, but this was huge, and romantic. A second room had glass windows with doors on sliders all around. In the center was a big whirlpool or large hot tub . . . or was it a swimming pool? The place was sexy.

I don't think Dane realized how sexy. I don't think he'd even seen the room. With the snowstorm gaining speed and the high tourist season in the Poconos, it was "the only room left," Dane had said.

I giggled, embarrassed at the red, heart-shaped bed.

Jesus.

I'd only seen those on TV. Rob and I had told Dane we were tired, but we were beyond tired, too tired to sleep or even relax. We were jacked-up, wired. And now, *this* room. I wanted to celebrate, to shake off the past four days. Energy—contained and repressed on the road—suddenly emerged. The manic energy needed a place to go.

I rolled up my pant legs and sat, fully clothed, dangling my feet in the "pool." Not too hot, not too cold. I was in the middle of a sip of wine when Rob returned naked, looking as mischievous as a boy at summer camp. He laughed, called me sweetie, and jumped into the water, begging me to strip.

And I did.

Free of the drugs and now my clothes.

"Wooo!" I squealed.

Rob splashed water in my face. I twirled on tiptoes. Rob kissed me. I kissed him back.

Jumping into the water, drinking wine . . . finishing the whole bottle and opening another. Kissing Rob in the pool, on the edge, in the bed, back in the pool.

As if we'd wanted to kiss for years.

My initial attraction to Rob had cooled in the years since Maui. But in a way, I think I loved him. I certainly trusted him. In the midst of that crazy night, I took our tryst for what it was, a stress-relieving expression of the adrenaline we'd kept inside.

The amount of passion we exhibited that night was equal to the fear we'd felt on the road, as we drove our illegal load and crossed state lines. In the truck, hopping from state to state like Texas jack-rabbits, the state only three days ago, we'd left behind.

CHAPTER 16

A FRIENDLY COP

"My flight's been cancelled."

Rob and Dane knew I'd agreed to drive this trip *only* if I could return to San Diego by the fifth day—the day my guru would arrive, the day before the community's Christmas party. I *couldn't* miss her or the event. *No way.*

When I woke at 6 a.m., all I could see was the Pocono Mountains covered in snow. *Snow means my flight is cancelled. Snow means I won't make it back to San Diego.* As I hung up the phone, I looked at Rob mournfully, tears rolling down my face.

"Don't worry, sweetie. We'll find you another."

Sweetie.

The tone of Rob's voice was even more comforting than last night's touch. Still, I had a hangover. Rob looked rough, too, his eyes red around their rims. We'd been hot-wired until two in the morning when I'd finally nodded off, drunk and exhausted, wrapped awkwardly in Rob's arms on the heart-shaped bed. After all our years on the road, Rob and I knew how to "motor"—to buck up and do our job—no matter the circumstances. Like "the show must go on" mentality of my dance years.

But not now. Not this.

Devastated, I fell in a heap onto the bed, ready to give up.

But Rob took charge, packed my suitcase, and got us out the door and into the truck. He told me to call and find a new flight while he drove toward Avoca, Pennsylvania, and the Wilkes-Barre/Scranton Airport—a forty-five-minute drive.

The last-minute flight was expensive—over $1,000—but the marijuana conspiracy would pay. At the Krispy Kreme shop on the corner, I ordered Rob a coffee topped with one-quarter cream, like he liked, and a glazed doughnut for myself.

In between Marvin Gaye and the morning show on WBPO radio, Rob patted my leg to reassure me. A half-hour later, the truck's wheels spun on ice. We drove slowly through fresh snow that had fallen on last night's dirty piles like dandruff dusting old top hats.

I called the airline to check my flight's status.

Just in case.

Shit . . . cancelled.

Again, I broke down, my nose dripping.

"I'm going . . . *sniff* . . . to miss seeing her . . . *snort.*"

Not a pretty picture. I was crying like I had at seven when I'd lost my Raggedy Ann at the Houston Airport.

Rob, like Dane and every guy I knew, responded to my tears and tried to take care of me. "Call Philadelphia," he said.

"But that's two hours away. We're driving the *opposite* direction, *away* from Philadelphia."

I cried harder and wiped my nose on the sleeve of my blue cashmere sweater.

"I'll turn around." And, he did.

My flight would leave in three hours. Probably . . . maybe. I booked a train ticket into Jersey where I could take a later flight that night.

Just in case.

Rob did everything to get me on that plane. He drove fast on ice, rocking our SUV as he swerved to avoid trucks that splashed puddles of rain across our windshield.

He succeeded.

Barely.

I was ecstatic, just as I had been at seven when a stranger handed Raggedy Ann back to me.

"Go Jen, go!" Rob called to me as I charged into the airport lobby.

I pushed my way to the ticket counter, ignoring the angry pleas of the other passengers in line, and got on the plane.

Once in the air, I relaxed with a cup of orange juice in my hand. I leaned my head against the window. A thick film of steam blocked my view, but I imagined the grandeur of that world I knew was beyond the clouds . . . beyond the sky . . . higher than any plane could fly—and I prayed.

Thank you for getting me on this flight so I can meet her.

Once we landed in San Diego, I drove straight to the community center, changed my clothes, fixed my hair, took the basket of red roses Ian handed me, and set it beside the chair where the guru would sit. I'd made it back with twenty minutes to spare.

My mind stilled as I found a place to sit on the carpet, folded my legs, and relaxed into meditation. At times, my tranquility was replaced by excitement mixed with the metallic smell of air ionized by the room's purifier.

An hour passed. And then another. After seven hours, all of the faithful, meditating in the large room realized she wasn't coming. And a phone call confirmed it was true.

All that work preparing for her arrival. All that stress trying to get here in time.

Was it for nothing?

No.

When I thought about Rob's care and his efforts to make me happy, my disappointment faded. Rob's care was more tangible than a guru's could be, especially one I'd never met.

I was fully aware that my relationship with Rob was compartmentalized. He was involved only in the drug part of my life. Yet the intimacy we shared created a foundation, and every trip we had already made strengthened our bond.

Rob didn't talk about the fear of being caught, but I could see it in his eyes, in his hands that trembled as he gripped the wheel, in his silence when he didn't talk . . . for *hours.*

Few others even knew about this part of our lives. And no one else understood.

Rob and I had become a driving team. In this venture, we only had each other. He didn't meet my friends, and I didn't meet his. Aside from the drug runs, we were completely out of each other's lives.

But our bond grew as deep as the risk we took—the risk we ignored—as we drove the drugs.

During my involvement with the community in 1999, my self-motivation had increased, a motivation that I thought had disappeared from my life along with dance. The more I volunteered and staffed the monthly intensives, the more I was inspired to do.

I'd have an idea and act on it—right then. Like the Tuesday "rest day" in the middle of the seven-day intensive when I saw an audition notice in the newspaper for dancers in a Pilates/kick-boxing video. Instead of resting, I pulled on a leotard and drove to the audition. Although I hadn't danced for two years, I was one of three women chosen, out of sixty, to do the video.

Styling came next.

Ian, who'd been a movie scriptwriter in LA, urged me on. I found a photographer who was looking to build his portfolio, and began my new career. I found clothes, set up shots, and assisted as a model ran barefoot on the beach with a shawl and cowboy hat, kicked a ball on the soccer field, walked in Balboa Park wearing a yellow gown and leading a teacup dog we'd borrowed from a passerby. The gig didn't pay, but I imagined the money I'd make later when I secured jobs with my new portfolio of pictures. I felt creative and useful.

A modeling agency in San Diego connected me to a photographer in Los Angeles, who connected me to a stylist in Newport Beach, who connected me to Billy—a man who rode a motorcycle and worked for *Teen* magazine. I liked Billy and I liked his pictures—a lot—so much that I gave him money to buy a new TV when his old one broke.

That summer, Dane called to tell me the trips wouldn't be happening for a while—the marijuana was all "dried up." The pot they did have, they just "couldn't get across the border." So I took a job teaching Pilates, the first real job I'd had in five years.

My new endeavors never lasted long. I'd made the one exercise video that paid $900. I'd worked as an assistant stylist for Target, but that job faded away for reasons I can't remember. My Pilates job ended after three months when a Speed Racer trip came up.

Sure, I was gaining motivation from my hard inner work in San Diego, yet I knew something was missing. I either didn't know how or didn't believe it was possible to transform the magic and creativity growing inside me into something tangible—and legal.

Maybe I wasn't good enough.

Plus, I didn't know what I could do, besides driving the marijuana, that would make such large sums of money. Maybe that was my excuse to avoid a permanent job, a career.

Why should I work?

Only *I* could tear myself away from the illegal business, and I didn't seem to care. At least not enough. Then there was the risk . . . the excitement.

And the money noose, like an outdated-necklace, tightened around my neck.

Rob and I stood on either side of the highway patrol officer as he swept his arm from left to right, tracing the highway in the air. "You know," he said, "right now there's a million dollars driving by us."

Rob and I stared at him, and we stared at the highway. We may have stopped breathing. At least I did. To us, it sounded like the cop was saying the black suitcase in the back of our white Suburban was filled with "over a million," which it was. But the cop didn't look at our faces. He just continued his tale, watching the cars as they passed: the red truck, the green SUV, the Penske trailer . . .

A back tire on our white Suburban had a blowout, leaving us trapped alongside the highway outside of St. Louis with this cop. Luckily, we weren't hauling drugs this time, just drug money, from Detroit to Phoenix.

A lot of it—the most I'd ever driven. So much, I couldn't even lift the bag.

As soon as Rob had pulled the SUV to the side of the road, he'd opened the back doors of our vehicle so it would look like we weren't hiding anything. All the officer could see were clothes, laundry baskets, plastic hangers, toys, and that big black suitcase.

"It's either cash or drugs," the cop continued.

I looked at him, eyes wide . . . innocent . . . shocked.

"Really?" Rob asked.

"What do you mean?" I chimed in.

"The trafficking. . . . We can't keep up. Yup, money or drugs," the cop repeated.

Rob guffawed a hearty "I know what you mean" kind of man's laugh I didn't understand.

I stood between them, feeling invisible in my blue jean skirt and bobby socks, twirling the tail of my French braid.

"So, you got a million dollars in the back of that vehicle?"

I was stunned, paralyzed. Unable to speak.

Rob gave another hearty laugh. Only I saw the color drain from his already pale face.

The cop looked stern at first, but then he laughed, too.

I smiled at no one in particular and, for no reason at all, except that I was so nervous—beyond nervous. I looked down, watching my feet trace swirling patterns in the rocks.

Distracting myself.

"Wow," Rob said, ignoring the question. "Really? Millions of dollars on the road?"

The cop's chest seemed to expand, probably with pride at his insider knowledge.

Now, Rob had him.

"Really," the cop replied. He hooked his thumbs in the top of his brown leather belt. "You wouldn't believe how much we found last year. . . . Yup, money and drugs. Where're you from?"

I continued to let Rob talk, perspiration dripping down my armpits.

"Phoenix."

"Well, I've never been to Phoenix."

The men started chatting like two old friends.

Tap, tap, tap, went my heart.

"You should come visit," Rob continued. "Here's my card." He handed the cop his pharmaceutical rep card from Abbott Labs.

Jesus.

Another patrol car pulled up behind the first, and a female officer got out, walked over to join us.

Oh, God. It's a party.

But she merely checked in with *our* officer and drove off.

"Phoenix, huh," said the officer.

"Sure, come visit my wife and me," said Rob, stroking my back, like a husband, I suppose.

Get me the fuck out of here.

My heart felt like a ticking time bomb. *Tap, tap, tap . . . tap, tap, tap.*

I kept smiling.

Static came from the cop's radio, and he held it to his ear, then his mouth.

"The tow truck's on its way," he said to his old friend Rob, without even glancing at me.

Am I that unimportant, even to a cop?

"Fantastic! I mean it, buddy. Phoenix, okay?" said the all-American male, the golden boy.

Buddy? Finally, after a few more male exchanges, the officer left.

Rob loved that story. He told it over and over to me and then to Dane, who said with reflected pride. "Really? You gave him your *business* card?"

I was disgusted by their "I'm too cool" laughs. But I had that feeling, too, that I was too cool to get caught. It just wasn't going to happen. *Ever.* We had escaped again, just like Dane and I had the time cops swarmed the restaurant parking lot in Indianapolis.

And, just like the cop said, if *we* didn't drive, someone else would.

Wouldn't I rather it was me?

CHAPTER 17

THE GURU

In January 2000, just over two years in the community, I finally met my guru. I would learn. I would grow. And I would leave.

In between, I'd fall in love. My life became more intense as I grew closer to the guru through her tight-knit circle. Now that she was back in Hawaii, people in San Diego often received last-minute calls to pack up and join her. They had no idea how long they'd be gone or if they'd ever return to the mainland. It was another experiment in letting go of choice, of control.

My turn came during a rare ten days off. I was in Chicago on a Saturday night, sitting alone at the bar in the House of Blues Hotel where I'd booked two nights. I'd already seen my parents and my friends. I was tired, not used to going out, not used to people outside the community.

Signaling the waiter, I ordered another glass of wine and continued writing poetry on napkins, a ritual from my Detroit trafficking days. Though I was wearing all black—pants, sweater, heels—I felt light inside. My head was down, focused on my writing, and I wanted to be left alone. Nothing about me screamed "available."

Still, I looked up at his bright twinkling eyes when his tan arm slid against the back of my chair and the other—decorated by a big silver watch—reached for my poetic napkin.

But I didn't respond.

Was it his persistence that pulled me in . . . or was it those eyes?

Eventually, he got me.

"Hi, I'm Casey."

Even though he was *really* good-looking, if he hadn't continued the pursuit, I would have let him go. I didn't realize yet that once Casey made up his mind, he was even more determined than I was. He never *ever* let go—unless his prize isn't as pretty and as perfect as he'd thought.

I shoved the napkins into my purse, then we danced to the band next door and into his bed that night.

When I said good night and turned to go back to my room, he grabbed my arm. "Where do you think you're going?"

I woke to bright sun and messy tangled hair. On the navigation program of his computer, Casey showed me where he lived—West Palm Beach.

Florida?

One man. One night. That's it. I'd successfully executed a one-night stand. I'd dated only one man for a few months the last two years. My life was different now. I wasn't looking for a relationship. I wasn't looking for anything beyond my spiritual seeking. I'd been called back to the community in Hawaii the next day. And that was the end of Casey, I thought. The ringing of my cell phone woke us up, followed by Georgia's voice.

"Jen, you have to come back."

"I'll be back in three days."

"No, now. We're going to Hawaii again. She wants us there for a think tank."

"Okay, I will."

Once I'd hung up, I sighed.

But I want to go. Urgent she'd said. I liked urgent. It felt important, like something was happening, and I was important, too.

The day before I left for Hawaii with Georgia, I dyed my hair black—witchy, pitchy black. I don't know why.

Usually my drastic hair-changes were a sign something was not right.

Was I unhappy? Discontented?

Georgia gasped when she saw me at the door. Ian laughed, saying my new hair looked like a wig. But I held my head high. I felt new, different. Bold like Casey's big silver watch. Secretly dark, sexy, seductive. Someone with secrets, like the marijuana tucked into a hidden place in my life.

Hawaii was intense. The guru's tough love taught us to release our egos, but it could be painful, and public. Asked to travel as secretary with the guru's daughter—an honor—I failed my first test. I wasn't a secretary, and I couldn't fake the skills.

After the second evening of waiting for a response from the guru, I cracked a Heineken and marveled at a caregiver who circled the table, seeming to float with happiness and contentment. I asked how she could stand being on call—always—for the guru.

"I *love* it." Looking at her face, I knew it was true.

I didn't love it. I didn't float. Why not?

What's wrong with me?

Rational Jenny answered immediately: maybe nothing was wrong, or right. Maybe I just didn't want to be tucked away in the community any longer. Maybe I wanted my life back.

Maybe this guru wasn't really my guru.

I decided the next morning that she wasn't. It was a painful decision, devastating after two years of devotion. Was I refusing the *gift* of being with the guru? I knew the positives: my inner growth speeded up, illusions dropped away, layers of my ego peeled back to expose the genuine and loving places inside.

But at what expense? *My life? My freedom?*

I prepared to leave Maui once again. But the guru ordered me to the other side of the island, where the younger members— including her daughter—were working out their problems. I felt punished—grounded—like I had when I was fifteen. Then, I'd smashed my favorite tongue-shaped Rolling Stone phone into the wall. Now, I just felt fucked-up, disappointed at failing the guru, not knowing if she was my guru. But if I broke free from the community, was I destined to live a life covered over by my ego, trapped by material desires?

At first, I'd enjoyed the solitude on the other side of the island— the house near the ocean, the peace. I didn't have any responsibility except to spend time with the guru's daughter, Saja. The first time we'd met she'd been cute and small, in overalls, and bold. She'd asked to borrow my ID. "You know, to go to a bar."

Now I felt trapped, confused. I was held captive on the island with no way out, unless I took a stand.

After a week with "the kids," Saja and I were instructed to clean the kitchen. She wasn't used to physical labor and left the work to me. When I asked her when I could go home to San Diego, she just nodded, turned the radio up and walked off, the yellow broom twirling in her hand. I felt dismissed.

Screw it.

I sprayed Formula 409 in the bathtub and then called the airlines.

I couldn't wait. I wanted off the island right then . . . that day.

I'll buy my own ticket. I don't care about the money. I want off this fucking island.

I called a taxi. Back at the house, bags piled at my feet, I waited by the gate to be picked up.

Standing in line at the airport, I received the call from Judy, the guru's assistant. "She said to take a few weeks off. Then, you can come back to Saja."

No, I'm not coming back, I thought, but all I said was, "Okay, Judy."

I'd thought my goal was enlightenment. Maybe it wasn't or

maybe the community wasn't my path. I was skipping town. Out of here like rocket-fire. Bailing. I'm Audi 5000.

Two days after my exit, I headed for San Francisco. I needed time to think. Something I couldn't do clearly in San Diego where the community was embedded in my life. The guru's assistant had suggested I take a few weeks off to contemplate what I wanted. Instead, I gave myself three days to make a decision.

Do I want to travel with Saja or not? Stay in the community or leave?

In my confusion, I felt weak, not strong like the trees of my childhood. Still, when I stepped off the plane and rode the train into San Francisco I felt ripples of excitement. My emotional turmoil and the stringent spiritual guidelines of the community were already beginning to slip away.

I don't have to answer to anyone.

I felt strong and free as I walked San Francisco's streets. Like a carefree child, I sampled pastries, browsed bookstores, tried on vintage tops and sparkling crescent pins. The bark of the ferry horn and the brisk wind were welcome distractions and took me far away from the warm tropical air of mixed-up Maui and my confused spiritual callings.

On the ferry, sea spray misted my face as water churned with each lap of the ferry's paddlewheel. How quickly the tall buildings shrank as the boat moved offshore, how quickly my worries about my future diminished as well.

When the ferry docked at Pier 33, I walked with no direction or plan except to make a decision about my future.

I want to take charge of my life.

With gusto, I hiked up a steep stairway surrounded by gardens. Near the top, the view was expansive. *The city—the world—is so much bigger than I am.* Standing on the top stoop, my gaze jumped from church steeple to high-rise to ships at port, and my mind darted, scanning the different directions I could go.

I felt liberated. I had a choice.

I wanted to reach out and dive into the city below . . . or fly like the finch I'd seen in Sedona. In that moment, I felt *really* alive. I'd made my decision.

I called Georgia. "I'm not coming back."

Georgia paused. "Okay."

That was it. She didn't even try to convince me to stay.

Why not?

"Jen, if you're confused, you *should* leave," she said.

Now, *I* was upset.

I felt discarded, a feeling that overshadowed the liberation only minutes before. I liked being needed. Needed felt safe. I'd felt that way years ago when Dane told me he was scared and he needed me. Now, I wasn't needed. If Georgia had begged me to stay, I would have felt better. I hated that selfish thought, but it was true.

Better to dump than to be dumped.

My mind spun, tormented.

The community had been my home. Am I still a serious spiritual seeker? What the hell am I going to do with my life? Maybe I don't want to break free. Maybe I want to play in the world—fulfill my material desires.

No, I wasn't just playing. I wanted to create my own life. I needed to *do* things in the world. I just didn't know what they were yet.

But I did know I wasn't supposed to be locked away, living a monastic life—a prophetic thought, given my not-too-distant future. But on that day at the intersection of Market and Octavia, I swore I wouldn't let anyone's opinion or judgments—even my own—get in the way of my decision.

I raced down the steps, taking three at a time. I jaywalked, crossed streets on a diagonal, and dodged honking taxis. I was strong. I would find a way to continue on my own path of inner growth and learning.

I didn't need the community for this.

I'd welcomed the spiritual rules and restrictions of the community, but now they seemed rusty, old, and stale.

Now I was free to make my own life. I could go anywhere, be anyone I wanted to be.

But go where? Be what?

Shit.

I had no idea.

Leaving San Diego happened fast.

I moved my belongings out of Georgia's apartment and shoved everything into a storage unit. I didn't have much time. Dane had called. "You need to be in Detroit *now* to pick up the money and drive to Phoenix."

Quickly, I went to my default plan. I'd move back to my home base, Chicago. I didn't know where else to go, and I was swayed by my friend Lane. He'd found a six-month sublease one floor below his in a loft building next to Oprah's studio. Living next door to the superstar talk-show host had to be a good thing.

Who knows what I'll do next, where I'll go.

My future was wide open.

In this openness, this gap—not knowing what would come next—my feelings switched from excitement to fear.

I didn't realize it then, but the feelings I thought were at odds were the same, just the flip of one coin.

The drive from Detroit to Phoenix was smooth, no hiccups until Albuquerque when Dane stepped in to replace the boy driver. Dane and I rarely talked any longer, and we hadn't driven together since his marriage to Aaron. I smiled as I drove with Dane, remembering old trips when we were a perfect drug-driving machine. Except *this* Dane was married and Aaron was pregnant.

Inside, I was frowning. *He's not mine. Don't be fooled, Jen.*

On the outskirts of Phoenix, Dane took a call from Aaron on his cell. As I drove, I could hear him lie to her. "I can't talk Aaron. I'm going to a meeting." He huffed, rolled his eyes. Then he hung up the phone. "She *never* can work the remote." Another sigh.

I was embarrassed, thinking back to when we were together.

Had he rolled his eyes about me? Complained behind my back?

I wondered if his excuse to Aaron was routine for Dane, one more lie added to a mountain of other lies. All those years of making excuses, making things up.

Dark corners never exposed.

Or was I projecting my feelings onto him.

My own lies had taken me far from the place I was looking for, far from the peace I wanted to feel. The place the stars had whispered to me. That feeling of peace—that inside place called home—slipped out of my grasp so quickly I could hardly touch it some days.

When I told Dane I was leaving San Diego and needed to get my car and belongings back to Chicago, he saw it as the perfect opportunity—and cover—for our next marijuana trip.

This time, I really did work hard for the money.

In Phoenix, Dane dropped me at a hotel and we went our separate ways.

The next morning, I flew to San Diego and packed my clothes, a few belongings, and the hidden box of illegal cash into Dane's Suburban and drove to Chicago. In Chicago, I passed off the cash and unloaded my belongings from the SUV into my new loft.

One quick look out the big windows of the loft—*I love it, I do—* and I drove the Suburban to Detroit, parked in a hotel lot and hid the keys. I took the first plane to Tulsa where Rob was waiting with the loaded U-Haul—around 2,500 pounds this time. He'd driven halfway with Dane and my furniture as decoy.

I knew about decoy furniture. Many times I'd bought used items from Chester's on University in San Diego—a table, kitchen chairs, a mattress—and then driven the U-Haul or Penske truck to Tucson to be loaded with marijuana. "Never rent a truck in

Phoenix," Dane had said. And *never* Tucson, an obvious unspoken fact.

When I arrived in Tucson, Wheto—my favorite drug smuggler—would meet me at Ina's resort and take the truck to be loaded. I liked Wheto, and he liked me back.

He'd laugh, and I'd giggle. *Just a normal meeting*, I'd say, fooling myself, as his eyes twinkled and he talked about his Mexican Mariachi band. He and three other brothers—two on guitar and one on a horn—played the circuit in Tucson and were all involved in the drug business.

Behind my back, they called me "princess," with endearment, Dane had said.

Wheto was in charge of the men who worked in the stash house.

By now, I'd earned enough trust to go the white house on Ina Road, a ranch with a circular driveway hidden by trees. I'd been inside, too. It was a marijuana factory. Here, the men wrapped ten- or twenty-pound bales of weed piled in odd angles on long tables, and packed the bales into hockey bags or cardboard boxes.

Windows were covered with blackout paper or white sheets so no one could see in, but I still didn't like to stand inside with all that marijuana for very long. After five minutes, my palms would sweat and I'd look over at Dane or Wheto, wordlessly begging to be taken back to the hotel.

Dane had told me years earlier that once the marijuana was loaded in the van or truck, you could smell the sweet sticky odor a mile away. But Dane came up with a system, a specific way to wrap the bales.

By now, the men had *almost* gotten it right: plastic wrap one, two . . . ten times around the green bale, a triple shake of carpet freshener—plastic wrap and carpet freshener again—and finally, sticky shelf paper at the end. The bales were neat, perfect—beautiful oblong packages wrapped smooth as burritos.

Much better. Less scary. When faced with the naked marijuana, I found it impossible—well, almost impossible—to justify trafficking the drug.

Now, the sweet odor barely leaked out, but I was oversensitive. It seemed to permeate the truck, come through the A/C and settle in my clothes.

Dane was right. Rob and I had a great cover for our trip. This time—October 2000—I was *really* moving to Chicago not like the other trips when I pretended to move as I transported marijuana. My furniture from San Diego was layered in front of the boxes that filled the twenty-four-foot-long truck. An open car carrier, attached at the hitch, towed my BMW. Rob and I drove from Tulsa to Detroit, dropped the drugs, and dropped Rob at the airport for his flight back to San Diego. Immediately, I drove the U-Haul—now empty of drugs, but still towing my car—to Chicago.

Whew.

It was dark—way after nine—and raining when I was done.

I was fried. Like so tired I could barely see. *The type of tired where nothing feels right. the type of tired that makes you weep.*

When I tried to unhook the car trailer, I started to cry. *Which way do you turn the wheel to make the carrier go the way you want it to go?* My tears turned to rain—a girly, blubbering mess. Thank God the men in the drug business couldn't see me. In my head, I heard Rob's frustrated voice telling me, "Turn the steering wheel the opposite way, Jen." Always blaming me—the girl—when he'd done no better than I had backing up to unload the marijuana, I stifled my laugh and didn't say a word. I didn't want to deal with a ruined male ego.

Let him swear; let him shake; let him think he's great.

As a woman, maybe *I* was really the one in control.

At the end of this trip, I was close to falling apart. Driving the money and the marijuana at the same time as I moved out of the spiritual community *seemed* like a good idea, but it left me exhausted and tense. Still, I was $30,000 richer and my belongings were back in Chicago.

By the second week of November 2001, I was completely moved in. Unpacked.

The Chicago loft was clean, neat, pristine. Large bright windows, wood floors, white curved walls. As I fell asleep, I looked through open French doors to the lit gas fireplace. I felt peaceful, like I belonged here.

Twenty silver-hued pillows lined the curved wall in the meditation room I'd created. Kitchen drawers and cabinets were labeled like I'd been taught in the community: "cups" in the left door, "silverware" in the middle drawer, "pots and pans" in the cabinet below the stove.

Again, matching my hair to my moods, I wanted a fresh start. I changed my black hair to childhood-brown, a bob with a flip tucked behind my ears.

Now, it was time to shop.

For two years, I'd scarcely bought anything. I told myself I deserved new gifts: a 42-inch TV, couch, new linens and kitchen items from Crate and Barrel—following my old pattern of buying new items for each new home. I cheerfully matched items to space. Now I needed clothes. Items in boutiques cried out my name: the tie-dyed shirt on North Avenue, red camisole top on Wells Street, leather trench coat with camouflage on Oak Street.

I knew I'd have money to spare, especially after talking with Rob. He'd called while I sat at the bar at the top of the Chicago Four Seasons. For the first time, Rob was coordinating the entire trip.

"How much?" I asked Rob.

"Forty."

My pulse raced.

"That's what you usually get, right?"

It wasn't.

Dane usually gave me $30,000 for a Speed-Racer trip, but I stayed silent. I mean, *Hell, lots of people are making lots of money. Why shouldn't I?* I wouldn't be going home to see Mom and Dad for Christmas, not this time. I couldn't miss this trip. No way.

Rob and I smiled when he got the money for all of us who made the trip. It was the perfect Christmas gift.

I was asleep by eight, snuggled in safe, knowing Lane was close, upstairs—only an elevator's ride away. At 6:30 a.m., I had a Pilates session at my friend Ceci's studio. Then groceries, shopping, and home to write poetry on my computer, sear tuna on the stovetop, drink a glass of red wine, and then another.

I felt delicate, cocooned in my new home, living a simple life. For most of the '90s, I'd taken full advantage of social Chi-town— out most nights dancing, talking, drinking with friends—frantic at times, needing to distract myself. Now, I didn't welcome such action. I wanted quiet, contemplation.

I was glad to leave the strict routine of the community behind. Now no one was telling me what to do. But I still didn't know my mission.

What the hell am I going to do?

Again, I turned to volunteer work. For three months, I met once a week with a nonprofit agency to receive my hospice certificate.

Other than that, I felt like I was starting from square one. *I want a life, a career.*

Thank God, Stephen and I talked regularly on the phone. Being physically alone was one thing; being emotionally alone was another.

Stephen lived in San Diego. We'd been friends ever since Ian introduced us at a transformational workshop in San Diego in 1998. Stephen had belonged to the San Diego community, too, until a bad blowout. He'd left before I arrived.

"The guru *hated* me," Stephen said, but I wondered what really had happened. He didn't say, exactly, but I liked Stephen anyway. After all, he was Ian's friend.

I don't want to judge.

Ian had told me Stephen owned a real estate investment firm and was a master businessman. The previous year, I'd traveled with Stephen on Maui to see his properties there, so I knew it was true. He had money—a lot.

Stephen knew how it felt to leave the community, so he was the perfect listener on our early morning calls. I shared my confusion about my life, the world, material things, and my feelings of being outcast, misplaced—scared.

Stephen held my hand long distance, hugging me with his wise suggestions to take it slow and give myself time to integrate the new changes I'd made.

"You're a different person than you were before the community," he said, "and the world will feel different, too." He told me it would take time before I'd find where I fit in.

Despite Stephen's wise words and Lane's sweetness, I had no idea what I was going to do. I had ideas, but still no motivation or direction.

At this point, Casey called. I'd only seen him that one time two months ago in Chicago, but we'd stayed in touch by phone. I'd thought about him, but never dreamed he'd be back.

His visit to Chicago set off fireworks again.

When he asked me to move to Florida one month after his visit, I hesitated at first. But the "yes" didn't take long, given our passion and Casey's persistence.

In April, at the end of my six-month lease, I packed my BMW once again and drove the three days to West Palm Beach—a place I'd never been.

CHAPTER 18

MY ALL-AMERICAN BOY

Casey had my heart.

We didn't even have to talk about why we were together; we just were. When I agreed to move to Florida, I even disregarded my first rule in a relationship—to find my own place. Our quick courtship, his fast-talking, and his sparkly *knowing* eyes attracted me. Now I was in a serious relationship with a man *and* living with him. After all my spiritual yearnings, I was ready to settle down into a traditional relationship, a real commitment.

Wasn't I?

My life went from faith to fish, literally.

Casey had grown up around lakes in Virginia, knew about boats, and owned a company that imported Japanese fishing lures. He cast lines and caught fish, and he wanted me to learn, too. Growing up a farmer's daughter, I wasn't squeamish like some girls might be. I fished in the ocean with gusto. I caught sharks offshore, learned to watch birds and swirling water patterns to locate schools of baitfish. I snagged bait on a sabiki rig—a chain of ten tiny hooks—wore a fishing belt and reeled in a tarpon off Key West. Casey was thirty-three—just one year older than I was—

charismatic and good-looking. When he talked, people listened—a characteristic of my father as well. Casey took charge, whether he was on his boat, in his car, out to dinner, or with friends. He was ambitious in bed, something I hadn't had in years. Sex on his boat, in the kitchen, on the couch. He was a go-getter man who matched the go-getter girl part of me. He was my all-American boy.

We were perfect together.

Weren't we?

Living with Casey was a radical change. Only five months ago, I'd been living an interior monastic life. Now Casey expected me to drink and socialize on his boat and at the waterfront bar, which turned out to be exhausting for me. Everything about Casey was *outside—exterior.* Still, he worked as hard as he partied, which showed me he'd be successful at getting anything he wanted. And if I stayed, I'd be successful, too. I'd earn the all-American white picket fence, house, kids, and fancy car.

But I didn't fit that mold any more.

In the mornings, I'd sit on Casey's deck overlooking the waterway and cry—tears falling in rhythm with slow-moving boats. I didn't understand my tears. *Is this a natural outpouring at losing my community and birthing a new life?*

I'd apologize, and Casey would be accepting of me just as I was. "You just cry, that's all."

The second week I moved in, I found the photos—sexy photos, from Casey's past—in the box under the kitchen cabinet. Casey with different women in his arms, smiling on a beach, on a boat, in a club.

Was the one with big boobs a stripper?

When I asked him about it, he nervously laughed. Yes, his ex-girlfriend—the blond in the pictures—had been a stripper. "You'd like her Jen. She's sweet and big-hearted."

What about the other darker woman?

The pictures proved he had secrets from me. I didn't like that.

Drew had kept secrets and lied, too. I'd told Casey *my* biggest secret, about my marijuana trafficking. I shut the box and tucked it away, right beside my intuition.

After four good months together, Casey must have wondered what I was going to do. He didn't ask out loud, so I didn't give him my excuses: that I didn't have my own life, that I couldn't find my footing, that Florida was so new.

I wanted to scream with frustration.

I haven't had a job in over six years. All I've done is follow a guru and traffic marijuana. Wake up, Jen.

On the outside, I looked like I had my life together—sassy short hair, classy clothes, fit and tanned body. But on the inside, I felt open, and vulnerable. After my exit from the spiritual community, I wasn't functioning very well in the real world. Plus, I'd never lived with a man. The quick change in lifestyle had shaken me loose from my foundations.

I had to take responsibility for my choices. My money was diminishing. I'd blown through almost $40,000 in eight months. I didn't have extra to spend any more, and Casey was paying our living expenses. I felt trapped, tied to Casey.

Did he feel tied to me?

Finally, Dane called.

Finally, something familiar.

"I want you to meet Harvey, Matt's new New York man."

I could make more money, coordinate trips. I felt in control once again. I flew to San Diego, rented a U-Haul and drove to Las Vegas. When I dined with Dane, we held hands across the table like old times. Later I met Harvey, who drove a snazzy green rental PT Cruiser and wore a bright Hawaiian print shirt. My U-Haul and I were ready, but the trip didn't happen. The shipment didn't make it across the border.

"Another three weeks," Dane said. I took the $2,000 I'd earned back to Florida and my new life with Casey.

Touching Casey's body, I felt like I'd known him forever, but something was wrong. I looked into his eyes, no longer bright and loving, and saw the distance growing between us.

Two weeks later, I flew to San Diego—again. Harvey's shipment had arrived.

Thank God.

I was ready for an escape and ready to make my own money—illegal, or not. It was my job.

I rented a U-Haul in San Diego, packed it with decoy furniture from Chester's, and drove to Las Vegas. The next two days I felt like a prisoner of my anxiety and the hotel as I waited for the drug shipment to arrive. I quickly tired of room service and lounging by the pool. I talked to Casey and other friends on my cell—wasting time, wasting words.

Time slithered and slowed—out of my control until the drugs made it across the border. Then I was back on track, focused on my goal to deliver the drugs safely and on schedule at the end of our three-day trip.

When the phone rang, it wasn't the message I was expecting. My dad's voice was soft. "Jenny, I think you should come home." He choked on his words. "Your mother has suffered a stroke."

He was right. I had to leave. Tears came to my eyes. My mom hadn't been well for years, but I couldn't face losing her. She was my rock, my best friend, my biggest advocate.

Even with my detour to see her, I could *still* help by "flying" money owed from an earlier shipment. Johnny would drive from Detroit to meet me in Ohio for the pick-up. We were criminals trusting each other in an untrustworthy business.

When my plane landed in Ohio, I took a taxi to the mall and bought a pair of Converse sneakers. I didn't try them on; all I needed was the box. Later, in my hotel room in downtown Columbus, I recovered the stashed bills, placed them neatly in the Converse box and put the box back in the store bag. Outside the hotel,

I handed the bag to Johnny. Talking with him in the back of the SUV felt normal, familiar. We smiled and laughed, but inside I was impatient. I was worried about my mother. I needed to get to the hospital *now*.

Damn, just give him the money.

My life didn't make any sense. In a couple of days, I'd be driving a load of marijuana through Ohio, only 200 miles from my hometown.

Just keep moving, I told myself.

My brother and I were walking Columbus's Brewery District near the river when Dane called. "Jen, you've got to come back. Now!"

I wanted to be responsible—I did—but to whom? My mother needed me. But I had a job to do. A lot of people were relying on me, taking a risk by holding the marijuana an extra two days.

"Give me one more day," I told Dane.

He promised to clear my request with Harvey. This would be our first trip coordinated by Harvey, and half the load of marijuana was his. The other half was New York's. Delaying the trip was not a good way to start a new business relationship.

"Who was it, Jen?" my brother asked.

I snapped the phone closed. "Dane. He's just worried about mom." Another lie.

After three tense days at the hospital, my mother's condition stabilized. The doctors diagnosed the stroke as a migraine. A *migraine?* I was worried, and I could see the concern on Dad's face, too. Mom looked tired, vulnerable, sick. But her vitals were fine, good enough for her to be released, the doctors said. I was relieved, but nervous that she was going home so soon. My mother was strong emotionally, but fragile physically. She'd had a kidney transplant when I was ten. Since then, she'd been on high doses of the steroid Prednisone. After the transplant, I was always afraid I'd do something to make her ill . . . or worse.

My escapades might upset her so much she'd reject her kidney.

I pushed the old worry aside. Now that my mother was going home, I wanted to leave without guilt.

I told my brother I was going back to San Diego—another lie—and he dropped me off at the Southwest terminal. As I lifted my bag to my shoulder, I left behind family loyalty and headed in the opposite direction. I had to catch my flight back to Las Vegas. My focus had returned to the marijuana waiting for me there.

When I woke at the Treasure Island Hotel after a deep, six-hour sleep, I was disoriented. I'd arrived so late the night before that everything was a shock—the early hour, the unfamiliar hotel room. I shook it off, dressed in my programmed attire—Brooks Brothers preppy pants and a white sleeveless shirt—and joined Rob downstairs. He looked as tired as I felt. He'd flown in two days before to coordinate loading the truck. Then he'd flown back to Missouri for a pharmaceutical convention, leaving the load overnight for Harvey with the keys on the U-Haul's front seat. He'd arrived back in Las Vegas this morning on the red-eye.

It was time to perform. Rob and I were a couple now. I purchased two coffees in the hotel lobby, extra cream for Rob the way he liked—just like couples do.

Outside, a short seedy man stepped out of a blue SUV. He was loud, flamboyant, friendly—and the top of his left ear was missing. "Aren't you the all-American couple," he smirked approvingly. "Hi, I'm Cliff. And this is Bob." He pointed to a big man in the driver's seat.

From the back seat of the SUV, I couldn't help staring at the silhouette of Cliff's quarter of an ear. I was uneasy. The frayed fragment of flesh seemed to symbolize the ugliness of our drug trafficking, that dark part I preferred to ignore.

I like things pretty.

I compulsively smoothed the wrinkles on my cotton pants. I calmed myself with the comforting words my mother had always used. *There, there. It's all right. Everything is going to be okay.* When I was a child, those words would stop my tears. I thought back to her hospital stint when she'd looked so vulnerable hooked up to the IV. But she'd been released. She'd be okay.

Yes, all better, I told myself, looking down at my smooth unwrinkled pants. *Yes, all better.*

Or was it?

Keep it simple, Dane would say, think of everyone involved as family. This was not simple. I didn't know these people. I glanced at Rob for his reaction, but he stared ahead, mechanically stirring his coffee. My stomach knotted, but I stayed silent. The boys—Harvey's boys—were taking us to the loaded truck.

It was early—around 8 a.m.—when we met Harvey and the U-Haul. I knew we'd make it to the pass in Colorado, maybe further, before nightfall. I waved good-bye to one-eared Cliff and Big Bob and drifted off to sleep with my head against the truck's vibrating window, my pillow in my lap.

Hours later, Rob's swearing woke me. Smoke billowed from underneath the hood of the truck. I felt a wave of heat roll through my body, as though the smoke had entered the cab.

I wish I could stay asleep.

Rob turned off the next exit into a dirty old gas station. I knew we were in Utah, but where?

Bumfuck Egypt . . . nothing but desert for miles around. Even though Rob and I traveled these dusty roads year after year, nothing looked familiar.

At first, we were fresh, hopeful, anxiously wired. We thought a tow truck would come right away when we called. But the day inched along, the hours feeling like years. Patience dripped away from my bones, emotional droplets drenching my body along with my sweat.

The heat, the worry.

The white camisole I wore was no longer white—smudged from my dusty fingers. Rob didn't look so good, either. His white-collared shirt and khaki pants were sweaty and wrinkled now. He stepped down from the rear of the truck, looking frazzled and even a little desperate. Secretly, I enjoyed watching his usual poise unravel.

Twice I snuck away to call Casey. He listened to my travails, but he didn't really get it. Although he often smoked marijuana to relax after a hard day's work, he was like the majority of pot smokers. He gave no thought to the precarious voyage his quarter bag of weed made before it came to his dealer and then to him. My role as a drug trafficker made him nervous. I'd expected more understanding. Casey seemed strong and calm—on top of his game—but wild, too. A risk-taker. But trafficking was different, dangerous—out of his league.

Rob and I circled the old pay phone attached to the wall and jumped when it rang. "The truck's coming," the operator said. Two more hours passed as we waited in the dust and grit, Rob complaining off and on.

Fuck. I alternated profanity with silent prayers, willing the truck to come.

No tow truck appeared. I didn't understand how this was going to work anyway. We had a truckload of marijuana, damn it. And Rob wasn't offering any solutions. We still weren't talking, so I didn't know what Dane had said when Rob called. I knew Dane couldn't really help. Even if he sent a man with another truck, it would take hours—days. Time we didn't have.

We were stuck, with no way out.

My nerves were a wreck. I couldn't think of any alternatives. I could read Rob's mind. He was thinking the same thing: *we've got to get out of here soon. We're sitting ducks for the cops. Nothing about this trip is safe. We're trapped.*

I unlocked the back of the truck and checked it myself, at Rob's request. A familiar odor was festering inside—boiling. Hours earlier, we'd opened a can of coffee to camouflage the smell. Then, the scent of the roasted beans had stung my nose, settled inside the truck, and filled the air.

Now I couldn't smell the coffee. Alarmed, I walked over to Rob. "The truck *stinks*."

Rob bought packets of air freshener at the mini-mart—a paper evergreen tree, a lemon cutout, and an orange. My stomach sank. These flimsy bits of fragrant cardboard were our salvation?

No way they'll cover the smell of 3,500 pounds of pot.

I focused my anger on Rob. I had no one else to blame. He blamed me back. He was glaring when he came out of the truck. I jumped down and stomped away.

"What's up with you?" Rob shouted. I ignored him and went back to my milk crate throne like Marie Antoinette awaiting her beheading. I counted ten cars, two trucks, and one tractor. The churning fear was building inside me. I was tired of being a victim. I wanted to break down—blow off smoke and steam like the broken-down truck. I kicked the blue crate, feeling foolish at the tiny thud of my sandaled toe.

Rob walked aimlessly around the U-Haul, looking as depressed as I felt. *A man with a problem he can't fix.* His cell battery had finally died. So had his patience. He threw the phone. *Crack.* It landed on the truck's bumper and bounced into the dirt.

"Jesus, Rob!" I was more disgusted.

I sat back down on my crate. The fluorescent light buzzed. A swarm of bugs flew around its yellow glow. It was getting dark.

At least with the fading heat, the smell won't get any worse.

Morning had turned into late afternoon. At twilight, the sky turned bold, projecting angry orange-red slashes above my head. The sky's colors mirrored my building frustration. I was tired— bone tired—of watching and waiting for the tow truck that was supposed to come. The buzzing of the florescent lights merged manically with my thoughts.

There is no way out. There is no way out.

Whether I meant this trip, this business, my life, I didn't know.

Stalking rows of Pringles and nachos in the mini-mart after dark, I passed Rob going the other way. After seven hours, there was nothing left to say. We'd both bought tuna kits and dined al fresco, him standing beside me as I sat on the crate he'd brought for me to sit on. The gesture had been endearing at the time. Now the crate dug into the backs of my legs. I'd torn the plastic from a tuna container and bitten off the corner of the relish and mayonnaise packets. My stomach turned over as I stirred the concoction with the wooden spoon that came with it.

I looked at my watch. *Nine hours since the truck had broken down.* I prayed for the tow truck to come. The meditative inner peace I'd learned in the community had sustained me the first four hours. Not now. *Was God testing me?* If so, I failed. My foundation of balanced calm was not as strong as I'd thought.

Rob was inside the back of the truck, checking it for the tenth time and swearing. I stayed silent. *Someone needs to stay calm.* Inside, I wasn't calm. The gas station attendant offered me bottled water with a sympathetic smile. "For free." But I only felt worse, dirty and unattractive—an object of pity.

At least we had a bathroom, the only one for miles. We were surrounded by desert on all sides, sand and brush and an occasional scraggly tree. A beat-up truck pulled in for gas, leaving a cloud of sand in its wake. A man with pointed, gilled cowboy boots exited the blue fifties Chevy, dust shadowing his weathered face. I could smell the booze from where I sat, still perched on my milk crate. *I wish I had a drink.* At this point, even cigarettes were no consolation.

The gas station seemed a beacon of light at the final nod of day. When the moon rose, I felt a moment of hope and possibility in the grandeur of the expansive Utah sky. Still, by 10 p.m., I felt sorry for myself.

I hugged my knees as I sat on my blue crate, dipping my head to stretch my back. When I looked up, I was blinded by approaching lights, lights that illuminated and distorted Rob's silhouette.

Up close, the flatbed trailer looked huge. I let Rob take the lead, while I took the supporting role I'd learned well over the years. I knew he needed to be the man after his inability to take care of the day's business.

The driver looked the part—bearded, burly, competent—and quickly attached a hook to the U-Haul's front end. After all that waiting, action felt good, even though it was vicarious. The driver turned a crank and magically the truck rolled forward onto the bed's flat surface. The driver had no idea what was inside; nonetheless, he was now an accomplice.

"He's taking us over the pass into Denver," Rob told me.

I was shocked. *We never drive through the night.* The odds of making mistakes increased in the darkness. Yet this time we were being driven—taken—with divine protection in the guise of a tow-truck driver.

Rob told me to sit in the U-Haul while he rode in the cab with the driver. I looked at our truck, high on the flat bed.

Why?

The request was weird, was it even legal? When I asked Rob, he said there wasn't room for all three of us in the front seat.

I didn't say it out loud, but I must have looked pained. "Jen, it'll be fun," Rob said, coaxing me.

The wind whipped powerfully through the Utah plains, violently rocking the truck. I couldn't sleep, and I knew Rob wouldn't either. He'd watch the speedometer, the trucker clueless that he was hauling drugs. Our cover was a reality: We were a couple with a broken-down U-Haul. No one would look inside the truck—not tonight.

I hope.

From my elevation, I looked down on passing cars. It was 650 miles to Denver; 1,596 miles to Detroit. I stretched out on the seat, my coat covering me. I felt cold and alone with the marijuana, especially when rain pellets began rapping on the window, especially when the U-Haul dangerously swayed back and forth.

Hours later when we stopped to refuel, I told Rob I was getting in the cab. He didn't argue, and I fell asleep wedged between the two men, the heater blowing on my face. I leaned my head on Rob's shoulder, snuggled.

We were moving. My heart was calm. The trucker was taking us over the pass.

I woke to a bright morning and the voices of Rob and the truck driver. Denver lay just beyond a stretch of flat land. My head felt turned inside out, my inner clock disturbed. I was tired, grouchy, and hungry. The driver dropped us at the U-Haul location where our new truck waited. Rob came back with the keys.

"Just act normal, Jen," were his only words of advice.

We had no choice and paid the U-Haul employees to help us unload the old truck into the new. I smiled, trying to distract them. *Did they even speak English?*

"O, Mamacita," I heard one of the men whisper.

I smiled again, but I was shaking and sweating as I passed the wooden end table into a man's hands. Hand-over-hand, a table and a lamp left the truck. The dresser was last, exposing thirty-five unmarked boxes. Neatly taped and in a variety of sizes, their cardboard sides enclosed the marijuana—our responsibility, our future money.

Do the men smell what I smell?

The men moved the boxes as directed.

Do I see a knowing smile?

No one said a word in Spanish or English.

Sitting in McDonald's, I dug into my sausage McMuffin and rocked side-to-side squeaking my orange plastic chair. Rob glared at me, too tired for words. We both were shaken into silence, exhausted by the rush of not getting caught. One of Johnny's boys would meet us in an hour. He'd drive behind, protecting us until we reach our destination.

We had two more days on the road.

I wish I may, I wish I might, never have to drive tonight.

But I wanted the money. And, having started, I didn't want to fail.

Somewhere outside of Detroit, four men I didn't know unloaded half of our boxes into another U-Haul van parked off to the side of the road.

It was night—dark and raining—and the men were headed for New York. Always another truck, other men, another exit, and a new drop-off location. The motion, the stress of the drug trafficking was beginning to make me sick.

The familiar lights of Detroit's airport signaled the end of a successful trip.

Almost.

Rob and I would stay at the Ritz-Carlton. In the morning, I would get the money I'd earned. The $20,000 would rest peacefully among my clothes—the hundreds and twenties vacuum-packed and sealed to hide the smell of cash.

As the ticket-taker at Northwest scanned my ID, my hands trembled as always. Walking away, I almost allowed myself a feeling of relief.

At the counter, I chose green mint Tic Tacs, Dad's favorite. Vanishing inside normalcy, I thought about my own childhood when Dad and I drank Dr. Peppers he'd hidden in the stream, when I sat on the toolbox inside the combine. These were my favorite times when I—a girl—felt included in my dad's world, a world where my brother fit so naturally.

When I look back, I wonder about my marijuana conquests. Besides the money, why take the risk? Maybe I was trying to prove that I—the token girl—could go head-to-head with the men. As a woman, maybe I wanted to hold my own.

I didn't hold my own on the farm.

Growing up, my dad *did* pay me to work. I picked rocks out of fields, mowed our half-acre lawn. Once, I cut corn stalks out of the beans with a sickle, but accidentally nicked the top of my head. By the time I was thirteen and Jerry was fifteen, he chose to do the farm work while I girly things: gymnastics, dance.

Some nights, Jerry would beg me to feed my 4-H steer down the road.

"I don't want to go," I'd whine, tired from gymnastics, cozy on the couch.

No one *expected* me to work on the farm. Still, I feel guilty, now, about my disinterest. I wish I could take back those days and feed the steers, help out during harvest season, be with my dad. Would I have been less tempted by the masculine world of drug trafficking? But whether it was trafficking or later, real estate, I competed just the same.

I sighed and broke the seal on the green Tic Tacs. I was tempted to bite into the mint, but I allowed it to slowly dissolve. Melt. Disappear. Like I wanted to disappear after the last seven days.

A sweet taste filled my mouth.

Yes, all better, as my mother the comforter and protector would say. My mother believed in me. When I excelled, she was there to point out the next open door, future possibilities, and successes. Even as I took on the role of smart high school student and leader—honor roll, president of Future Teachers of America, and captain of the cheerleading squad—I led a secret, double life, sneaking out of my house with the wildest boy in school.

A good girl going bad?

Sure, illegal money was stashed in my purse, in my pockets, and in thousand-dollar bundles in my suitcase. Sure, I was still leading a double life, but still I had to reassure myself. *There, there all better.*

When I reached Florida again, I knew that Casey and I were in trouble. I couldn't keep up with his lifestyle, and he wasn't as accepting of mine as I'd thought. I did take steps toward a life of my own, though. I began working as an assistant in the events department of a nonprofit agency, a job I loved immediately. My experience working events for the community helped on my resume and on the job.

A month later, I made a hair decision—always a signal of change in my life, for better or worse. The previous week, a colorist had already ruined my hair, turning it a cheap hooker blond. On this ill-fated, awful hair day, another colorist convinced me to go red. I called Casey before, just in case he said he'd hate it.

"What do you think about red?"

"I'd love you any color, any which way," he answered, and I beamed. The stylist saw my face and smiled.

I was loved—but not enough.

My hair was now fire engine red. *Too late, I can't go back. My hair had been colored twice in two weeks. Change it again and I'll have straw for hair.*

Casey didn't comment on my awful cartoonish hair, but I was embarrassed. I knew how I looked. At the beginning of the week, I sensed something was wrong—something beyond hair.

"Is everything okay?" I asked him.

"Yes, Jen, you're like family. I'm not going anywhere."

But that Friday night, he didn't come home.

When he returned the next day, he held me close and cried. We both knew our relationship was over. But neither of us talked about why or what the hell was happening.

Three weeks later—November 2001—I was in back in Chicago.

I used to blame my bad hair color for my failed relationship with Casey. Even now, even though I'd had misgivings about our relationship, I'm not quite sure what happened. I'd been sure we'd work it out. I'd been sure he was my future husband.

Did he want someone more like he was? Did he want the all-American girl I used to be?

All I know was that it was over, vanished, as if our love had never been.

CHAPTER 19

I NEED SEXY

I couldn't stop the pain.

I shuffled as I walked to the Diner Grill with my friend and ex-roommate, Bud. For the past week, I'd slept on his couch saying very little. Even talking took too much effort.

I couldn't eat. All I wanted to do was sleep, but not in my bed . . . not alone.

I miss him.

I'd moved to Chicago again because I didn't know where else to go. But the city seemed darker than I remembered. Lakeside fog enveloped couples as they walked in the park along the lake. Everyone else in twos, everyone else attuned to the beauty around them.

I finally found a rental at West Burton's Place. *Something familiar—but was it?* I was alone in my dark back unit, situated where light barely seeped through the stained glass window. I took a couple of steps onto the private deck that everyone coveted, but the roof was covered with snow. It was cold—32 degrees—nothing at all like Florida.

I missed the sun like I missed the lighter places inside myself.

Only one experience calmed me: a skilled stylist on fancy Oak

Street had extinguished my flame-red hair. The chocolate brown was better than red, though not natural-looking, not blond. I still felt ugly inside and out. My heart, which I'd worked so hard to open, had snapped shut.

Wanting help turned to needing help, but no one could ease my pain. After six weeks, Kelly, Bud, my mother—even I—had grown tired of my story.

I was stuck.

I couldn't move on. And I couldn't stop calling Casey.

"Why don't you love me anymore?"

His answers were vague and gave me no relief.

In my apartment, alone, I danced the cathartic meditation I'd learned in India. I screamed like the Hindu goddess Kali trying to force out the pain, the past . . . and Casey. Shopping, buying CDs, eating-out—nothing lifted my mood. For the first time in my life, not one distraction worked.

The pop had gone out of my snap-crackle life.

I was scared.

What's wrong with me?

I had one thing to hold onto. The next week—mid-December—Casey would be in Chicago on business. He had promised to call when he arrived. I couldn't wait to see him.

How would I act?

How would I feel?

What would I wear?

Feeling rejected had only strengthened the memories of my good times with Casey. I was desperate to hold onto the good and the pretty. To avoid the dark emptiness of my pain.

I fantasized Casey would come back to me. For the first time, I wanted a do-over with a man. This time, I would do it right, whatever "it" was.

When Casey called from his Chicago hotel an hour before our meeting, my excitement faded.

"I should tell you I've met someone."

What? When?

I held onto the kitchen doorway to steady myself.

"Jen, she's the *one.*"

I paced in circles, the phone pressed hard against my ear.

Jesus. I've only been gone six weeks.

I used my old tactics: I whined, I defended my point of view, I cheered for *us*—for the relationship that no longer existed.

I gripped the phone. Somewhere within the silence—in the gap between our words—I sensed relief hovering just within reach. But when Casey said he was cancelling our date because "it wouldn't be fair to Courtney," a sudden rush of power emboldened me.

"NO. You ARE coming." The pain in my belly melted away as I said those words, words that reclaimed my power as a woman.

I gave him one hour.

My heart beat fast.

I discarded tan suede pants for black fishnets and a mid-length black leather skirt.

Urgent: I need sexy.

When Casey knocked, I opened the door to those hazel eyes. Quickly, he looked away but extended his arms for an awkward hug.

At the Chicago Chop House—a Chicago favorite—the waitress seated us in the window, next to the piano.

Romantic.

Casey ordered for us, cut the filet mignon on my plate and smiled at me across the table with twinkling eyes, like he used to do. His gaze felt weird—like I was his and he was mine—like what I thought I wanted. As we sipped our after-dinner drinks, I pretended we were a couple holding onto our last hour together. In the cab returning to my apartment, he kissed me.

Or did I kiss him? With a gentle hug, we said good night outside my door. That was the last time I saw him . . . held him . . . kissed him.

Sleeping in sweats with blankets layered over me, I burrowed into nighttime.

Yes, the pain is still there, but so is the relief.

Some missing bits of self-knowledge appeared like flotsam in the wake of our breakup. I saw my inability to communicate with a man, my reluctance to ask for what I wanted.

I knew.

The dance took two.

I left Chicago shortly after Casey did. But I cried twice more: buckets of tears with a bottle of wine on New Year's Eve and, later, as I circled the city alone in my BMW for two hours—Lakeshore Drive to lower Wacker and back. My weeping blended like an Indian chorus with the husky tones of Eddie Vedder, lead singer of Pearl Jam.

In the new year—2002—I returned to poetry, cooking, and something new—e-mailing Elizabeth.

We'd both worked on the community's intensive management team in San Diego, and she'd left soon after I had. Now Elizabeth worked for Stephen in his real estate investment company. Faith—another ex-disciple from the team—worked for Stephen, too. Faith had trained me back in 1998 when I'd first been invited onto the team.

Faith's white skin, heart-shaped-face, and sweet motherly tones were opposite to Elizabeth's narrow face, clipped English accent, and sharp tongue. Yet, by coincidence or sheer luck, Elizabeth appeared at a critical time in my life, so I emoted to her online, night after night, on a recurring theme: "I have no direction at all. I'm worried about my life." Night after night Elizabeth responded with tender loving care.

After speaking to Stephen, Elizabeth offered a life-saving solution.

Stephen wanted to hire a third person, she explained. "Come to San Diego."

Stephen knew me as a friend, not as a future employee, and he knew about my trafficking. How would that affect a business decision? Elizabeth and Faith knew how hard I'd worked on the intensive management team, so they advocated for me, advising Stephen I'd be a great addition to their current team—and to his business.

Stephen agreed.

The next week—mid-January—I flew to San Diego for an interview.

By now, I was an avid traveler, a frequent flyer. I'd never counted the trips. But *this* Northwest flight was a trajectory to new locations and new vocations.

I am taking charge of my life.

I chugged the remains of my orange juice, satisfied. Mom and Dad would be pleased.

In some ways, my accomplishments had already exceeded my dreams: I'd danced professionally in Chicago, traveled to exotic places all over the world, devoted myself to a spiritual journey. I'd held my own alongside men, made thousands of dollars—never mind that it was the marijuana business.

Now I was ready to *do* something, to start a real career.

My mom and dad's approval would be an extra-special rotation on the symbolic wheel of my life.

I rested my head on the airplane window, watching tiny brown squares of farmland below turn to finger-length mountains. I was flying West to opportunity, to something different, and to the possibility of breaking out of marijuana trafficking.

Finally . . . a solid job . . . a career.

I looked down as Stephen spoke, my fingers tracing the zigzag pattern in my skirt. The pattern was complicated, but Stephen's words had been clear. "I'll hire you, as long as you're not involved with *the business* any more. You aren't, are you?"

"God, no. NO."

Am I? Dane hasn't called for months. Neither has Rob.

If Stephen hires me, I'll quit driving the marijuana.

I sat across from him on the couch, my brown boots crossed at the ankles. I crossed my heart, and I didn't cross my fingers behind my back. I wanted to keep the promise to Stephen. I did.

Stephen made a promise, too. If I did well training for the project management position, I could quickly work my way up. When Faith left mid-summer, I would continue in the business as co-supervisor with Elizabeth.

I smiled.

Not a huge smile. My break-up with Casey was still too fresh for that. Stephen had offered his condolences, but we were talking business now. We kept our distance. I would be his employee. He would be my boss. Soft looks and supportive phone calls were not appropriate.

Will Stephen still pursue a romantic relationship?

I hoped not.

We shook hands on our promises. I had one month. Just enough time to move. Just enough time for *one* more trip . . . and a broken promise.

I felt strong when I returned to Chicago with my new plan. San Diego was far—as far away as I could get from Florida.

Casey and Courtney can take a hike.

I was back.

I saw the Jenny I knew in the mirror after a stylist colored and cut my hair into choppy, sexy, radical-streaked blond. In the dressing room at Barneys, I twirled in front of the mirror in designer Seven jeans, left to right.

I was thin, but not too thin.

Downstairs, purses displayed on open wooden shelves caught my eye. *Cool.* The Kelly green was unusual. I looked for the tag.

Hidden tags mean high prices. A thousand dollars. Jesus.

I'd never bought an accessory at this price. My blue Paul Smith coat and Dries Van Noten skirt had been expensive, but those were articles of clothing. I walked out, past the doorman in his top hat and striped tie—and then returned.

Screw it. I deserve a treat. I'd been dumped, dammit.

Okay, I felt a little guilty.

Yet, more money was coming, and soon. A trip was happening—already in place—once again, perfectly coordinated with a move across the country.

The last trip for me, cross my heart and hope to die.

I laid out cash for the Marc Jacobs designer bag as casually as I'd tossed the twenty on the counter for Bobbi Brown rum-raisin lip liner last week, as casually as I'd pushed my guilt aside at breaking my promise to Stephen.

The green bag would be my favorite for years, as bright and bold as the next chapter of my life promised to be.

CHAPTER 20

I SMELLED DEATH

I said my final good-bye to Chicago en route to Vegas.

I couldn't wait to deliver the cash stashed in the trunk and then to head for San Diego. But Vegas was the first leg of a ten-day route that would end, not in San Diego, but New York.

Damn.

Still, I sang as I drove. I hummed along with country songs on Midwestern stations, grateful I was out of my Casey-dumps. Crossing the country, I crossed weather patterns as quickly as I'd moved from state to state the past two years.

In New Mexico, the heat burrowed into my car, and I exchanged my new jeans for shorts. I discarded my sweater until mid-afternoon when I hit Flagstaff's cool. After nightfall, I arrived outside Vegas to dry desert heat and a truck-stop neon sign where I met one-eared Cliff and Big Bob. We said few words as I passed off the cash that I assumed they were taking to Harvey, who lived part-time in Vegas.

But where did Cliff and Big Bob live?

The rumors varied. Cliff lived in Colorado and Big Bob in New York, or was it Las Vegas and San Diego? Harvey's boys were always on the road, either driving decoy cars or driving money from East to West to East.

Cliff and Big Bob seemed as homeless as I felt. After my long drive, and after I dropped the cash, I couldn't *wait* to reach San Diego.

Once there, I couldn't rest.

I checked into a bed-and-breakfast in Mission Hills—a historic section of San Diego—and fell asleep surrounded by unpacked suitcases. As I slept, my dreams turned pages like a multi-colored flipbook, from blue to green, to bright-engine red.

The next morning, I flew to Las Vegas for my *last* marijuana trip.

Cliff met me at baggage claim wearing sunglasses, looking thinner than he actually was in dark jeans and a navy jacket. His voice bounced with inflection as he talked, like his chatter was important, like he was my friend.

Still, I didn't feel safe.

Why, because of the imperfection of his ear?

Yes, but it wasn't only the ear. Cliff seemed *unhealthy*. Like he smoked two packs a day, dined on frozen potpies and pizza. Standing next to Cliff, I felt unhealthy, too. Not fresh and pretty like the white ruffled socks I sometimes wore. Not neat and efficient like Dane. As we walked, I was aware of the unclean places inside myself.

I don't eat three meals a day, sometimes overindulge when I drink, don't budget my money, don't really save any money at all, and . . . I fib. I remembered what I'd learned in the community: secrets kept hearts locked.

I want to come clean. Don't I?

Cliff was quick to brake, so I bounced in the back seat of the SUV, trying to hold my cell steady as I called Rob. He was already at the house with the loaded trailer. With Dane in Europe and Johnny coordinating this trip, I had questions.

"How much am I going to make?" I asked Rob.

"I don't know. Call Johnny."

Johnny was a nice guy, educated, not a thug like his brother, Frankie. He fared much better at the Detroit business than Ray, who'd had problems with drugs and stealing money even before he served time.

But I felt nagging discomfort. Johnny lacked common sense.

"How's it going, buddy?" he asked when I called. He over-emphasized the "B" like we had in sixth grade when we pronounced letters and rhymes on the wall.

B—beating heart, beating heart. B-B-B—Buddy.

I rolled my eyes. The men in the business called each other buddy in case someone was tapping our phones.

How inventive. As if their secret code would keep us from getting caught.

"How much am I getting paid?"

The amount of the drugs and the distance determined the price. This was no Speed Racer, but the setup was long—a Suburban, U-Haul trailer, and open carrier with a car. We were hauling close to 3,000 pounds, and our final destination was New York.

Johnny spoke with conviction. "Twenty."

I knew it. He's trying to screw me out of $10,000.

I was ready to throw a fit, but I didn't want to give Johnny a reason to complain about me. On an earlier trip, he'd heard Dane reprimand me in a McDonald's parking lot in front of our loaded U-Haul. "This *can't* happen on a drive."

Plus, I didn't want this trip taken away. I knew I'd lost others. Trips happened without me: after I cheated on Dane, after I got a ticket for speeding when I was driving the marijuana.

I knew I could be replaced.

"Jen, we'll work it out," Johnny said.

Was he trying to cheat me? Was Rob?

I wanted my fair share of money. Yet what was " fair?" No one told each other what they were paid, so I tried to figure it out and make sure they didn't take advantage of me.

After I hung up with Johnny, I called Rob. "Don't worry, sweetie; we'll work it out," he said, repeating Johnny's words.

Although Rob's words were the same, I believed him.

Rob had my back.

Didn't he?

Once we arrived at the house, I sat at the breakfast table while the men hitched the trailer, checked the taillights, and other men-preparing-for-drug-trips stuff.

I felt nervous, uncomfortable without Dane, uncomfortable in a sparsely furnished stash house in a development with twenty other houses close by. We weren't hidden.

Anyone can walk by and see the truck . . . see me.

Cliff walked into the kitchen, and I couldn't help it, my gaze went to his fragmented ear.

"It's a death-house you know," he said.

"What do you mean?"

"There was a murder—a double one." Cliff sat down, put the palms of his hands on the table and whispered for dramatic effect. "The husband and wife were both found in the master bath in puddles of blood."

We're doomed.

Later, I refused to go in the master bath alone and asked Cliff to stand outside the door. Tingles ran up and down my arms.

I swear I smelled death.

I was sitting at the breakfast table, looking preppy—not sexy—in my striped Brooks Brothers shirt, khaki slacks, and new green bag, when Hunter walked in.

Ta-dah.

Surfer blond hair and a bucket full of energy filled the room. A stylish leather jacket was slung over his shoulder.

Hot.

For the first time since Casey, four months ago, I was attracted to a man.

Hunter gave me an up-and-down look along with an aggressive

smile. "Hi, I'm Hunter. I'm riding with Cliff." He eyed my purse, "*Nice* bag. Is that Marc Jacobs?" So, Hunter had an eye for fashion, and he didn't hide his feminine side.

Suddenly, I was excited about the trip.

I waved good-bye to Johnny as Rob backed out of the driveway. The three men—Cliff, Big Bob, and Hunter—led the way in a dark blue Cadillac. The trio would stay fifteen minutes ahead to guide us to safe truck stops, mini-marts with no cops, and to hotels—a Ramada Inn or Holiday Express—where we'd find morning coffee and half-eaten doughnuts flirting with Special K and Sugar Pops.

Appropriately, Harvey brought up the rear.

Harvey wanted the load to arrive safely. After all, the bales had come from *his* Mexico connection. The Detroit men were paying New York for their share of the drugs, and Rob and I were contracted to drive.

See? It's just like any old business, officer.

The six of us were a mixed-up lot. When we stopped for dinner, everybody ignored Dane's rule to be low-key and not create a scene. But this wasn't Dane's trip; Harvey was in charge.

Big Bob looked tough, but he spoke softly. One-eared Cliff was the chatty one. Rob and I were quiet—the good-boy, good-girl team.

I moved out of quiet as the trip wore on.

Harvey's eyes were on Hunter and Rob's eyes were on me when Hunter and I flirted in New Mexico, laughed in Oklahoma, gossiped in Missouri, and got drunk in Ohio at a cowboy dive bar.

The night we hit the snowstorm, I was behind the wheel.

I could barely see the Pennsylvania road as I followed the grooves of Cliff's tire tracks. I zigzagged on ice. Cars pulled off to the side. Mini vans spun on the road. My high beams illuminated snowflakes suspended like a baby's mobile hanging in the sky.

Inside I shook, but my hands were steady on the steering wheel, my focus heightened by the danger of the dark, snowy night.

We can't have an accident, not with the drugs.

A trucker passing our truck lost control. *Shit.* I did a quick fierce maneuver, turning the steering wheel hard to the right. Rob looked like I felt—white as the falling snow. But I did my job well and stayed focused on the equipment trailing behind me—the SUV, trailer, and car carrier.

We stopped before the snow did.

It was late—11 p.m.—way later than late, past our road-time bedtime. We were all quiet, stunned by the exhausting three-hour drive.

Hunter was impressed. "Damn, girl. I'd trust you driving *any time,*" he said, flipping his blond hair, and offering a movie-star smile. Although I was tired, I blushed. But my pride, my sense of "winning in a man's world" quickly died. What good was the *coup* if I couldn't tell anyone outside this secret world?

In this world, everything was kept secret—accomplishments, too.

Hunter invited Rob and me to stay in New York for the night. He'd called on my cell while Rob drove us—and the marijuana—through Jersey, over the Verrazano Bridge and into Staten Island. Harvey and the other men were staying in a bed-and-breakfast in the village that catered to gay men, where they "always stay," Hunter said.

Rob refused to come.

Actually, he seemed upset, almost angry as he drove, rolling his eyes and changing radio stations as I shifted to look out the window.

Why? Is he jealous of Hunter?

Although our trysts had ended and Rob was married, on the road I felt like I was his and he was mine.

After fifteen minutes of silence, I asked Rob to drop me at the mall while he and the other men unloaded the truck. I knew I'd only be a distraction there. I couldn't unhitch the trailer, and I didn't want to deal with all that waiting, plus . . .

I need something to wear tonight.

I wanted to look good for Hunter, and I had nothing but a Ralph Lauren sweater and my Seven jeans—no shoes with heels—and I *needed* heels to wear with my too-long jeans.

Rob agreed to thirty minutes.

Forty minutes later, he called, and though I was still in the middle of a purchase—a leather coat at Guess—I told him I was coming. Another 20 minutes passed. Instead of rushing to the truck as promised, I rushed to Nordstrom's to purchase high-heeled boots.

Rob's voice seethed on the cell. "Where the hell are you?"

I was defensive, trying to cover my embarrassment. "I'm coming—*Jesus.*" I rushed toward the exit. Face tense, I tried to hide my purchases, but Rob saw the shopping bags and shook his head.

On our drive back to Newark, he was silent again. He wouldn't talk—not to me, not even to Cliff who sat in the passenger seat.

I took a deep breath. The day was a final rolling credit on a life that sometimes seemed no more real than a movie. Tonight, though, my job was finished.

The trailer had been unhitched, the car carrier dismissed.

Rob is mad at me.

The distance between us was a weight on my heart. I dragged my feet as I followed him out of the truck at the Newark hotel parking lot. Rob turned around, gave me one last look, and left without a word.

Rob is the only person who really understands "drug-trafficking Jenny." *I need us—Rob and me—to exist.*

Eventually, his friendship would disappear like a mirage, like Casey, like other parts of my life that now felt unreal.

Hunter consoled me as I cried.

Crossing bridges, driving through tunnels, I snuggled next to him. Champagne uncorked, beer bottles tipped—that night the boys and I had fun.

Maybe I should have stayed in Newark with Rob, but I'd given in to the temptation of Hunter. I imagined his magic wand could turn me back into an attractive woman—the woman I'd been before I met Casey. In Hunter's bed by the fire, I was that woman.

Was the moment of fun worth being cast out of the business?

CHAPTER 21

A DIRTY BUSINESS

Once back in San Diego, my life fell into a methodical rhythm. I moved in stride with my new job, ocean waves, and easy weather. The routine was soothing and took me out of my Casey-pain like the trains in Chicago had lulled me to sleep back in 1994. The click-clacking of their wheels as they passed outside my window had been like steady good-night kisses.

Now I was consumed with real estate.

Stephen's company purchased distressed property, and I renovated foreclosure homes. Faith taught me to negotiate with trustee and mortgage companies, while Elizabeth trained me to manage contractors and escrows.

On the weekends, I browsed bookstores and coffee shops. Sundays, I enjoyed the local farmers market where I chose fresh vegetables and cut flowers.

Mondays I began another work week. The nine-to-five days were sometimes eight-to-seven, but still a novelty after the frenetic 24/7 schedule in the spiritual community and the intense four-day drug-hauling trips. When I wasn't involved in those activities, I'd had no schedule. I'd done whatever I wanted whenever I wanted to do it. I didn't mind, even though my only free time was after work or weekends. Some nights I hung out with Dave, an ex-CEO of the spiritual community who now purchased property for Stephen. We'd drink wine and talk about life, relationships, the pitfalls of spiritual masters and, of course, we talked about real estate. My work was my life, and my co-workers—Faith, Dave, and Elizabeth—my friends.

I loved my daily routine.

Every morning at my bed-and-breakfast, I set my coffee on the bathroom sink, dried my hair, and applied mascara and pink lipgloss. I was beginning to like myself again and to like what I saw in the mirror. Sometimes I'd imagine I saw my family and my family's family standing behind me.

My legacy.

My father's father had built a farming empire and my mother's father had designed bridges and houses. "They were all hard workers," my dad said. In my mind's mirror, I saw them judging me, expecting me to make more out of my life.

I judged myself and expected more, too.

Sometimes I woke with a winning attitude. *I have a job—a career.* My family lived inside me, walked beside me. On those days, they didn't judge and neither did I.

I felt *right* in the eyes of the world.

Right, or not, I still teetered between two different worlds.

In one world, I bought Juicy sweat suits and Gucci sunglasses at Saks Fifth Avenue and red Prada sandals I threw into the back of my closet after only one wearing. I stored the illegal cash like a Russian nesting doll inside a box in my closet in my bedroom.

In the other world I budgeted my weekly $750 paycheck, shocked at how much the IRS took out of my check. "Is this right?" I asked Stephen's accountant. I couldn't believe it. I'd made "tax-free" money for years.

Still, I cherished the security of my job like I cherished memories of my childhood, but I feared I wouldn't be able to budget my legal money once the drug money ran out. And sometimes my life felt mundane. I missed the days I could travel and take off on a whim. Now, I worked hard—sometimes late into the night. My efforts showed, and Stephen rewarded me by increasing my hourly pay.

I was seeing a side of Stephen I hadn't known. He was a top-notch investor who'd had "next to nothing but ambition" in his twenties, his ex-business partner told me. For example, fifteen years before, he'd bought an older, quality sailboat and spent a season refurbishing it. He sold the boat for $20,000, which he turned into $50,000, which became $100,000. During the next ten years, he bought property on Maui, eventually turning his initial investment into millions.

I respected this businessman Stephen.

And, Stephen respected me. He invited me to important meetings, gave me important tasks, trusted me with his money.

At one point, Stephen was hot on the trail of a foreclosure property going to auction. We had only one hour, and Stephen needed extra cash.

"I have $10,000," I said.

Inside I felt proud, like I was special to have cash lying around. I admired Stephen. I wanted to be special to him.

Stephen never questioned me, just borrowed the cash. He never bought the property and quickly gave the money back. I thought for sure he'd ask where the cash came from. I thought for sure he'd be suspicious. But he never said a word.

Did he still believe I'd kept my promise?

Though I'd wondered if our relationship would change now that Stephen was my boss, our friendship continued.

Then, one night after work, he invited me to the movies, then kayaking. Weeks later, we shared pasta and wine at his favorite Italian restaurant, Arrivederci. When we arrived back at the office, I parked my car. Behind the koi pond and tall bamboo, Stephen *almost* talked about "us" as more than friends, more than employer-employee.

A place I didn't want to go.

I was confused. I wanted Stephen's approval and cherished his friendship, enjoyed cuddling and holding his hand, but I wanted nothing more. Rejecting his overtures might jeopardize our friendship. But he didn't really say how he felt about me. If he had, would I have said yes?

With a stuttering uncomfortable good-bye, Stephen left. I was almost relieved when he shut the car door. Whatever happened that night in my car—whatever Stephen said or didn't say—unconsciously I'd made my decision when I dodged the issue.

Weeks later, embarrassed, he avoided me, wouldn't talk. I was confused at first by his response, but then accepted the shift away from our previous comfortable relationship. Stephen never asked me out again.

After six weeks living in Mission Hills, I found a permanent place to live. The early 1900s cabin was only one block from the office, at the bottom of a canyon that overlooked a suspension bridge.

Every night I parked my car at the top of the steep rugged hill and walked down to my new home. In the morning, wearing heels and loaded with paperwork, I climbed back up. I soon tired of the daily up-and-down climb, but I knew I was in the right place because of *the sign*.

When I signed the lease, the landlord had shown me the alarm. "Choose four numbers," he'd said.

I spontaneously picked 1017—my birthday—October 17.

He chuckled, eyes wide. "I don't have to change *anything*." The date was the previous tenants' anniversary. I felt heard by God. Confirmed I'd made right choices. So, how could I negate *anything* that happened next?

It was June and the birds were chirping sopranos. The canyon walls that surrounded the cabin amplified all the sounds: woodpecker tapping, airplanes descending, coyotes howling. I tried to ignore the howling by covering one ear with my blanket.

Immersed in my new life, I felt as peaceful as the birds sounded.

All I thought about was real estate, property, and profit. My thoughts about business skipped one over the other like the crisp leaves that shadowed Chicago's sidewalks in the fall.

Then Dane called. "Jen, we *need* you."

I held my breath.

I like being needed.

"No, I can't."

I'd made a promise, a promise I want to keep.

Dane continued with convincing drug-talk: he wanted me to buy a new vehicle—a truck—and to drive with Hunter.

"I'll give you $20,000 extra if you buy a new truck."

Fifty thousand. *More than I'll make in a year with my job.*

And just like a druggie who can't let go of one more high, I convinced myself it was the right thing to do. The next week, I traded in my BMW for a new Discovery Land Rover.

Where did sweet *Jenny go? I don't know, but she's lost—*
She's lost in the heat of the kitchen,
cookin' up trouble,
a'misbehavin' and a'cheatin',
a'lyin' and a'stealin.'

Would she ever *come home?*

Dane wanted me to pick out the pot.

"I *barely* even smoke," I told him.

Dane didn't either, but he always picked out the bales for Detroit. I found this hilarious.

"Look for red veins," he said.

Look for the yellow brick road, I thought.

His last suggestion was to choose bales that were sticky to the touch. *Okay. Okay. Okay.*

I flew to Tucson and to Wheto, with his mustache and mirrored aviator glasses. He chomped gum as he drove us to the house on Ina Road.

I was nervous.

No Dane to hold my hand.

Most of the Tucson men didn't speak English. Wheto barely did, but he never admitted it. Most times he answered with a nod and a smile, like "Yes, yes, yes."

Did he *really* understand?

Inside the house, Wheto directed me to a back room—a bedroom turned drug-storage area. He left me alone with a man I didn't know who nodded and smiled just like Wheto did.

I'd never seen so many bales. Metal shelves were stacked with over a 100 three-foot-by-two-foot bricks clothed in plastic wrap that glimmered from the light of a cheap florescent lamp.

I felt like I was standing in a house of mirrors. Feelings of dread, fear, and shame came over me. And I remembered . . .

Blocks of modeling clay had been stacked just like this in my third-grade classroom.

At eight, I'd spent hours modeling a clay Paul Revere on a horse. I was proud until the skinny tall girl with the black hair made fun of my pony-tailed figurine.

She stood looking at it, her hands on her hips. "It looks like a girl."

I started to cry and told the teacher, who reprimanded me. "Now, you don't want to be a tattle-tale, do you?"

Then, I felt worse—a sinking in my belly that continued down my legs and into my toes.

Though I'd been innocent then, the feelings were the same now. Plus a pain like a golf ball had lodged below my sternum.

This felt *wrong*.

But I couldn't leave until I'd chosen the full load—2,500 pounds—*140 bales.*

I rolled up my sleeves and got to work.

My job was to say yes, or no: yes, we'll take it or, no, the quality isn't good enough and we don't want it.

Jesus, who was I to judge?

Honestly, I didn't know what the hell I was doing. At first, I tried real hard when the man-I-didn't-know dropped the first bale on the table and tore through the plastic wrap with a box cutter.

I took my time . . . felt for stickiness, investigated for red-veins—anything at all that would tell me the bale was a "yes."

My good-girl wants to do everything right.

An hour later, I wasn't even halfway through, so I just took a guess. As soon as the man plopped the bale down, I made my decision and he whisked the bale away. Like a blackjack dealer passing out cards, he slapped another bale down.

Hit me again.

Again and again . . . and again.

Droplets of sweat gathered in the crook of my back, dropped into my underwear, hid beneath the wire of my bra.

Damn it's hot.

After two hours, my vision blurred, my heart beat fast.

I was freaked out, anxious in a room alone with this man and all this pot in a place I didn't want to be.

Get me the hell out of here. This isn't pretty. This is dirty business—drug business.

Three hours later, I completed the task.

Wheto drove me back to the airport.

Home. I want to go home.

But, I couldn't click my red heels together like Dorothy. I couldn't wish my way out of this bad witch-of-the-west mess. I had to keep going.

Fuck.

Hunter, acting like Hunter, immediately put me on edge. He was to drive the Land Rover Discovery with the attached U-Haul trailer to Tucson to be loaded.

I wore my expensive drop-waist, flower-print dress when I met him near downtown San Diego. "Hey girl," he said as he hugged me. "Wow—*look* at that dress. You look like *Breakfast at Tiffany's*." He laughed, swung back his curls, and beamed.

I didn't have time to be impressed. I had one hour to finish at the office; then I had to pack for my flight to Tucson.

This was business, but Hunter was distracted.

He got into my new truck. "Yum. It smells like teenage girl and bubblegum in here."

Jesus.

I needed to show Hunter how the truck worked—important details if he was going to drive to Tucson. Although there were no drugs, the truck was in my name, and so was the trailer I'd rented. Driving from San Diego to Tucson with an empty trailer could look suspicious to a cop.

Yet Hunter peeled out, spinning tires in the gravel.

The night in Tucson was no better.

At first, I'd felt special during dinner at the hotel restaurant. I smiled over my plate of enchiladas as Harvey and Dane riffed about my being the best-and-only girl. The other men—Hunter, one-eared Cliff, and Big Bob—listened as I told stories about my new real estate job.

After dinner, Dane and I went back to our room. I didn't question why he'd gotten one room, but I was annoyed.

At least there are two beds.

I remembered his routine: the tan dopp kit, the toothbrush from Costco, even the boxer shorts. When Dane slid into my bed, I said no. "NO." I repeated firmly. "You're *married*."

I wouldn't want my husband to cheat on me.

"God, Dane. Aren't you happy with Aaron?"

He didn't have much to say, just scowled and went to sleep in the other bed, his back turned away.

In the morning when I woke, Dane was gone. Outside the loaded trailer, Dane ignored me and got into Harvey's car. The two men would follow from behind, while the boys took the lead.

On the road, things got worse. The truck couldn't carry the load over the steep elevation of the Colorado Pass, not with the snowstorm. Instead, Hunter and I took a side route, a small road through flatland and small hills. The driving was slow and we lost time, almost an entire day.

Sheep blocked the road, delaying us further, and I honked, laughing and crying hysterically.

Hunter swore.

My new Discovery was a V8 but, because it was smaller, it had less towing power than a Suburban. Dane had urged me to buy a bigger truck—a Chevy Suburban—but I told him only horse-girls drive those. "People would think I was crazy."

My decision had come back to haunt me. I'd bought the *wrong* truck.

Outside Chicago, my bad luck continued.

I watched the red light spin in my rear-view mirror as I ran through a toll. Harvey and Dane passed on my left, Harvey mouthing a silent "What the hell?" at me.

In Detroit, after the trailer was unhitched, I wasn't invited to dinner or for drinks. Instead, I cried alone in my room feeling like an outcast and a failure.

Lost.

Until Dane knocked on the door.

"Is everything okay?" I asked.

He smiled, patted me on the back, and handed me the cash. "Yeah, sure Jen."

I didn't believe him and, eventually, I was proved right. When he walked out and the hotel door shut, I cried.

Why did I feel betrayed?

For now, I was richer by $30,000, plus the $20,000 I'd used toward the new truck. I was tempted to spend all that extra cash. Plus I had the salary from my job, which was only increasing.

Feeling antsy, I decided I needed to move again. Climbing up and down to get to the cabin was exhausting, and the raccoons were freaking me out at night when I slept, rolling across the roof like bowling balls, then launching off into the canyon.

The move wasn't far—just ten minutes—but I was moving from the "country" to a downtown view—an artsy loft with a deck overlooking a new baseball field the city was building.

Suddenly, I'd elevated my lifestyle, upgrading from an easy $1,200 per month rent to an exorbitant $2,600.

Was I unhappy?

If I can't change my feelings inside, I'll change the outside. Despite all my spiritual work in the community, I was still good at fooling myself.

I didn't see the big picture—I didn't want to—not when I had a desire to satisfy. Why did I think life would look the other way while I did what I wanted?

As if I could get by being pretty and nice and clean on the outside.

As if I could look in a magic Romper Room mirror.

CHAPTER 22

THE BUTTERFLY EFFECT

I had butterflies in my stomach.

I was always excited when Ian called. During the past two years, we'd stayed in touch by e-mail and phone. In February, after my interview with Stephen, Ian and I saw each other for the first time in two years at Ono Sushi, a corner Japanese restaurant.

Over sashimi, my fingers had tapped nervous rhythms on my leg. With each stir of miso soup, my stomach flip-flopped.

I'd giggled, embarrassed I was acting like a schoolgirl.

I was surprised, too. I knew I was attracted to Ian, but I was still healing from my break-up with Casey, and Ian was off-limits again. During a hiatus from his girlfriend, Minka, Ian had slept with my friend Elizabeth.

When he hired me, Stephen told me Elizabeth wanted a relationship with Ian. "I told her if you moved to San Diego, you'd pursue Ian."

Ian and Stephen were close friends—almost like brothers. They'd met in the '70s on the same commune in India where *I'd* had gone. Both were fiftyish, English, and skilled soccer players who'd grown up in the town-turned-city of Leicester.

During the interview, I'd negated Stephen's comment. "My heart's *broken*. I can't even *think* about another man."

Six months later, I could.

As Ian talked, my body burned. The sun's rays were strong and warmed my back as I watched koi swim in their pond behind the office, but Ian's words over the phone were . . . *warmer.*

"Stephen's offered me a job," he told me.

My heart beat fast.

"Stephen wants to expand his business," he said. In a few weeks, Ian would move to Los Angeles to purchase properties for Stephen. But I knew the offer was more than that. Stephen liked to help his friends.

For me, Ian's most important news was he'd broken up with Minka. They'd grown apart after a yearlong separation on community business, Ian giving intensives in Germany, and Minka in Hawaii working on Kalindi's team.

Four years ago, I'd felt the magnetic pull between us, but he was taken then.

Now, he wasn't.

Weeks later at the San Diego office, I invited Ian to dinner and he accepted. The following Saturday, after dinner and drinks at my loft, we woke in the morning to our decision: we wanted to spend more time together.

Our new relationship created distance from my work friends. Stephen wasn't surprised, but Dave acted like I'd abandoned our friendship and Elizabeth walked around with an empty smile. My good-girl status fell to the bottom of *my* ocean. In addition to our growing friendship, Elizabeth had helped me secure my new job and she'd introduced me to my new spiritual teacher, Darrell, an American who lived in France and gave seminars in the States.

Aside from the wounded friendships, the first six months I dated Ian were fun—and easy. As planned, Ian moved to Los Angeles to an A-frame house below the Hollywood sign with filmmaker Cornelia and her boyfriend, Tom.

This was not the first time Ian had lived in LA. Before the spiritual community and his move to San Diego, he'd owned an art gallery in Santa Monica, brokered art deals, and attempted to make a career as a screenwriter.

On most weekends, we investigated the movie-star city. Our list of favorites grew: brunch at Hollywood Café 101, hipsters at the store American Rag, and lamb chops at Figaro Café.

Other weekends, Ian traveled to San Diego to my city-view loft.

Ian sautéed pasta in my black shiny kitchen as we debriefed our week. We listened to music or made our own, Ian creating beats on my *djembe* drum—a skill he'd learned in India—as I hummed off-key. The light from the skylight was dim, the music jazzy or Afrobeat. I could feel our relationship falling naturally into place, as if Ian and I were honoring a predesigned agreement.

Occasionally, I'd wake to the sound of wind whistling through bulldozers and cranes. They'd been deserted on the construction site outside my window only yards away. I'd never been so close to anything being built, but given my work schedule, I had yet to see the equipment move. The crane's arm never angled the other way, nor lifted metal beams or wooden posts. Even so, my back-deck view was grand, filled with possibility.

One day a set of bleachers appeared—as though constructed overnight.

Like magic.

From March 2002 to March 2003 seemed a magical year, especially with Ian's entrance into my life. I didn't see the year as prequel to a coming storm. I didn't see the foundations and footings being poured for a *self* that would have to withstand a typhoon.

And Ian, like a singular concrete pylon, would be the strongest support of all.

In June, Elizabeth softened.

I treated us to two nights at the fancy Mondrian Hotel on the Sunset Strip where we dined "*el* room service" and watched movies after a day of consciousness work at Darrell's seminar.

The next day, beside the pool, we talked.

I don't remember what we said, but I remember how Elizabeth listened and watched with both eyes clear and focused, not looking away until she was sure I'd finished speaking. The more we talked, the more I relaxed. I wanted to trust Elizabeth, and I wanted Elizabeth to trust me.

First, though, I had to trust myself.

I didn't.

I still felt the control of the marijuana money. If asked, would I drive again?

The last day of Darrell's seminar, I was chosen to pass the silk ribbon to another person's bamboo pole. In the moment it took to catch the ribbon and throw it back, time slowed. Once again, a space appeared—a place where everything was possible. In that space, the distance between Elizabeth and me dissolved. Later that night, as we drove back to San Diego, a warm feeling filled the car. The sweetness of our earlier friendship returned.

My life fell back into a flow.

I felt a rightness with Elizabeth, with my job, with Ian.

A rightness where nothing goes wrong.

In October, I treated myself to a birthday gift—ten days in the South of France and Darrell's annual retreat. Darrell was different from Kalindi: he didn't declare himself a guru or even a teacher. His students did.

Darrell encouraged us to look at life from a larger perspective. There were consequences to our actions, he said, and to the choices that we couldn't see or didn't want to see—hundreds of thousands of consequences as in chaos theory or the butterfly effect. After hours listening and dialoguing, I wanted to make conscious decisions in my life. I wanted to be aware of how the choices I made affected other people. Not just people close to me, but people I didn't even know.

But I didn't want to look at my trafficking. I didn't want to stop. *I can't,* I told myself.

After the seven-day retreat, I met a charismatic man who owned an art gallery and invited me in for tea.

I liked Paris. I liked tea. I liked art.

I was tempted to stay, but I was a new woman with a new man and a new job, and I'd just finished a workshop about responsible decisions. This was a good time to practice what I had learned. I might not be able to resist the money, but I could resist this man. Like a good girl, I came home.

In December, a week before Christmas, Rob called.

I'd already received my gifts: two sparkly purple skirts from Ian and two new additions to my loft—a roommate and a kitten.

Katie worked as an aide to a soon-to-be district attorney and needed a place to live. I offered my loft, which was large with an extra room. Then Gloria, who owned the building and lived below me, handed me a six-week-old kitten.

The kitten and I needed each other. My life wasn't as chaotic as it'd been with my dog Stacia. I wasn't traveling every three weeks trafficking money or drugs. I was thirty-four and settled enough to take on the responsibility of a pet. I named him Zoey.

Rob's call was a "no-big-deal" deal.

"You just need to rent a storage unit in Tucson. Oh . . . and a U-Haul."

No driving—no three or four days away—no worry about cops.

"I'll meet you in Tucson to drop the truck and the next morning we'll pick it up, loaded."

"Then what?"

"We'll unload the boxes into the unit—fifteen minutes."

"Who's picking it up?"

"An Atlas Van truck."

Rob said I'd make $10,000. I didn't ask who would be in the truck or how they were connected to Dane. All I knew was, *I* didn't have to drive. *Easy,* I thought to myself, *a piece of cake.*

Right away, I made a mistake. I went to the wrong rental facility, one I'd been told to avoid. Someone in the business had used it before, and Dane and Rob didn't want to increase our odds of attracting suspicion. Too ashamed at my stupid mistake, I didn't tell Rob and I didn't cancel the unit.

A few hours later, I found a better facility in a prime location. *Perfect.*

Then I rented a twenty-four-foot Penske truck. *Easy.*

Later, I met Rob and we dropped off the truck. "See you in the morning—early—6:30 a.m.," he said.

I nodded my head and went back to the hotel and to Dave.

The job was only two days before Christmas. *Why not have fun, too?* Ian was in England visiting his mum, so I invited my friend Dave.

He'd bought his ticket to Tucson, and I'd paid for two nights at the Tucson El Conquistador Golf and Tennis Resort set back against the Santa Catalina Mountains.

Dave didn't ask why I was in Tucson, and I didn't tell. Instead, the night before the Atlas truck pick-up, we celebrated *our* Christmas with steak, lobster, and wine at the fancy hotel.

The next morning, I woke at 6 a.m.

A half-hour later, Rob picked me up.

Unloading forty boxes out of the loaded U-Haul took less than an hour. As scheduled, fifteen minutes later the Atlas truck and trailer pulled in, and two men got out. We all introduced ourselves, using phony names. The men loaded the boxes. The truck left.

"The operation was a success," Rob said over the phone.

It was true. The "deal" was as smooth as my feet after my pedicure at the hotel spa.

Two days later, I flew to Ohio for Christmas on the red-eye, $10,000 richer and 10,000 ways more stupid.

Like puzzle pieces falling into place, my foolish choices—as Darrell had warned—were designing an unrelenting year for me.

By March, Ian and I were officially a couple. Zoey had grown from a kitten into a teenage cat, and my roommate Katie spent most of her nights with her boyfriend near Balboa Park.

After a year with Stephen's company, I'd worked my way up as he'd promised. With Elizabeth, I managed renovations, sales, and escrows. On my own, I reinstated defaulted loans—a high-pressure, think-on-your-feet type of job.

There was nothing wrong with my life. I was happy . . . balanced. When Rob called again, I saw no reason *not* to do the job. I still had the unit. All I needed was the truck. The only difference: Harvey would join us in Tucson.

New York was piggybacking off Detroit's deal. The Atlas Van truck would deliver boxes to Detroit for both operations, and Harvey's pot would come from another source—to be delivered by his men before the Atlas truck arrived.

I didn't mind seeing Harvey. I was happy I wasn't driving across country, even though I knew Hunter's girlfriend, Tiffany, had replaced me. I didn't want to hold a grudge. Plus, Dane and I had made up.

Dane has my back.

The next morning, I dressed in my favorite Juicy blue sweats, and Rob drove the loaded truck into the facility. Then we unloaded the boxes—filled with 1,500 pounds of pot—into my unit. An hour later, Harvey's load arrived—driven by two men in a white truck—which Harvey helped unload.

Rob pointed out the orange stickers that meant the boxes were designated for New York. Although Rob was calm, I was nervous.

Extra people and extra activity might look extra suspicious.

Rob turned to me, while we waited. "Do you remember what names we used last time?"

I didn't.

"Shit. So you be Lori, and I'll be Bob."

Sounds good to me.

The flippant decision created aliases we'd be stuck with for years—two white-bread '80s names.

When the truck came, only *one* man got out. The other man wasn't feeling good. "The flu," said the other man, peering out the passenger-side door.

The other man looked confused and tired. "Hey there, what's your name?"

Come again?

"I'm Bob," Rob said, and then pointed at me. "This is Lori."

The man loaded the boxes with the dolly. He was jumpy, not calm like last time.

Is he on drugs?

I brushed off my edginess.

We were finished. Done.

A piece of cake.

Two nights later, cooking dinner for Ian, I got the call.

Dane.

"It's not good Jen—not good at all."

"What?"

My heart went *pit-patter, pit-patter.*

"The load was intercepted," he continued. "Someone got caught."

"Caught? Who—I mean *how?* Was Johnny? . . . Shit!"

My eyes widened, and so did Ian's. He knew about the marijuana, and he knew I was talking to Dane.

"Is *anything* in the unit?" Dane asked.

"Boxes—unused—and some decoy furniture. Should I get them?"

"No, stay *away*. I'll call with an update."

"Dane, I'm scared."

"I know, Jen."

"The unit's rented in *my* name."

"Shit!"

But Dane wasn't surprised. None of us had ever used a fake ID. I was too stunned even for frantic thoughts, so afraid, I felt myself disappear.

No one was here to protect me.

The next day, I ignored Dane's orders, rented a car, and drove to Tucson to get the unused cardboard boxes.

They'll look suspicious. I can't just sit around waiting for Dane to call.

The rain was an ominous sign. A raincoat concealed my girly body and a baseball cap hid my short hair.

After two attempts at the combo lock, I rolled up the door. Paranoid, I looked around. Ten unused boxes, stiff and new, faced me.

Ten unused U-Haul boxes accompanied me home. I'd left the furniture. Rain pellets, swishing wipers, no music on my radio. *Numb.* I wanted to stay this way. I didn't want to feel.

I dumped the boxes somewhere.

Can't remember where.

My functioning level—my brain—had shut down, extinguished by paralyzing fear, the kind where you don't feel anything at all.

CHAPTER 23

WHO'S YOUR DADDY?

The next four days I worried.

Worry made me sleep. Worry woke me up.

I couldn't focus on anything. I shuffled papers on my desk, then left work early and drove aimlessly in my car. I paced my apartment, waiting for Dane to call. When he didn't call, I called Ian, then called again. All I could think was, *people have been arrested*. The thought was foreign, unreal.

But, it was real.

Finally, the phone rang—Dane. We would meet Joseph-the-attorney in downtown Los Angeles.

During the three-hour drive, my mind was as gridlocked as the traffic. I blared the radio, wishing music would block out my fear. Yet, no matter what played, the lyrics in my head were the same: *what's going to happen to me?*

Dane would come up with something. He always did.

I arrived in LA, frazzled. Cars honked as I drove, circling downtown streets looking for Figueroa. Once I found the glass high-rise and parked my car, I could breathe.

I slouched low in the driver's seat, wiggling out of my conservative office attire into something less frumpy—a long jeans skirt and white blouse. Changing clothes in the car was a skill I'd learned as a dancer—all those quick costume changes and costume bags for performances at outside venues. But this performance was unscheduled and unknown.

The white tablecloths, chandeliers, and tall ceilings in the first-floor restaurant were fancy. This was a place where I could pretend everything was okay. When Dane greeted me with a big smile, the tiny helixes of tension spiraling through my body relaxed. This was the first time I'd seen Dane in six months, the first time since he'd told me people had been arrested.

Dane's like family, protecting me. Isn't he?

I'd only seen Joseph once, three years ago, when we'd driven the marijuana. He'd worn jeans and checked shirts then. Now he wore navy pants and a striped tie, looking the part of high-powered attorney.

Joseph stood and smiled, too. But when he sat back down, his gaze was jumpy, his hands unsteady on the table, compared to Dane, who calmly signaled to the waiter.

"The house chardonnay," he said, gesturing toward me, "and I'll take the same. Joseph?" Casually, he slipped a white envelope of cash to me under the table.

Dane knew I wanted money. No more trips would be happening anytime soon, if ever. My name was on the storage unit.

How could I—we—be so stupid?

I didn't count the bills, but my hands could feel the amount. I guessed $3,000—the last of the funny-money. I felt like I'd failed myself and everyone in the business.

Dane didn't mention mistakes. He kept the meeting light, touching my leg with an it's-okay pat.

I was hopeful, waiting for Dane's solution. But the longer I sipped my wine and the more Dane smiled, the more I saw the meeting for what it really was. A check-in.

Dane's job was quality control. He needed to report back to Johnny and Harvey that I wasn't freaked-out, that I was strong and solid like he was.

For a moment, I felt like the tarpon I'd caught off the shore of Key West, except I was hooked on a marijuana-business line that stretched from Detroit to San Diego. Dane, holding Detroit's end, needed to hook me, reel me in . . . and not let go. That's what it felt like and, later, the facts would confirm it.

Dane *had* hooked me nine years before, with his need and his love. Later, it was about the money. But we still were *family*. I wouldn't hurt Dane, and Dane wouldn't hurt me. So, why did I feel unprotected? Why did I feel caught? I wanted to torpedo my frustration toward Dane, to bombard him with questions he couldn't answer, like what was going to happen to me . . . to my life. Instead, I asked Dane questions he could answer, but questions he couldn't answer over the phone. "Who was arrested?"

"One of Johnny's men. He's a stand-up-guy. Johnny said he wouldn't talk."

"But, what happened?"

"DEA and SWAT teams raided the house and then the truck—as soon as it arrived. We don't know how, but they *knew* it was coming." Dane tugged my leg, squeezing more firmly than before. "Try to relax." But I couldn't relax. I was frozen, numb inside and out.

I thought back to my first date with Dane. The clean white tablecloth and the perfect breadsticks in their perfect jar seemed lifetimes away. Now the fancy restaurant disgusted me. The cold, perfectly sliced butter annoyed me as much as Dane's touch. There was nothing perfect or pretty about this situation.

"Am *I* okay?" I asked.

I didn't really want to hear the truth, and Dane didn't tell. Maybe he didn't know. He danced around my question with a jig and a smile. "Wheto said 'the princess' should come to Mexico."

Was this my only back door, my only escape?

"They have a place for you to stay until things cool down."

I felt worse.

No way, I thought. *No way in hell.* My mind went to Tucson, to bales of pot, to eight years ago when someone had been *taken* by the Mexican drug-dealers.

I stared at Dane, then down at my plate. When I realized he wasn't going to answer, my stare turned as cold as the restaurant's décor: mauve silk curtains, stark white marble floor.

Dane told me not to call him. He'd call me. "*Never* mention anything about marijuana or money over the phone." He said he'd give me more money next time, and that Joseph had a connection—some ex-governmental official with experience in cases like this. Dane would set up a meeting soon, "real soon."

He hugged me. "Don't worry, Jen, okay?"

But, I was worried.

I walked away carefully, trying not to slip on the floor's polished tile or on my worry. I looked back at Dane and Joseph, who were engrossed in conversation.

Are they talking about me?

For the first time, I doubted Dane. Doubt rushed my mind with the frenzied energy of a mob at a sold-out concert.

Does he care about me, or is he lying?

If I can't trust Dane, who can I trust?

My dad had taught me to trust people, so had my mom. I'd carried trust in my backpack for years. Now, I felt naïve and silly.

And paranoid.

Twenty minutes later, I was sitting across from Ian at our favorite French café, both of us chain-smoking. I fantasized that I could leave, take a break from Westminster and play-pretend in Mexico that I had another life . . . that I was a *different* Jenny. I put my head in my hands and said it out loud: "Maybe I should take the offer and go to Mexico. . . . But I can't just leave my life."

Ian's words were vague, comforting. "I know, Jen. . . . I know."

This time, not even Ian had answers. No one did.

Confused, I took the easiest way out. I didn't do anything at all.

The next week I continued my routine. I applied mascara and pink lip-gloss, took Pilates class on Tuesdays and Thursdays, cleaned Zoey's litter box, and bought iced-mocha coffee with sweet-stick cookies. I met contractors, called agents, and laughed with Elizabeth and the newest employee in our office, Zulyia.

Hidden in the camouflage of my routines, I thought maybe awfulness wouldn't see me, would pass right through and go away.

I *almost* felt better when I saw Rob in Los Angeles the next week. *Sweet Rob.*

I hadn't seen or talked to him since we'd left Tucson, when we'd thought everything was okay. Still, I was normal enough to see that Rob looked good, tall next to Dane. He was the high-rise at 1900 Avenue of the Stars where we met and Dane was the squat two-story shopping center next door. Both men were dressed sharply in white shirts and crisp slacks. *Clean.* The clean that used to make me feel safe. But, *damn* Rob was nervous.

Then again, Rob always was.

He walked straight ahead, focused, as we followed Dane into a small room connected to an office. Dane had set up this meeting with a man who was supposed to give us an answer to our question: were Rob and I going to be okay?

Dane was playing jovial when the man with the sandy blond hair walked in. "Nate," Dane said, introducing Rob and me. "He's been on the other side of the game and knows a lot."

Rob and I sat in two stiff-backed chairs facing good-looking Nate. I was curious. Waiting. Hopeful.

"I've confiscated pot and prosecuted criminals. I know what they're looking for," Nate said confidently.

Dane told him our story.

Once upon a time . . .

When Dane had finished our tale, Nate asked what we wanted to know.

Rob spoke first. "Can they arrest us?"

"Not unless they catch you with drugs."

Perfect—just what I want to hear.

"Really?" I asked.

"Sure. All you've got is a unit with nothing but some furniture. Nothing's going to happen."

"He's your man," Dane said. He looked at us like everything had been resolved.

Drum-roll please.

"If *anything* happens, anything at all, Jen, call me," Nate said. "You'll only be in overnight."

In?

I felt the blood drain out of my face. Did he mean in *jail?*

He handed Rob and me each a business card. "I'm your man."

I'm your man. I'm your man.

The words echoed on the marble tile as Dane walked away . . . from me . . . from our beginnings.

I'm your man. I'm your man.

I wouldn't see him again for two years.

Rob pulled me aside. "What do you think, Jen? Do you trust him?"

"I don't know, Rob. . . . I don't know."

I want to. It's all I have.

"Jen, if I hear anything, I'll call you. If you hear anything, call me." Rob was desperate, and I could tell from his stuttering voice that he was scared.

So was I, Nate or no Nate.

Later, I realized I had believed Nate 110 percent. I'd mixed him up with someone else, someone I could trust.

Who's your daddy?

I'm your Daddy.

The night before my arrest, I had two vivid dreams and wrote them in my journal. In one, there is a character like Gumby with a hole in his center. Something is missing, but what? In the other dream, I'm in a small boat at night and we're moving very fast on dark stormy waters.

Both true. Both prophetic.

Both dreams foretold answers to questions that were brewing, questions I wrote once again in my journal that morning: Should I move? Should I quit? Should I commit?

I hadn't heard from Dane or Joseph for weeks. I was tired of not taking action. Later that day at work, I called Joseph.

"What should I do with the unit? It's still in my name."

"Cancel it."

I was relieved, tired of the unit hanging over me. I wanted off the lease. The tops of the tall bamboo outside my office swayed back and forth in an invisible breeze as I tapped in the number.

I gave her the number and told her to trash the furniture inside the unit. She asked why, and I told her "because I don't want it." When she asked *why* I didn't want it, I thought, *Why is she badgering me—God, just let it go,* and then I blurted, "Because I'm going out of the country."

Oops.

From the moment I woke on April 23, 2003, the day felt important—special—in ways I couldn't fathom. Looking back, my dreams, journal entry, and thoughts seem to be one continuous thread—a direct line of information from God or my unconscious—reaching toward what was to come—as if what happened next had been forever written in stone by ancient gods, lifetimes away—and finally, the time had come.

"This month feels familiar," I wrote at the top of my journal.

I could smell it.

Is it someone's birthday?

Next I wrote, "Just because you can't hear them doesn't mean they're not screaming."

The trees?

Just a few days before, Ian and I had talked about the old philosophical riddle: if a tree falls in the forest and no one is there to hear it, does it make a sound? I'd felt sorry for the trees. "They are alive and they feel. Just because you can't hear them doesn't mean they're not screaming."

On this morning, the screaming seemed closer.

What am I forgetting?

Still, the workday began like any other: personnel discussions, a possible move to the LA office, lunchtime Pilates, logistics.

Then Stephen's assistant interrupted our meeting. "Someone's here to see Jen."

But a man in white tennis shoes had already pushed his way through the doorway. "Jennifer Myers. I'm from the DEA. You've been indicted by the Eastern District of Michigan."

Did Stephen and I walk toward the man?

Did we meet halfway?

I can't remember.

Did I die?

Am I still here?

If so, God, can you please make me disappear?

I was somewhere in downtown San Diego.

The wind moved around the corner of the alleyway, chilling me as I stood with the agent. I shivered and looked up at double metal doors. The building extended high in the sky. Up and up, so high I couldn't count the levels.

I couldn't see any windows.

I was shaking from more than the wind.

Mug shots and fingerprinting had taken hours. I was worn out, my strength thin. It was now evening, the light dim outside where we stood.

"You seem pretty calm," said the DEA agent, an older man who'd driven me there.

Silence.

I didn't even look at him.

"I guess you've done this before," he continued. "You sure are acting like a pro."

He couldn't see inside me, inside where I was frantically praying.

I turned my head to look at him, pausing before I spoke. "No . . . never."

I could tell he felt sorry for me. I was beginning to feel sorry for me, too.

I was totally frightened.

The unknown behind the double steel doors was freaking me out.

I can't stop shaking.

"Someone will be here soon. Don't worry."

I didn't respond. I liked him. I did. I just couldn't give *anything* away right now. Nothing. I was protecting myself, and I had to remember he was the enemy.

I looked down at my toes, past my hands cuffed in front of me, feeling incredibly alone.

The agent pushed the intercom button again.

"Yeah," someone finally said, the voice faint through the speaker.

"I have a commit here: Myers."

The doors, when they finally opened, scraped rusted metal against concrete, about to lead me into the unknown, a passage into my imagined hell.

When the woman appeared in front of us, my mind resisted

going through those doors with her. I looked back at the agent, who suddenly seemed safe and familiar.

I did *not* want to leave him.

I felt a piece of me break off and separate as I was led through the towering doors.

I am not going to cry.

As I looked back at the agent, I imagined a young girl behind him. She stood motionless, sad. In my mind, I waved good-bye to her and silently mouthed, *I'm sorry.*

And the doors closed.

CHAPTER 24

DOUBLE-DUTCH TROUBLE

I heard a *slam,* and the steel doors closed behind me.

I was locked in.

Has the earth stopped moving, or have I?

I could still feel my heart . . . *thump-thump* . . . *thump-thump* . . . a beat that quickened as I looked around.

The change was a visceral one.

Bright, glaring lights.

Steel cages lined both sides of a hallway, gleaming under florescent lights. The glare of the lights was as unforgiving as the agents had been, the steel cages as empty as I was.

I was disoriented, standing next to a female uniformed officer I didn't know.

With a tug, she directed me into a small room where a three-ring plastic binder lay on a metal table. She opened the binder and wrote something. I didn't see what.

I felt like I'd died and she was writing in God's book. I thought of my grandma and her large Bible, always open on the living room table. But I wasn't listening to my grandmother singing from a hymnal or reading from the scriptures. I hadn't died and this wasn't heaven.

I was in hell on earth.

A hell *I'd* created.

The officer unlocked the handcuffs. "We don't need these right now. Take off all your jewelry."

I felt vulnerable when she placed my pearl earrings and cross necklace into a plastic bag and opened a wide drawer. One side held ugly synthetic bras and full-cut panties. The other side, pairs of navy blue canvas shoes.

"You're so small," she said, almost sweetly. She shuffled through the drawer like a sales clerk at a seriously twisted Victoria's Secret. Lucky for me the size "small" panties and bra were brand-new, not well worn like the others, and not discolored like the white jumpsuit she pulled from somewhere, I don't know where.

I suppose I looked as new as the underwear. New to prison, or was this a jail?

Where am I?

The officer handed me my new bundle of clothes and directed me into a cell across the hall.

Click. She locked the door.

Nothing fit right. The new panties reached up to my bellybutton and the rolled-up hem of my white jumpsuit covered my shoes. My designer outfit lay on the floor, the blue Juicy sweats corrupted twice—first at the storage unit where the drugs were picked up, and today, behind bars.

My arrest.

Despite the dark and ominous aura surrounding the clothes, I was reluctant to hand over the last of the familiar, the last of *mine*.

Everything went into a white mesh bag tied at the top with a string—clothes, jewelry, and flip-flops. The officer carried the bag like she was taking out the trash.

I felt like trash.

She unlocked the door and, on command, I followed. My feet shuffled along the concrete floor, slow in despair, awkward in new canvas shoes. We walked an endless hallway past gray and empty cells.

I didn't know what came next, and no one was telling.

At the end of the hallway was a metal door with a tiny window, not a door I wanted to step through . . . one I *had* to. Behind the locked door was a five-by-five-foot room where I sat alone on a small metal bench. Silent and oddly calm, I waited—whether I liked it or not, whether I wanted to or not.

No dignity. No choice. Time distorted.

No windows. No clocks.

I shuffled in and out of the cell again for more fingerprinting, another mug shot, and an assigned number on my jumpsuit that reminded me of a kindergarten nametag.

This is Tammy . . . and Stephanie . . . and Robby.

But I wasn't a name. I was a number.

My ties to my past threatened to break. Then where would I be? Lost at sea, far away from my beginnings. Far from the protector trees of my childhood. Far from the comfort of the white barn on my parents' farm.

If the trees had whispered words of truth, I hadn't heard, or hadn't listened.

They had failed me.

Or had Dane?

Possibly *I'd* failed me.

After hours—or was it minutes?—I circled the small room. On tiptoes, I peered through the tiny window.

I feel forgotten.

I was right. Sometimes the officers *did* forget. I heard voices later and an officer said, "There's someone in there!"

Keys jangled as he rushed to open a metal door—mine.

This time, another female officer directed me and three other women to a semi-private concrete area, like a divided shower stall, but no shower.

"Okay, girls, you know what you got to do . . . bend down and cough."

What? I had *no* idea. I stood, mouth open, motionless—like, *huh?*

"Don't give me any funny business," the officer said, looking directly at me. A bolt of fear tore through my body.

"She's new," I heard one of the women call out. "She's never done this before."

"Turn around, bend down, spread your butt cheeks and cough," the officer said sternly.

Jesus.

I wanted to disappear.

I wanted to melt like the bad witch in *The Wizard of Oz*, or fist-bump like the wonder twins in the cartoon of the'80s so I could transform into another shape and get the hell out of there. I did *not* want to pull down my pants or bend or *spread*.

I did it anyway, but not right. "No, you gotta hold it. I need to see you aren't hiding somethin."

Like what?

I was horrified. What could I want bad enough to hide . . . *there?*

On the third try, I did it right—and every time after that.

Bend down and cough? Sure, no problem, officer. I ain't hiding anything. Not in my a—hole, not in my che-che . . . and definitely not in my mouth.

A tiny girl—under five feet—sat on the bench in the corner and sobbed, unleashing the tears I couldn't.

How could I cry? I was frozen.

She looked even tinier than *I* did in the white jumpsuit. The sleeves hung past her fingertips, the legs rolled double at the bottom. She finally lifted her head, her plump cheeks tear-stained. *Did she even speak English?*

I wanted to wrap her in my arms, to console her and stop the tears, but I couldn't.

Or, could I?

I was in unfamiliar territory. I didn't know whom to trust. What I could and couldn't do.

Better not to talk at all.

I stayed silent.

The gangly woman wanted to talk. "I'm a coyote," she said to no one in particular, after the cell's door slammed shut and the officer walked away.

What's a coyote?

"They caught me with two Mexicans in the gas tank."

I was shocked. *They were* in *a gas tank?*

She turned to me. "Why are you here?"

"Marijuana trafficking."

"Oh, you mean a mule."

I was ashamed. I'd been more special than that, hadn't I?

Her chatting switched to Spanish when she turned to the other girl, who suddenly began to talk.

The gangly woman reported back in English. "She was caught in her boyfriend's van—crossing the border. He had drugs—a lot of drugs. She swears she didn't know." She turned to the girl and then back to me. "She has no money for an attorney. Her little girl's in Mexico. She doesn't know how she'll get out."

I didn't know which felt worse, hearing the girl's problems or worrying about my own. At least I was feeling something. I was no longer numb.

For the past six hours an animal instinct had kicked in, numbing my feelings like Novocain. The Jenny I knew had skipped town. A different part of me, like a big sister, had taken over.

Was I protecting a lovely and innocent girl . . . or a shameful and guilty one?

I don't know.

What I did know was, I felt shattered. Fragmented, like millions of tiny dancing lights snuffed out. Like the shooting lights from the sparkler my dad had lit on the Fourth of July when I was seven.

I'd stepped on that smoldering sparkler fifteen minutes later.

The excruciating pain stopped in hours, but the scar—a long dark line like a tattoo embedded in the sole of my left foot—was so deep, I imagined it would never disappear.

But it did.

Maybe *this* pain would stop. But what about the scar?

Hours later, I was handcuffed and escorted by a male officer into an elevator with a man handcuffed like me.

I stared. He was the first man I'd seen in handcuffs—except on TV. I wondered who he was, why he was here.

Was he dangerous?

"Face the wall," said the officer.

"What?" I asked.

"Don't look at him. Look at the wall."

Oh—

That's what troublemakers had to do in fifth grade, face the wall.

I couldn't stop the shame.

The man was dropped off before I was. Two floors up, we exited, stopping in front of a metal door. The officer turned. "Are you ready? This is the *crazy* floor."

I looked at him, eyes wide. I could hear noise through the closed metal door—a steady hum of ruckus. "I'm *not* kidding," he said. But he smiled.

When he uncuffed me and opened the door, I didn't want to go in.

Loud.

Noise bounced from porcelain tile to windowless wall like a Ping-Pong ball; feet were thumping; fingers were typing and shuffling cards. Girls sang, laughed, and yelled. Two women were even chasing each other around the room.

"HEY!" the officer yelled, "Calm it down!"

They ignored him.

He gave me no further directions, just walked away, with a jingle of keys and side-to-side jaunt.

For the first time since I'd arrived, I was unattended.

Immediately, I was swarmed. The women's words rushed over me: "Hey, you want to do aerobics with us in the morning?"

"We do it every morning."

"Why are you in?"

I didn't know whom to answer first, so I didn't answer at all.

The past four hours of lock-down in a small cell seemed like a luxury now compared to enduring this crowd of unknown, female *prisoners*.

But, I'm a prisoner.

I collected items the women offered.

"Here, use this shampoo. Here's some toothpaste, soap, conditioner." I was the new girl on the floor, and they wanted to help— an honor system among inmates I'd learn later.

I was hesitant, shy, sort of checking things out like I had the first day of seventh grade. But, the more items I had to call mine, the better I felt.

The women's care surprised me, and melted away the ice inside. I began to see something soft in this hard locked-down world. We had *each other*.

This had always been true, but here, in the midst of crisis, locked inside a new world with new systems and rules, the connection felt like a brilliant sunset after a dark June-gloom day. I told one woman I hadn't gotten "my phone call."

"Girl, you deserve to have a call. Fight for it." And I did, walking over to the officer two more times before he finally escorted me to the phone.

I patted the pocket of my jumper.

Still there.

I'd protected this card ever since I'd been arrested.

"It's a business card," I'd told the agent when he arrested me, "an attorney. I need his number."

Now, I pulled out the crumpled card—my lifeline.

I'm-your-man Nate.

After the third dial, still no answer.

When I realized I couldn't leave a message from a prison phone, I was frantic. My fingers shook as I randomly punched keys, desperate to remember *anyone's* number.

But, I couldn't. I was confused, and my fingertips tingled. My confusion turned to fear and then tears I brushed away. Then I heard the knock. "Your time's up."

"But, I didn't get through to anyone."

Was I whining?

I was.

Shit. Double-dutch trouble.

Everything had happened *so* fast.

Does anyone know where I am?

At least *I* knew where I was now.

One of the girls had told me we were in San Diego's medium security correctional facility where the government housed federal offenders who were serving short sentences, or those who were awaiting trial and hadn't been granted release, which is where I fit in.

A few women had been here for *years*, I was told. They waited with an unknown future, living on a floor the size of a small cafeteria with no outside view.

No outside at all.

An officer directed me to a cell—a two-person room. She pointed to the top bunk. My bed. The metal toilet was exposed, open to the room, to my cellmate.

I refused to go.

The first night, I felt empty anyway . . . barren.

By midnight, the desolation gnawed at my insides. *No one knows where I am.*

When the guard locked our metal door and every other cell-door that circled the main room, I felt claustrophobic for the first time ever.

A *slam*, the clinking of keys, bolts turning. The sounds repeated like an endless echo. The eerie musical discord unlocked a floodgate of tears I wiped with the corner of the scratchy wool blanket.

I can't believe this is happening.

I wanted to renegotiate with God, to reverse life's order, to take it all back, and make a new Jenny plan.

I'm sorry, God. I'll do anything . . .

I was scrambling, begging.

Desperate.

I woke up to the guard unlocking our door. "Myers! Get up. You've got court."

The metal mirror was warped. All I saw was my face distorted, wavy.

I dragged the plastic comb through my hair. The same way I tore the foil off the top of the orange juice from the breakfast box the guard handed me, disjointed and slow.

Not in control.

Going to court took hours, and there was a group. We were processed in and out, pictures taken, strip-searched, and other logistics I can't remember.

I do remember the marshals. Big, burly, tall, *good-looking* men wearing navy T-shirts with M-A-R-S-H-A-L printed in bold yellow. Even in devastation, I noticed. Marshals—like paramedics and firemen—such a sense of manliness, control.

I was not in control, especially handcuffed and chained to a prisoner on either side, wearing a metal chain that linked around my belly like a Gothic accessory belt.

The marshals led the train of us into a long, dim tunnel that ran underground and connected the prison to the courthouse. "Keep your head down," one marshal would say every now and then.

We shuffled, awkwardly trying to find unison in our forced two-step dance. Yesterday had been awful, but this chain gang was worse. I felt stripped of my rights, of respect. Every step was taking me closer to somewhere I didn't know, but didn't want to go.

Choo-choo . . . choo-choo . . .

We were a human train going nowhere, in never-ever-again land.

I promise, God . . .

I was negotiating again.

Underneath the courthouse, I waited in a cell that felt like a cage until I was taken upstairs to "normal." The expensive wood and fine lights of the courtroom seemed beautiful—extraordinary—compared to where I'd been . . . cages and tunnels and cells.

Lions, and tigers, and bears . . . oh my.

The minute I saw Stephen and Ian, I cried with relief.

I was no longer in this alone.

The prosecutor argued I'd flee the country.

The words I'd said to the woman at Sabino Self-storage two days ago rang in my head: *I'm going out of the country.*

Those words had gotten me arrested.

The prosecutor showed the judge the unused seven-year visa to India in my passport.

Were they kidding? I'd gotten that visa *six* years ago.

Stephen stood up and spoke on my behalf.

The judge paused before he spoke. "We'll have a hearing. *But,* Mr. Watts and Mr. Ross, you'd better come prepared. Bring letters from co-workers, family, and friends. You'll need to *argue* her case."

For the first time, I heard the live sound of a gavel hammering down.

The ice inside cracked a little.

I felt hope.

The next six hours were busy. I was called off my floor three times: first, to meet a public defender, then Stephen's attorney's assistant, and finally, Joseph.

The one-by-three-foot sliver of a window in the room where I met the attorneys saved my sanity.

After twenty-four hours, I could see out. I could see a sailboat in the bay so far away it looked like a toy boat.

It's true. The world is still there.

I wanted the sailboat to stay in my view as long as possible to remind me that everything was moving out there, even though I was in here, locked up. I wanted the moment to last.

Everyone wanted my case: Stephen's attorney, the public defender, and Edward—the attorney Dane and Joseph had found.

Joseph looked scared as hell.

"Are you going to *give* her anything?" the officer asked Joseph before we stepped into the room.

"What?" He looked confused.

Frustrated, I blurted out, "Joseph, if you give me something, they'll strip-search me after our meeting. I've already been strip-searched *once* tonight after I met the first attorney. Say 'no.'"

"Sure—no, of course not," he stammered, pale.

I don't remember what Joseph said. Something about promises, that Dane cared about me, things like that. All I remember is how he looked: shocked and pale with cheeks so red they looked like he'd been slapped.

Prison was freaking *him* out.

I bitched about "I'm-your-man-Nate" who was *not* "the man." Then I pleaded with Joseph to get me out."

Dane had an attorney.

"He's the best, Jen, just the best. He's known as the 'pot guy.'"

I had mixed feelings—relief and unease.

Could I . . . *should* I trust Dane when everything he'd told me *wouldn't* happen *had* happened?

The next day I waited in a holding cell with the girl who'd cried the day before.

I smiled. This time, since no one could see, I patted her back when she cried again. We weren't allowed to touch in prison, but the touch felt good, alive.

Through a Plexiglas panel, I met Edward, Joseph's attorney. "Don't worry. We're going to get you out." He reached his hand through a small opening to grab mine.

I looked at my hand, half covered by a white jumpsuit.

Is this my hand?

I could barely tell.

The judge released me, on three conditions.

I was to wear an ankle bracelet and live in Stephen's guesthouse. Until my parents' property was posted as bond, Stephen would take financial responsibility, guaranteeing I would not flee.

My parents' property?

They didn't have much money.

I can't believe what I've done . . . the magnitude.

When the court reporter brought the papers to sign, I began to cry tears of relief that I was getting out, tears mourning my past life, my present pain, and the pain of hurting the people I loved the most.

My new life was going to be very different.

But this was only the beginning.

When I first realized how my actions had affected others, my tears turned hot with shame and slick with lies that burned as they slid down my face.

The judge looked up from letters my friends and family had written and met my gaze. "I don't know how a woman such as the one I'm reading about could have ended up here."

I opened my mouth, but before I could answer, he said, "That was a rhetorical question. *Don't* respond."

But I wanted to shout out my story, tell him what a good woman I really was.

Wasn't I?

That afternoon, two officers drove me to Stephen's house.

I sat in the back of a normal mid-sized car, feeling grateful— almost elated.

A trip to prison for three days will spark anyone's life.

My *grateful* included the sky, the clouds, the traffic, and even the smell of exhaust. To me, they were all the same.

I was happy to be outside. Still in shock, I felt both older and more childlike. Hurt, like when I'd stepped on that sparkler.

Scarred, this time on the inside.

I was just different, that's all. A different that held all of the letters of the alphabet, named every part of me and my life—where I'd been the past ten years and who I was now.

From A to Z.

Nothing was hidden anymore.

Or was it?

CHAPTER 25

BUT I'M A GOOD GIRL

My senses were alive.

The orange-red sky was like no sky I'd seen before, the officer's blue jacket as rich in color as a sapphire.

Through the window, I saw Stephen's house lit up as bright as the Christmas trees my brother and I used to trim with white twinkle lights. A glow climbed over the canyon and stretched high across the sky.

I was almost surprised when I pulled the lever and the car door opened.

I'm free.

The feeling was unfamiliar—alien—after three days in prison.

Freedom didn't last long.

As soon as the officers led me through glass sliders into Stephen's guest quarters, they attached a two-inch wide rubber band—a new accessory—around my ankle.

The unwanted ankle bracelet sent a signal to a two-pound box shaped like a small car battery that sent a signal to a government computer. I'd carry this GPS unit with me, keeping it no more than fifty feet away from me and my tether.

This was house arrest.

An officer explained the new rules: "You can't leave the house until 7 a.m., and then only for work. You have to be back home by 6 p.m." He pointed to a stand they'd connected to my phone. "If you don't place the box on the stand by then, a red light will light up on the box." The light means a signal has registered on the government computer.

His final words: "Report to pre-trial on Tuesday."

I felt like I'd gone from one prison to another. At the same time, I was relieved I wasn't actually locked up.

Still, I was petrified. *If I made a mistake, would they lock me up again?* I knew the judge would.

I'd signed my name on a piece of paper agreeing to adhere to the government's rules. There would be no more secrets, no fancy clothes, no exotic vacations. My inner concierge had locked down luxuries and thrown away the key.

This time, there was no back door.

After the officers left, all I wanted to do was crawl under a blanket like a tired five-year-old and hide.

Still numb.

But my welcome home dinner was waiting. Ian had cooked the roast, and Stephen and Larissa, his new wife, were anxious to hear what had happened.

Larissa slid curious looks at me as Ian told what had happened on their end. "We didn't know where you were the first night."

I knew it.

"Stephen's attorney called the prison, but they told us you weren't there."

Half true, since I wasn't officially *there* until I was "processed in" at midnight.

"Stephen spent the last three days scrambling to get you out— collecting letters, making calls. He didn't even *work*." That was unheard of for Stephen. Ian didn't mention his own sacrifices.

For the first time in my life, I'd actually been saved. The plastic silver knight I'd kept since I was five had finally come to life. Was Stephen the knight? Or was Ian?

Possibly both.

After dinner, Ian gave me a gentle reminder. "Jen, you have to call your parents."

No. I can't.

But Stephen had asked for my parents' number after I was arrested.

Jesus, they already know.

After Stephen called my parents, my mother called her brothers who were both attorneys on the East Coast. Tom and Mark had been in daily contact with Stephen since my arrest.

"Jen, your family's been great. They care," Stephen said.

Now I *did* want to call. I wanted to cry on my mother's shoulder like I had at ten when I'd crashed my three-wheeled ATV into a tree. Stunned and crying, I hadn't been able to walk at first, and my mother had run toward me with outstretched arms, calling my name. Frantic, she'd scooped me into her arms. I'd already stopped crying, but her tears wouldn't stop.

"Mom, I'm okay," I'd said. Embarrassed and comforted at the same time, I'd rolled my eyes and disentangled myself from her tight embrace. To prove I wasn't hurt, I'd cartwheeled and pirouetted toward the front door until she smiled.

This time I knew it would take all of my strength to convince my mother I was okay.

Because I *wasn't* okay. My cartwheels didn't turn and my pirouettes didn't twirl. They'd been slammed in the prison door.

I told myself I didn't want to deal with my mother's fear. The truth was I didn't want to face mine.

I don't remember making the call; it's been hidden under shame too long, tucked inside painful places I still don't open.

I do remember Mom's tearful, "We love you, Jenny," and Dad's words of strength and support.

My brother was the outspoken one. "I knew Dane had to get his money from *somewhere.*"

All I could think of were my own mistakes, my imperfections, so obvious now. But my family didn't seem to care whether I was perfect or not. In their space of no judgment, I felt love.

I cried, grieving a loss I didn't understand. Like something was being taken away that could never be replaced.

Like a part of me was dying.

But, what part?

Having sex while wearing an ankle monitor wasn't sexy.

The thick rubber ankle band clunked awkwardly against Ian's ankle a few nights later in Stephen's bed.

Ian didn't seem to mind, but I did.

The government band was a constant reminder of my new restricted life: I was on house arrest, on pre-trial, waiting to be sentenced for a crime I *had* committed.

I'd sought freedom for the past five years. Now I was farther away than ever.

Wasn't I?

I woke to a gorgeous Saturday. Normal. The sun shining and the cup of coffee Ian made in the press. Not like prison.

On numerous occasions, I'd been to Stephen's two-story house on an acre of land in east San Diego, but I'd only once gone down the spiral stairs that led to the guest quarters. With a two-sided gas fireplace and sliders opening to a pool, the one-bedroom was not a bad place to be. Even on house arrest.

My release from prison had made me feel light, free and alive, except for the weight around my ankle. The over-sized rubber bracelet hung low, making a clunking sound like a belly dancer's ankle bell gone sour.

The excitement of leaving lockup had dissipated and I walked aimlessly, dazed liked I'd been in an accident, irritated by the light film of dust on the floors and countertops. *I need to clean this place,* I thought to myself. Stephen's guest quarters had been empty for months.

I also needed my belongings.

Every task felt impossible.

I was climbing my way out of shock, trying to catch up to the reality of the last four days. I couldn't leave the house until Monday, so Ian brought everything to me from my loft. He rented a truck, packed what I needed—including Zoey—and moved it all to Stephen's.

That evening, cocooned in Ian's arms and surrounded by my cat, my sheets, my pillows, I felt safe.

When I rolled over in bed, Ian cuddled tighter. The square metal box embedded in the bracelet hit my bare ankle with a *thud.*

Reminding me again.

Not safe.

Monday morning, I woke to a slow mind and slow movements. Tears of frustration flowed when I couldn't find an outfit that covered the bracelet. I was not going to show up at work exposing *that.* Being arrested in front of everyone five days ago had been shameful enough.

Finally, I chose a long patterned skirt and tucked my tether into black, soft suede boots.

I could see the lump through the suede, but would *they?*

The DEA had confiscated my SUV. I had no idea where it was or when I'd get it back. When Elizabeth picked me up, I didn't want to leave Ian or the safety of the house. I felt exposed, my secrets revealed. If I left, I'd be vulnerable to suspicion and attack from others.

But I had to go to work.

Ian kissed me good-bye with a promise to call. He was off to Los Angeles and wouldn't be back until the weekend.

Elizabeth's hug was gentle, but not gentle enough.

I wanted to feel good like I had as a child when I ate rainbow sherbet on a cone, ran barefoot in warm rain, and listened to a symphony of crickets on a twilight-fading night.

I feared my lifeline had snapped. Would it ever grow back?

Call 911. I need reviving.

Once I was at work, the day seemed like any other day. I called agents and escrow officers, wrote budgets, and made schedules.

But, *I* wasn't the same. A part of my brain was missing.

I couldn't calculate numbers. The word "paper" slipped out when I meant to say "pen." Eighty percent of my brain was occupied by my trauma and legal case, leaving only 20 percent to maneuver everything else.

How will I ever get by?

To my amazement, life continued.

On Tuesday, I met Jeffrey.

His curt voice, crew cut, and military style seemed appropriate for a pre-trial officer and federal government employee. His job was to make sure I obeyed the judge's rules and stayed in town until sentencing. This involved his knowing way too much about me, so much that I felt tied to the government like a lover caught in a morbid seduction.

He even had my pee.

A woman watched while I squatted and peed into a cup. Efficiently snapping on gloves, she placed a litmus card into the cup to test me for drugs.

"Negative," she said, and threw the gloves into the trash along with the cup and my pride.

I wanted to scream, *I don't do drugs!*

But I was muted by government rules and didn't say a word.

Instead, I got used to the peeing routine.

Jeffrey gave me more rules: Visit him once a week. Ask his permission if I want to go anywhere but work.

I was concerned about my coffee. "What about Starbucks?"

"Drink coffee at work."

"Seriously? I buy a Starbucks *every* morning."

"Fine. Leave me a voice message where you are."

So I did, every single morning.

"Hi, Jeffery. It's Jennifer Myers. Monday, umm, 7:45 a.m. I'm going to Starbucks, located at 3150 Sixth Avenue." Starbucks at 2300 Broadway. Coffee Bean at 2000 Washington Avenue.

As for the weekends, we'd "go slow," he told me.

The first weekend I couldn't leave the house. The next, I could leave only for a few hours with his approval. Every weekend after that, if things went well, he'd approve my faxed itinerary.

The second Saturday, I made a mistake.

With the gas tank empty and the needle past red, I pulled into a station. Ian reminded me that I should have been home twenty minutes ago.

"I know, but *they* won't."

Then I heard a loud *beep . . . beep . . . beep.*

"What's that noise?" I looked around, then down at the box in my tote. *A text* showed in a window I hadn't noticed on the box before: "Call me. Jeffery."

Oh . . . that's how it works.

I was never late again.

To survive the insanity of my restrictions, I made it a game. I told myself I would be the *best* woman on pre-trial ever. I would do everything 100 percent right, just like my mother had taught me with my fifth-grade science fair project.

Back then, I'd spent hours researching, designing posters, and memorizing my report. I was determined to win the county competition—to beat everyone. And I had, in both fifth and sixth grades.

Now I created extensive weekend schedules for Ian and myself. Since I could go out, we did. Garden walks, brunch, and walks on the beach. Museum exhibits, movies, and street fairs.

During the week, I left work at 5:30 p.m., earlier than my normal ten-hour day. Rushing to make it home by six, I tailgated cars and wove through traffic. Once home, I sprinted into the guesthouse like a runner on a relay team, sweating, nervous, heart pounding, to set the box on its stand.

Even Jeffery, with his neat desk and curt talk, grew tired of my precision—all those faxes and calls.

"Geez, Myers, you sure like your coffee."

"Am I the *only* one that calls?" I asked, feeling silly that I'd done it wrong for weeks.

But I hadn't done it wrong. This time my good-girl perfectionism was paying off. If I followed the rules, my restrictions were lifted, and Jeffery paid less attention to me.

I mean, Jeffery had to keep watch on hundreds of people on pre-trial.

Where was this going to end?

I didn't know, and God wasn't telling.

I ached to talk to Dane, but that wasn't allowed.

My only news of him came from Joseph when we met in downtown San Diego the first week after my arrest. "He's okay, Jen. Are you?"

I could have asked Joseph the same. He didn't look good. Was he tired, hung over, or afraid for himself?

He handed me a white envelope of cash. "Here's five, and there's more coming." Joseph was my spokesperson to others in the conspiracy, the man in charge of keeping me happy so I didn't talk. And he was my link to Dane. "Call Edward, okay?"

"Okay."

Stephen was vehemently opposed to my hiring Edward to represent me. "He's *Dane's* recommendation."

Stephen didn't trust Dane. He was afraid if I accepted Dane's money to pay Edward, I would be tied even closer to drug dealers.

But Joseph was right about this. I'd done my research. Edward was one of the best. Plus, I didn't have extra money of my own to pay an attorney. When I was arrested, I'd been on an upswing of spending and my credit cards were maxed out. Any attorney would cost, but one of Edward's caliber cost more—$80,000.

"Seriously, Joseph? That much?"

Seriously.

Edward's law office was downtown, close to the federal courthouse where cops parked for coffee. Parking enforcement carts circled the streets like coyotes stalked rabbits in the canyon behind Stephen's house.

Slender and tall, Edward walked at a clip, legs bowing as I followed him down a wood-floored hallway.

His desk was as full as the parking spaces outside his office. Stacks of papers—some a foot high—were strewn this way and that.

I immediately fell in with Edward's Harvard law ways as well as his signature ties. The ties were slim and deco or quirky pink and bright yellow. He was witty, chaotic, sometimes pompous, and usually late. His hurried look said, "If I could only find that file. What's going on?"

Still, Edward was a master when it came to the federal system. He'd negotiated many lighter sentences in pot cases, but times had changed.

When he told me I was facing ten years, I almost fell out of my chair.

"*Ten years?*"

"Jen, it's a point system, calculated by the *Federal Sentencing Guidelines Manual.*" He threw a heavy, green soft-cover book on his desk.

What? Dane had never mentioned anything about these guidelines. Nor had Joseph, and Joseph was an attorney.

I almost choked on the bile rising in my throat. "You mean there's *no* way around the ten years?"

"Not unless you cooperate."

Cooperate? "I'm not talking."

"My hands are tied. I can barely do my job. Even the judge's hands are tied by the guidelines."

The classification of the drug and the amount of drugs involved determined the sentence. Edward was right. Although pot was the lowest risk—Schedule 1—I was charged with conspiracy to sell and distribute 3,500 pounds.

Other factors applied: my role as a mule, victims of my crime, level of violence (none). A gun could have added another five years—a "gun charge"—the girls in prison called it.

Holy shit: ten years.

No way.

I can't.

I wouldn't survive.

Edward made calls.

He called the Detroit prosecutor—the first of many conversations—weaving his way through the government maze to negotiate a better situation. Edward smiled as he described me. "She looks like a school teacher. She's a *good girl.*"

Was he being sarcastic, or sympathetic? I couldn't tell.

Maybe I could look the part, but I didn't feel like a good girl.

I'd created a mess, and everyone was scrambling to help me out of it.

My parents were rushing to get paperwork for my bond. Edward was working to find my car, get me off house arrest, and keep me out of prison. Ian was traveling to San Diego every weekend, living with my restrictions. Stephen was still protecting me, but I could tell he was torn between his compassion for my predicament and his anger at my continuing to drive the marijuana after he hired me.

Now Stephen wanted me to work in Los Angeles—120 miles from San Diego.

"You can manage LA," he said a month after my arrest. Ian was buying houses, and I would be in charge of training men to supervise the renovations. At my first court appearance, I could ask the judge to lift my restrictions so I could travel outside of San Diego.

After the judge agreed, I made weekly day trips to LA with my box in a tote, and my tether under jeans.

Now, I *didn't* cry.

Most of my life I'd dripped tears as easily as I'd spent money.

For the first time, my grief was plugged up.

I was on auto-survive.

Every night before bed, I'd review my life and my journals.

I'd wake in the night and open my eyes, knowing something was wrong. I'd run through my drowsy checklist: pillow, still there; Zoey, by the window . . .

In haze of sleep, I wouldn't remember until I did. *Oh,* ankle bracelet . . . *still there.*

I'd close my eyes and somehow fall back asleep.

I struggled to control a future that couldn't be controlled.

I couldn't eat. Lost weight. Smoked. Read my journals. Looked for back doors.

None.

"*Ten* years," I repeated to Joseph at his LA office.

His face turned white, and he stuttered as he told me Rob wouldn't stop calling him. "He's worried about *his* fate."

"Well, tell him I'm looking at ten years," I said, disgusted at what sounded like selfishness and weakness. Rob was thinking only of himself.

I could hear my voice rising. I was furious. "Joseph, don't you know about the federal guidelines? You know, the green book?"

He hadn't. He didn't.

Now, he looked sick. His face went from white to a chalky shade of gray.

"Well, see that office across the hall? The plaque on the door says 'criminal attorneys.' Go ask for the federal guideline book. I'm sure *they* have one."

I was disgusted. Frustrated.

Joseph told me he was freaked out, trying to get money to pay Edward's fees. He met men he didn't know in "weird places." His face twisted to grim. "Scary."

He was still wearing a Brooks Brothers suit, but he was no longer the suave LA man. He'd been replaced by a shaky, scared shadow of himself.

I liked Joseph. I did. I knew he liked me, too. He was genuine when he told me not to worry. His eyes would soften with a look of care and concern.

But Joseph really couldn't help.

The truth was, Joseph was in danger, too, and he knew it. But there was something *I* didn't know. People in the drug business were meeting in different states, and they were talking about *me*.

Later I read transcripts of their conversations. It wasn't pretty stuff.

But what *was* pretty? I couldn't tell. My "pretty" barometer was off. My rose-colored glasses, gone. They were tied up in a white prison bag, along with my blue Juicy sweats.

CHAPTER 26

EVERYBODY'S TALKING

I was having a meltdown.

For the past hour, I'd been trying to find something to wear. Rejected outfits and mismatched shoes were scattered on the floor.

I was running out of time.

Discouraged, I chose a cream-colored suit and brushed my wet, tangled hair with angry, frustrated strokes.

"Jen, we *have* to go." Ian's voice was tense.

I was stalling.

I didn't want to go to court.

Ian looked straight ahead, his eyes on the road.

The court date had brought back my bouts of crying. "I'm *ugly*." "Jen, you look great." He didn't say much, and his voice was clipped and terse. He was running out of patience.

"I don't *feel* great."

I wiped away streaks of black mascara, smoothed wrinkles on my suit. Looking out the window, I cried some more.

I didn't want to be in this car headed for court. I didn't want to be in my life. I wanted to disappear and let someone else take over.

But *who* would volunteer?

I felt a little better when I saw Edward. He was focused, his body relaxed as if the courtroom was his home. In a way, it was.

I wasn't relaxed. This was alien territory for me.

Standing behind the podium, I wrung my hands as Edward asked the judged to release me from house arrest.

The prosecutor brought up my Indian visa again. "She'll flee."

I felt myself crumble.

"Pre-trial?" the judge asked. He and I looked at Jeffrey, my pre-trial officer.

For a moment, Jeffrey seemed as comforting as my mother. "She's followed the rules," he replied, just like my mom used to say.

I thought back to the ethics my mom had tried to teach me. Like the time when I was thirteen when she'd angrily driven me back to Kings Island Theme Park to give back my prize stuffed sheep. I hadn't earned it, she said. I'd lied.

"I'll guess your age or your weight," the man had told us. "If I'm off five—one way or the other—you get a prize." He was only one year off, but wanted a prize, so I lied.

When we got to the theme park I told the attendant I was giving back the stuffed animal. I felt mortified when I handed her the brown crinkled bag and told her why. She raised her eyebrows but didn't say anything.

She probably thought I was weird, but I felt damaged, bad, a liar—a girl who didn't follow the rules.

Like I felt now.

I'd flee?

The judge began slowly and quietly. "You know . . . *sigh* . . . I've never quite understood the purpose of an ankle bracelet." Then he raised his voice and gestured like a circus ringmaster. "It's not as if she crossed the border into Mexico where a steel cage would drop down, like in that movie with Steve McQueen. What was the name of that film?"

He looked at the court reporter and then across the courtroom, as if waiting for an answer.

No one spoke.

"The point is, she could cut the bracelet off if she wanted to. I would."

When giggles ran through the courtroom, I almost giggled, too. I was amused and pleasantly surprised by his attitude. I'd expected a harsh and official judge. Instead, he seemed comical and casual.

And, *almost* on my side.

The next day Jeffrey unlocked the bracelet with a special tool.

"You still need to see me, Myers, once a week. You'll be tested for drugs, and if you spend the night in LA, call me. More than one night, you'll need permission."

Untethered, I walked out the high pre-trial doors like I was walking on pillows piled on a Tempur-Pedic bed—a lightness I wanted to feel forever.

When I exited the elevator, I saw a sales stand hugging the corner of the lobby. Designer knockoff wallets and handbags.

My heart raced. I was tempted to shop. And I did.

I inspected the bags inside and out, looked for tags, felt for linings and rough zippers until finally the *one*—a maroon bag with two handles and a double pouch. I paid $200, extra money I didn't have to spend.

Once home, I jutted my hips to one side and another, modeling my new bag in the mirror for Zoey.

Two days later, I hated the bag and threw it into the back of my closet, so embarrassed I didn't tell anyone, even Ian, about my purchase.

I felt silly.

I'm released from house arrest and I buy a purse?

The funny San Diego judge was not my real judge. My case belonged where I was charged, a place I didn't want to go. Detroit.

It was my time to plead "not guilty."

Edward bought the plane tickets and I paid for the hotel room at the Ritz-Carlton where Rob and I had always stayed.

I felt anxious, desperate for routine in my upside-down life.

Traveling back to Detroit on the plane the first time since my arrest, I felt nauseated. Once I left the airport, I was repulsed by the city's smell—a mixture of exhaust and burnt rubber from auto manufacturing plants.

Or was the foul smell only in my mind?

When Edward opened the door of a blue Mercedes, memories of past taxi rides on past drug trips leaked out, corrupting my mind like an oil spill: cash in wrinkled bags handed through windows, shoeboxes of cash dropped on beds, the green van, dark-haired men, U-Haul trucks and trailers . . .

I didn't trust this dark city.

But I knew, the dark I didn't trust was inside myself.

Jen's world.

The prosecutor scared me more than Detroit.

When Edward introduced us, I wasn't sure how to shake his hand. With a smile, like *thank you for arresting me* or with a blank look that said *I don't care.*

I decided to smile.

What's wrong with me?

He wanted me to go to prison. But my mother had taught me to be polite. Was I a good-girl-gone-bad or a bad girl trying to be good?

I didn't know.

What I did know was I couldn't find my inner bearings—not in Detroit, a place where I didn't feel safe, or good, or pretty.

The judge was black, and as I stood in front of her, I imagined her judgment: I was a white woman who'd brought drugs into her city.

After court, an officer ordered me into the back for "more fingerprinting and a mug shot." He treated me like a criminal, locking me inside a cell while I waited for the procedures.

The next forty minutes, my body shook. Memories of the San Diego prison were fresh in my mind, but this time, instead of my Juicy sweats, I wore a blue suit, Mary Jane heels, and pearls.

Although I was locked up behind shiny steel bars, I sat upright and proper like I was in church. My fear revved on high turbo-drive.

I felt exposed as men locked in cells across the hall leered at my bare legs, whistled, made catcalls and suggestive comments. Their male testosterone was in lock-up, too.

Why am I in a cell?

When the officer brought me back, Edward was livid, his face cherry red. "*Never* put my client in a cell." As he swung his briefcase and raged at the officer, I felt protected.

Walking down the courthouse hall we seemed out of place, though. My stylish blue heels and Edward's pink tie seemed to clash with the conservative, gray, rough-around-the-edges Detroit style.

We'd almost made it to the entrance when a skinny man in Levi's called out, "Hey, are you Jennifer Myers? I'm Erick—DEA—I'm handling your case."

He held out a hand, and I shook it, staring at his blond almost nonexistent eyebrows and beak nose. Who *was* this man?

"I spoke to you over the phone the day you were arrested."

Oh.

Now I remembered: "All your friends are talking. Wha'cha think about that?"

His threatening words had scared me, but he was no older than twenty-five. I could wrestle with him or hug him like a younger brother. "On the phone, you scared me."

He almost smiled as another man walked up. "Tell Todd here what you told me, how I scared ya."

Then I recognized his familiar Southern drawl.

"You did. I was *really* scared." And, I meant it. Erick laughed and puffed up his chest as he poked Todd in the arm. Like he'd won a prize, this agent who was only a kid.

He'd called the girl and made her cry.

I felt loss as I walked out the courthouse doors. As much as Detroit repulsed me, the city had been an important part in my life, for years.

My work was in Los Angeles, and it was time to move there. I'd already hired our first employee, and Ian and I had found an apartment for the office—the lower half of a duplex in Hancock Park—only a mile from where Dane had grown up.

I wanted a new city and a new life.

I wanted to be with Ian. I'd felt tied to him, since my arrest, as if he was a part of my legal case and one couldn't exist without the other. I felt grounded when I was with him. He spoke gently, weaving my story into lighter places on dark nights when I was anxious. I didn't want to untwine. I wanted to live with Ian every day, while I *had* every day.

With Edward's legal expertise, it didn't take long for the judge to agree to the move.

But freedom was an illusion. The waiting kept me imprisoned whether I was locked up, locked down, unlocked, restricted, or released.

Some days I felt good. When a restriction was lifted, even better.

But they were temporary feelings.

My life's foundation rested on my spinning legal case. Each day took me closer to prison or further away. I didn't know which.

The not knowing made me feel manic, out of control. I wanted off the carnival ride.

Other days, I'd wake and take a deep breath.

Still here. Breathe in . . . breathe out.

Something was happening. I could feel it. Maybe I was growing up—maybe I was more in control than I thought I was.

The truth was I was busy.

Not only was I managing the Los Angeles office, but I was also planning Larissa and Stephen's wedding celebration. During the four months I'd lived at Stephen's guest house, I'd gotten close to Larissa. She'd asked for my help, and Stephen had asked for Ian's.

Good distraction.

The long complicated criminal process was eating at me, but I couldn't eat. I was "too thin" as my friend Stefan used to say.

I meditated, screamed into a pillow, danced to loud music when I was alone but remained upset, especially after my last meeting with Edward.

"Jen, I have good news."

Great.

"I got you seven. It's called a safety valve." He was proud, but I was devastated. Seven years?

That was the *good news?*

I couldn't imagine going to prison. Somehow, I expected to get out of it. I didn't *feel* like a criminal.

"That's it, the best you can get?"

Edward didn't have to say anything. I knew the alternative. "*Unless* you cooperate."

I was silent.

Shit.

"I'll talk, but not about Dane."

"It doesn't work like that, Jen. They'll want to know everything. If you hold anything back, you won't get your deal."

"Then I'm not talking."

"Jen, *everyone* talks."

I was firm.

Seven years?

Someone was talking.

Edward told me that after he got off the phone with the prosecutor. "Jen, somehow they *know* a lot of details. Do you know how?"

I didn't.

They'd arrested a man from Detroit. I didn't know him. And Joseph had sworn he was a "straight-up guy. No way he'd talk."

So, who was talking?

Edward shuffled through piles of paper, distracted. "Jen, you should cut a deal. It's almost too late already." He made me feel like I wasn't very important. But his next words were *very* important. "Someone has *already* talked."

I met Joseph in Los Angeles at the Coffee Bean on Hillhurst Avenue. A place where hipsters dressed down in peg-legged jeans and Converse shoes, and women wore braids. Joseph looked out of place in the East Village vibe, but I felt at home, a feeling that had grown during my first month in LA.

Our meeting was quick, routine.

Joseph passed the cash, and I asked how he was, both of us pretending we had something to say.

I was still concerned about Dane, yearned to talk to him but couldn't.

"He's good, Jen. Don't worry."

Who's worried? Me?

I used to battle headaches and now battled an ache that gnawed at my insides, starting at three o'clock every day. My indigestion was so bad sometimes I couldn't sleep, knives shooting into my sternum and my throat. I felt sick, went to the doctor and swallowed chalky foul-tasting stuff. Nothing showed up on the X-rays. I guess it was stress.

Gone ill from my misbehaving, sick from my arrest and all this waiting . . . and what's going to happen next?

In two days, I turned thirty-five.

Happy birthday to me.

The weather suited my mood. As I drove from Los Angeles to San Diego, a cloud darkened the sky, hovering like my legal case. Seaside fog layered the coastal highway like the regret that stifled my birthday excitement.

I was getting sick of it.

Tired of waiting and wondering what was going to happen next . . . who was talking . . . and worried about *seven years*.

I'd made my decision.

I was cutting a deal.

Edward told me to "dress nice," so I did.

I felt silly in my black dress and pearls next to the men from Detroit in Midwestern casual—khaki pants or jeans with checked shirts. They were the prosecutor, Erick the DEA agent, and Todd who turned out to be an IRS agent.

Later, I asked Edward about the IRS. "What does *that* mean?" He didn't know.

Scary.

I felt torn.

On one side, I wanted to protect myself. On the other, I wanted to protect everyone else.

But *who* was protecting me. *Someone* wasn't; that was for sure.

I pointed at pictures: "Yes . . . Yes, him. . . . No . . . Yes."

They had *everyone*.

Edward was right. They did know, but how?

"Hey, you don't have to dress up next time, okay?" were Erick's last words before he left.

When I shook the prosecutor's hand this time, I was on his side. Still, the handshake didn't feel good.

Life seemed unfair and flawed. I felt desperate and dark, waiting in deep water for a bite as powerful as a shark's. My mind felt twisted, tired after a full day of talking, pointing, and answering questions.

I ached for all that I'd done and all that I couldn't reverse.

I felt angry, like I'd pushed aside my values by my decision to talk. I wanted to be a victim. I wanted to blame someone else.

But, how could I?

I *was* guilty. I'd wanted the trips, and the money.

And, now, I didn't want to go to prison.

I felt stilted and repressed, locked up inside.

Not the way I wanted to be. My sacred circle used to include gurus and seminars and dolphins. Now I was surrounded by prosecutors and pre-trial officers and DEA agents.

Erick would call and ask questions. Questions I couldn't answer, details I didn't remember. The more Erick talked, the more I realized there was a lot I didn't know—and they did.

I heard about loads I hadn't been invited to drive, the scope of New York's participation, and just how much money the marijuana was worth—billions of dollars. Each load I'd driven, maybe a million.

I mean, someone was making a shitload of money, and it hadn't been me.

"Always behind the eight ball, Jen—always in debt," Dane had repeated, and I'd believed him.

Had he been telling the truth?

I stopped calling Joseph.

I left a sweet message, thanking him for his help, telling him there was no reason for us to talk.

I wasn't supposed to talk to Joseph. If I did, I'd get in trouble.

Now, I wasn't tied to drug dealers. I was tied to the federal government, which was offering me a deal. I'd signed the plea agreement, feeling like I'd signed away my life. If things went well, the prosecutor would suggest a "downward departure" from the guidelines and the judge could legally sentence me *below* seven years.

Joseph called anyway. Then stopped.

The silence was foreboding.

CHAPTER 27

THE CASH SMELLS GOOD

I was standing outside my apartment in Hancock Park talking real estate on the phone when Hunter walked by with a little dog on a leash.

I stopped mid-sentence, mouth gaping.

He couldn't be here—not in LA in front of my apartment. And, what was he doing with a scruffy little Yorkie on a leash?

He took the lead, giving me his big movie star smile. "Hey there, darling."

At least some things hadn't changed.

Unable to talk to anyone in the drug business except Joseph, I'd felt alone. My bottled up words shot out like a stream of pepper spray. "Do you *know* what happened?"

He swore he didn't.

I was soothed by the reflection of blades of green grass that turned yellow in Hunter's sunglasses, but not by the tiny Yorkie. Frantic, the dog ran back and forth sniffing grass.

Behind his stylish smile, Hunter was as tense as the trendy little dog. When I told him about my arrest, Hunter placed his arm around my shoulder and flashed another big smile. "Wow, *really?*"

Both the dog and the man settled down then. Circling, the dog rolled onto its back. Smiling, Hunter slid his glasses up over his curls. In that moment, I trusted Hunter. He was someone familiar who understood the business, and he was handsome. But, when he asked if the duplex was where I lived, I lied. "It's where I work. What are *you* doing here?"

"Staying at a friend's, working in fashion." I could almost believe that.

When we exchanged numbers, I knew I wouldn't call. With a hug and a last flip of his hair, Hunter waved good-bye. As I walked up the driveway, I felt a slight hint of fear.

Should I be concerned?

When I told Ian about the encounter, he warned me that it wasn't a coincidence.

He was right. Hunter lived in Las Vegas. He wouldn't be in LA, on my street. But his casual manner and mock caring eyes had drawn me in. His walk-by had seemed natural, one of life's hidden plans. A synchronistic event like I'd experienced during my spiritual travels.

Now I was worried—frantic. And so was Ian.

He paced back and forth in our bedroom, as tense as Hunter and the dog. Ian whispered about my safety, and his.

Am I being watched? If so, why?

DEA Erick told me not to worry but to keep him posted if anything out of the ordinary happened. Nothing did.

Still, I felt stalked when Hunter called and left messages. I didn't answer.

One week later, I recognized a white Suburban with Midwestern plates parked a block from my duplex. Hunter and his stripper girlfriend had driven marijuana in that truck.

I snapped a photo of the license plate to show to Erick, *just in case.*

Hunter called three times and then stopped.

I could breathe.

Until, I couldn't.

Edward heard that Rob talked before I did. The rumor was Rob had hired a top-notch attorney from San Diego and turned himself in one month ago, thinking *I'd* talked.

I hadn't. Not yet.

Why was I surprised? Rob had always been scared. Of course he'd want to protect himself first. He'd thought of himself first when he kept calling Joseph, the way I probably should.

I didn't blame him for talking, but I couldn't understand why he'd turned himself in. I was glad I'd followed Edward's suggestion to cooperate. If I hadn't, I'd probably be locked up. It was clear to me now. No deal—*no* winner. If you don't make a deal, you end up a loser.

My next trip to Detroit, I traveled alone. No Edward.

The DEA's downtown office was dreary with gray tiled floors and a dropped T-bar florescent-lit ceiling. Deserted.

"More fingerprinting," I was told.

I waited, quiet and demure with a hair barrette and feminine blue designer coat. When the receptionist called my name and I stood up, a young man in jeans put down his phone and perked up.

"*You're* Jennifer Myers?"

"*The* Jennifer Myers who drove tons of pot across the country into Detroit?" His eyes seemed to pop out of his head, his mouth turned half a grin. He looked surprised, almost impressed.

He knew my case, but who was he? With his jeans, flannel shirt, and all that youthful masculinity, I guessed he was an agent.

Should I feel complimented or offended?

Didn't I look like I could drive that much marijuana for eight years? Did I look too innocent or too weak, like I didn't have the guts?

My old competitiveness flared, catching me off guard. I felt like a side act at a carnival show—a drug tell-all attraction. I was relieved when Todd the IRS guy walked in.

"Ready?"

On the way to the back, Todd checked his gun.

"*You* carry a gun?" Now I was the one impressed. "Why? You're an IRS agent, not DEA."

"Yeah, we get guns, too." He sounded proud, bantering about gun practice and targets. Wanting to find something in common, I brought up my trapshooting win with Casey, the only time I'd shot a gun. "Damn, she's good," the men at the club had said when I shot another clay pellet out of nowhere. I'd felt like a trickster, surprising them all.

This time I'd tricked myself; thought I could keep all that money and never get caught.

IRS Todd didn't seem tricky or complicated, but simple and nice, like he belonged on a college campus. He was calm with less aggressive maleness going on. Unlike Erick, he had no Southern twang when he spoke.

After fingerprinting, he flipped through mug shots on the computer.

For the first time I saw mine in pixel. It was an awful picture, really, no smile, a double tuck of my chin. I asked Todd to re-take it, and he did. Like a model at a photo shoot, I tilted my head to the left and beamed. I was pleased when he showed me the picture.

I looked good.

Why did I care? Looked good for whom?

My first mug shot was worse.

After Todd, I met with Eric who pointed at pictures again, "How about that one?"

"No."

"That one."

"Yes."

Then, "How about her?" And, he laughed as he pointed at my picture, the one taken when I was arrested.

It was horrible, really. I didn't recognize *that* girl.

Face long, sagging. Like I'm fifty years old. Defeated. A sad girl with an upside down smile.

I looked away, disgusted.

Later that day Erick and another agent picked me up. We drove on highways, then backstreets where gravel driveways led to concrete buildings and unfamiliar abandoned strip malls.

Erick pointed out drop-off locations I didn't recognize and asked me questions. Sometimes I thought a place looked familiar, but I wasn't sure.

"Ya recognize that one?"

"No."

Twenty minutes later we pulled up to a different address. "How about that one?"

"No."

As darkness replaced day, I settled into comfort. The drive almost felt normal like the agents were my friends, asking questions about the city.

I slipped out of my seat belt and leaned forward between the front seats to begin a conversation the way I used to when my parents drove my brother and me to the DQ on hot summer nights.

I directed my questions to Erick. "What do you think about marijuana? I mean, I never felt like I was *hurting* anyone."

He was quick to reply. "It's a gateway drug. Everyone starts with pot. You haven't seen the guns and shoot-outs."

"Marijuana?"

"You betcha. Some deal it all—marijuana, cocaine, *and* crack. It's a bad scene."

Like an armadillo protecting its underside, I curled up, defended myself. "Well, I never saw a gun, not *once*."

Still, I was disturbed about what he had said. If it were true, people could have been hurt by my crime. People I never saw, never knew.

Was he *right*?

I thought about Darrell who'd spoken at his retreat in the South of France about how even our subtlest of actions had a worldwide affect.

"Get some sleep," were Erick's last words as he dropped me at the Ritz-Carlton. But, I couldn't relax. Instead, I sat in familiar—the bar, Kir Royale drinks, salty peanuts—but *I* was unfamiliar. This time, the words I wrote on cocktail napkins were dark and dirty like I hadn't bathed in days.

Tomorrow was grand jury.

I tore up the napkin and dropped it onto the table like pieces of a jigsaw puzzle—except this puzzle had no box and no picture.

How could I fit the pieces together if I didn't know what the final picture looked like?

I was tipsy and in a bad mood when I called Ian. I was angry he hadn't come, angry at myself for not asking him to come, angry he hadn't insisted. I hadn't realized I'd want him with me—that I wouldn't want to be alone.

Abandonment followed me into sleep, and the Egyptian cotton sheets draping my head didn't help. *I'm alone . . . I'm alone* slipped out in my dreams.

I feel like a victim.

The next day, I felt out of place in my black suit with the wide pink Charlie Brown stripe. The prosecutor beside me in the elevator wore traditional dark blue.

Do I want to fit in?

I do.

I smiled at the other man in the elevator, and he smiled back—a smile that seemed to confirm we were on the same team.

But, we weren't.

Once in the room, the man took his place with the others in their jury seats, and I took mine—on the witness stand.

The prosecutor had a flow chart that listed everyone from the drug business—those I knew and some I didn't. Lines joined circles like the math brainteaser I'd mastered in sixth grade. Except this time, the circles enclosed names instead of numbers. Dane was in a circle labeled "Kingpin" and I was below labeled "Mule."

I wanted to answer honestly, so I tried my best to tell exactly what I *knew*, not relying on what I'd been told.

When I flew back to Los Angeles, I slept for days. Then I did a little detective work. I called the hotel that agents had recommended. "Can I have Rob Miller's room?"

"He checked out a day ago."

I'd been right, and so had Edward. Rob *had* talked.

We'd both been interrogated at grand jury. That fact brought us together. For a moment, I almost felt bonded to Rob, whom I hadn't seen since my arrest—even though I'd been irritated he didn't once ask Joseph how *I* was. Before I knew he talked, I'd been tormented by my decision to talk. I'd had dreams where we kissed hello or hugged good-bye. Either way, I was always crying. We'd been friends, hadn't we?

When I was a child, I'd thought friends were forever—a lifetime. I yearned for simpler times when I'd played house among the exposed tree roots with my best friend, Laura. We'd made platters out of leaves and cups out of maple seeds.

Not like now.

Who were my friends? Was Dane? Was Hunter?

The government knew a lot, things I didn't know, things Rob couldn't know.

Who else was talking?

Sammy called. "I have your *green* sweater."

I don't know a Sammy. I don't have a green sweater.

"Do I know you?"

"Dane told me to call. You left your GREEN sweater at my house."

Dane. That's all I heard. "How do you know him? How is he? Can I talk to him?" My words stampeded together, my emotions lassoed. I was frantic, caring about him, and feeling guilty at the same time.

"He's fine," the mysterious woman replied. "Let's meet so I can give back your sweater."

What sweater?

I didn't hesitate. "Yes."

I thought she had a message from Dane. Maybe—just maybe—he'd be there. Eleven months was the longest I'd gone in eight years without seeing or talking to him. This separation made me yearn for him, like I was a teenager forbidden to see my boyfriend.

I couldn't wait to see him.

She chose the time—8 p.m.—and I chose the place—another Coffee Bean on Beverly Boulevard, a block from where Ian and I lived.

I don't know how we found each other, but I remember how she looked, young with brown hair and freckles. She was nice, but not elegant or well dressed like the kind of woman Dane would know.

Who was she?

I asked about Dane.

"He's fine." She switched topics quickly, obviously wanting to bypass my Dane question, the only reason I'd come. "You met Hunter, right?"

"No. How do you know Dane?" I tried to redirect the conversation, but she ignored my question.

"What do you mean, 'no?'"

"Well, *yes.* I saw Hunter a few weeks ago. He called but I didn't call back. I haven't heard from him since."

"He didn't give you anything?"

"No. Like what?"

"Shit." Sammy shook her head. "I *knew* it," she said, softly.

I was confused, but she continued. "How are *you?*"

"Good—really good." For a moment it was true.

"Don't you have something coming up?"

What?

"You know . . . the date in December?"

Oh, my sentencing date. Just a date on a calendar, the court's docket.

Now that I was cooperating, I saw the time-line game. If you're indicted, you wanted to postpone the inevitable, the awfulness of prison. As if by stretching time, you wouldn't have to go to prison at all.

"Those dates always get postponed. It's not happening."

Within her silence, detail came alive. I noticed her navy windbreaker, her face bare of make-up. Behind her, a couple laughed, chatted and drank coffee by the fire. Normal.

"Dane and Harvey have names you can give the prosecutor if you need something to give, if you have to talk."

Names? Who is this woman? What the heck is she talking about? I feel like I'm in a movie.

"If you go in, they'll put money into your account. How much do you want?"

She was talking about prison.

Jesus. I was tired. Tied up with all this code-talk, soiled with the "let's help Jen out so she won't talk" stuff.

God, help us all. As if any amount of money is worth spending time locked up.

"I want nothing," I said. Sammy ignored me and handed over a crinkled blue Gap shopping bag. "Think about it. I'll call you later."

"What's this?"

"Your sweater."

When she left, I looked into the bag—envelopes within envelopes. The bag was heavy. Once home, I opened the bag and counted—$35,000 cash.

The cash smelled good. Familiar. My heart beat fast, like hundreds of people were applauding me after one of my modern dance shows. Like I'd felt when Dane and I counted piles of cash in his Arizona condo.

I wanted to keep the money.

"Jen, you have to call Edward." Ian was right, but I waited one night.

As I slept, I calculated ways I could keep the money—get away with it. Stash the money in a hole I'd dig in the desert or in the backyard by the fence or *somewhere.*

But I'd changed. I knew the consequences. I could lose my freedom, my family's trust and, most importantly, my trust in myself.

I knew keeping the money wasn't the right answer.

The next morning Edward was frantic, then exasperated. "Jen, why didn't you call me last night? Call Erick now!"

Like a good girl, I did.

I felt mysterious standing beside my car at a corner Chevron station.

Two big trucks pulled in and two young men in baseball caps stepped out, like a sting operation, like *21 Jump Street*—the '90s TV show.

As they sauntered, I felt silly, girly, with the Gap bag in my hand.

Quickly, the sting turned ordinary, innocent.

"Hey, are those Uggs? Real ones?"

I looked down at my short soft boots, a birthday present from Ian, and the jeans I'd tucked fashionably into the tops.

"Yeah?"

"My girlfriend really wants a pair," one boy-man exclaimed with passion. "Do you like them?"

God, is this a sign? But what would it mean, if it were?

"I love my Uggs."

I love the cash.

The pass-off was familiar, except this time I passed the cash to the Los Angeles DEA, not drug dealers and Detroit thugs.

The meeting felt like a mirage, except for the receipt in my hand. The agents left as quickly as they came, driving off in dark trucks with tinted windows, as if they'd never been there at all. For a moment, I wondered if the DEA men would keep the money.

It didn't matter.

I had given the cash back.

Ian and I moved to privacy.

Our new apartment was located behind the Hollywood Bowl, a popular outdoor venue. Faint rumbles of musical chords and tambourines floated like Ohio maple leaf spindles over the hill and onto our deck.

Outside, cobblestone streets led to white stucco houses that had each other's backs, while, inside, dark-stained floors contrasted with white plaster walls.

I loved our little home.

I loved Ian, and he loved back.

We talked at night over whiskey and wine or in the morning over eggs and toast, sharing Westminster stories, talking real estate, disclosing fears and joys.

Mornings were my favorite. The sun reached through the flax-colored silk curtains waking me as Ian slept, our arms and legs tangled together.

Still, even as we slept, my legal case grew dense as a cancer eating away at ideals, inspirations, dreams—and my relationship with Ian.

I wondered if we would survive, together.

Edward called with breaking news: The indictments were being handed down, tomorrow.

"Was everyone indicted?"

He didn't know.

"Even Dane?"

"Don't worry. "He's *okay.*"

Dane's okay.

EVERYONE said Dane was okay. What did that mean, and how did they know?

The next day the news hit the papers: "DEA Joint Investigation Halts Huge Marijuana Ring." We were all listed. Twenty people and a few of Johnny's men I didn't even know.

That night all I could think about was Dane.

How is he taking the news?

Like me, Dane was used to nice and pretty, too. He'd taught me to live the good life. All I could do was wonder until Edward received new news, another rumor through the attorney grapevine.

"Your boyfriend's a *rat.*"

Dane had turned himself in the same time as Rob.

"He wore a wire, Jen, on everyone."

Edward was disgusted and spoke in an I-told-you-so tone because I'd wanted to protect Dane. "He sure didn't protect you." Edward had read a document—a transcript—where Dane had talked about me. "*Not* nice things."

I brushed off Edward's words, relieved Dane was okay.

I called Dane.

Just picked up my cell and dialed.

He answered.

Had it always been that easy? I'd never tried to call.

Joseph told me not to.

Bottled up emotion came out. I think I cried. I talked like I never wanted to stop. I didn't want to hang up. "I've been *so* worried about you."

We both wondered if we could meet since we were on the same side, cooperating with the government.

Aren't we?

Aaron, Dane's wife, wasn't on Dane's side. She'd skipped town with their six-year-old daughter when things got bad. She was no "stand by your man" kind of wife. Ian had stood by me, and we weren't even married.

Dane said he'd ask Erick if we could get together. "He's a good guy. I think I can convince him." He sounded like he knew Erick better than I did. Like Erick was his friend, too.

But they're not our friends. They're DEA. They want us locked away.

When Erick said yes, I told Ian.

"I *need* to see him."

"Why Jen? Dane got you into this mess."

Ian was protective of me. He didn't understand why I'd want to talk to Dane, when all this was *his* fault. Ian loved me, wanted me safe. But, I didn't, I couldn't, blame Dane. We'd been through too much together. Finally, after nearly a year apart, I could see him.

I was ready for our rendezvous. I bought a ticket to Phoenix. I packed light and kissed Ian good-bye. I reassured him with a look that said *I'm okay.* Was Dane?

At the airport, he looked thin—worried thin. Our embrace was tight but gentle, his energy lower than normal.

Dane was no longer a man who threw cash around and made things happen with a phone call. The cash was gone and so was the power. I could feel the defeat in myself.

That night, as Dane leaned into the plush couch in the hotel bar, I could see it in his eyes. He'd been wounded, just like I had. He looked shell-shocked as if he were exhausted and frozen after climbing a high mountain. Like he was tense, but alert.

Our wounds bonded us. We shared DEA war stories, federal government jokes, and prosecutor stabs.

Was it still Dane and me?

Had it ever been?

The next morning I was by the pool with Dane when Ian called. He was upset. I could hear the hurt in his voice. Ian was my star, my guide, my protector.

And even though I hadn't slept with Dane, I'd left him to be with Dane at the spa in Phoenix. I promised to come home early, now, tonight. I changed my ticket, but I couldn't change the damage I'd done.

When Ian opened the door, I melted into his arms, relieved, thinking all was well.

I was home, back to my new life with Ian where I was supposed to be, back to safety.

That night in bed we had sex, the best I could remember. Covered in shadows, Ian cried, his body hovering over mine. He didn't say a word, and I didn't know why he was crying. But I knew why *I* felt bad. I whispered through his tears. "I'll never leave again."

Later I'd see that in choosing to see Dane I *had* left Ian. It was a choice I couldn't—wouldn't—take back. Somehow, I felt responsible for Dane. Like a mother tending to her child, I'd *had* to see him. Or, was I trying to ease my conscience about him? The moment I'd decided to cooperate with the DEA, I'd hurt Dane.

A mother wouldn't do that.

Yet, Dane admitted that before I'd even talked, he'd slandered my name to the prosecutor, saying I'd begged for the trips and funneled the illegal money into the spiritual community he called a cult.

"I *never* said anything negative about you," I replied, hurt.

Still, I felt guilty.

Did I need Dane's forgiveness?

Did he need mine?

No matter how it went down, we'd both turned our backs on each other.

The prosecutor had a need, too. "I *need* you to be honest, 110 percent."

So, I was.

For a while, the prosecutor and Erick thought I'd lied about Hunter. The prosecutor told me that at my next court appearance. "We thought you took money from Hunter."

"But, I didn't."

"Dane gave him money to give you—$35,000 cash. He recorded Hunter on a wiretap, saying he'd given you the money. You almost didn't get your deal."

"He *didn't* give me the money." I felt threatened, like I'd done something else wrong.

"We know that now, but only because of Sammy. Lucky for you, she told Dane that Hunter hadn't given you anything."

That had been recorded on Dane's wiretap, too.

If I hadn't met Sammy, who was a friend of Harvey's . . .

If Sammy hadn't given me the money and I hadn't had given it back . . .

If Dane hadn't worn a wire . . . *then* where would I be?

Looking at seven years.

Hunter had fooled everyone: the prosecutor, Dane, and me.

He'd kept the money. Played jester with my life.

CHAPTER 28

NO RIGHT ANSWER

I waited all day to pee on the stick I'd bought at the drugstore, delaying what I'd suspected was true.

I was pregnant.

For weeks, my tight belly had felt stretched, taut as a short thick rubber band. For weeks, I'd been hungry. Not a hunger I was used to, but a gnawing sensation like an animal was chewing my insides.

I shook the stick and felt sick when I looked at it.

No change.

The pink lines in the tiny test window wouldn't go away.

My head dropped to my chest. I was too stunned to cry.

Instead, I checked out. I felt as though I'd left my body and hovered over the toilet in our apartment, looking down.

I wished the woman holding a pregnancy stick would disappear.

I didn't want *her* to be me.

Should I call Ian?

Ever since Casey, I'd dreamed of having my own daughter who'd smell like baby powder, twirl in tutus, and skip in Mary Janes. A girl whose breath would smell sweet as a strawberry Jolly Rancher.

But I couldn't be pregnant, not *now*. Everything in my life was wrong for a baby.

I was going to be sentenced soon. I could be headed for prison.

Ian and I weren't married, and the longer we were together the more I realized he didn't want to be. He liked being single and alone.

He'd made "the comment" a few weeks ago as he stood in the doorway looking taller than his actual five foot six. I watched him from the sun porch, the porch where he strummed chords on his Fender guitar from time to time. A place I knew as safe.

I didn't feel safe. Ian was going somewhere and, again, hadn't included me in his plans.

"You're treating me like we're married." He stressed the word "married" with disgust as if it tasted rotten.

His hurtful words hung midair in my mind like a caption in a comic book I couldn't erase.

I defended myself, but what was I defending?

He was right. I did want to be married. The feelings had taken me by surprise. I felt guilty—wrong for wanting to have a family. Hadn't I rebelled against tradition and the "white-picket-fence" dream with my marijuana trafficking and my spiritual search?

Or was I was more traditional than I thought?

I threw the white stick into the trash and barely made the shot. This shot didn't win points.

Ian and I weighed our options. At age thirty-six, this could be my last chance to get pregnant. But what if I was in prison when I had the baby?

I'd heard the horror stories: incarcerated pregnant women were physically restricted, shackled during labor and birth, with a prison guard in the room. Then the baby was immediately taken away.

I couldn't give birth like that.

The reasons I shouldn't have the baby seemed endless. I didn't know when I was going to be sentenced. I didn't know if I was going to prison or, if that did happen, how long I'd be there.

There were too many unknowns. And Ian had told me he didn't want to be a single parent.

Nor did I, especially not in prison.

Back then, I didn't know about the special program some prisons offered called M.I.N.T.—Mother's and Infants Nurturing Together—a community residential program for women who were pregnant at the time of commitment. If an inmate was approved for the program, she could spend the first three months bonding with her infant in a specific facility before returning to the institution to complete her sentence.

My boss and friend Stephen was great. "I'll pay for a nanny if that helps you make your decision."

My attorney Edward wasn't, at least not in the same way. He saw my pregnancy as a sympathy card to play in court. "Jen, this is good news. The judge won't want to sentence a pregnant woman to prison."

I was mortified and angry, but not with Edward. He was just trying to get me the best deal. I was angry with myself.

How could I have allowed myself to get pregnant? I was irresponsible, foolish. And I knew when it had happened: the night I'd come home early from my visit with Dane.

Had Ian's tears of longing—or my regret at hurting him—fertilized the seed?

Long talks and walks in the canyon with Ian followed. No option felt right or good. The choices were nearly as bad as my legal case, when I'd had to decide between seven years in prison or cooperating with the authorities.

Together, and with careful consideration, Ian and I made our decision. My tears froze, turning into icicles that surrounded my heart.

I would have an abortion.

Edward told me to wait until after my next court appearance in Detroit in three weeks.

Wait?

I felt faint as Edward explained his hopes that the judge would sentence me soon, either to home confinement or to a short prison term. If so, I could make a different choice and have the baby.

I gripped the phone, trying to hide my flushed face. Stacy, a favorite first employee I'd hired last year, was sitting at her desk only a few feet away. She was pregnant, too. Unlike me, she was delighted to be having a baby. She'd looked down, when she told me the news, already rubbing her belly in circular, motherly strokes.

I was silent, grim, especially when my gynecologist explained the procedure and the timing. I should have the abortion in three weeks, no more than five.

I agreed to wait. After all, Edward was my attorney. He held my life in his hands.

I held a life in my hands, too. It wasn't fair to bring a baby into my mess. *Too much fear, too much trauma for me and the baby.*

With my decision, the life growing inside me felt like death.

During the next few weeks, Ian fed me and the baby. He brought home pre-natal vitamins and whole milk from Whole Foods. Was he in denial? Was I?

I scrambled eggs, sautéed broccoli, and boiled tomato soup that I couldn't eat. Nauseated, nothing but milk tasted good.

At work, I bonded with Stacy. I'd told her about my pregnancy, I guess because I didn't have any girlfriends in Los Angeles. Since my arrest, besides work and Ian, I'd locked myself away. I was too embarrassed about my legal mess to make new friends. Together, Stacy and I managed house renovations as we compared stories about our fatigue, swollen ankles, and too-tight jeans.

I hadn't realized how much thicker I was until I dressed to go to a concert at Disney Hall with Ian. When I tugged the sheer beaded tunic past my mid-section, I ripped a small one-inch tear on either side. I was too tired or too lazy to take the shirt off and, later, too tired to enjoy Luciana Souza's beautiful, wailing voice.

Next to the willowy blond in jeans, I looked fat in the bathroom mirror at the concert hall. But I felt thin and fragile inside, my heart as torn as my shirt.

The decisions I'd had to make the past two years were driving me to scary places. The choices felt like a war between parts of myself. One side had to surrender; but which side? Which choice was the *right* choice?

I'd taken my time and looked deep inside to try and find the right answer. Was there one?

Driving home after the concert, I looked out the Toyota 4-Runner's window into lighted homes—a favorite game of mine. I wanted to catch a glimpse of life, of other people, whether they were alone—watching TV or washing dishes. Or together—two lovers entangled on the couch or a mother and daughter laughing.

I yearned to be those people, to fall into *normal.*

"I'm sorry," I whispered, "for all I've done and can't take back, for what I'm about to do."

After my silent apology, I relaxed. For a moment, I forgave myself.

The melody Ian hummed as he drove sounded as tender as a mother's lullaby, soothing me . . . and the baby who wouldn't be born.

But underneath was grief. Was there something hidden beneath the sorrow?

If I were brave enough to follow my sadness like a thread, would it lead me to the deeper place I'd always yearned find?

No matter how awkward, ungraceful, and painful, how ugly my choices seemed—even to myself—*I* had made them.

My court appearance in Detroit proved non-eventful, my pregnancy irrelevant.

This was my second appearance in front of the judge who would eventually sentence me.

The first time in her courtroom, seven months ago, I'd been pleased and hopeful.

The Mardi Gras mask on her raised desk, the long decorative duster coat she wore, seemed like good signs.

She appreciates art, I thought to myself. *Possibly, she has a soft heart.* In my perfect world, she'd look past my crime and see the good woman I was.

My first impression was wrong. She shook her head and looked at me with dark piercing eyes. This judge now seemed tough, non-bending.

And I was guilty as charged.

After court, Edward chatted casually with the prosecutor, hoping for information that would hint at a sentencing date.

The prosecutor alluded to a long wait; the New York's federal district was now involved.

Edward said I'd have to talk to the New York prosecutor soon.

Everyone indicted in my case was talking except for one person, Edward told me. He didn't know who. The Detroit prosecutor and DEA had passed the information to their counterparts in New York. The federal district was opening another case.

More indictments would be handed out soon.

"Matt (the New York drug lord) and all of his men are guilty," Edward said. "They're going down." We walked at a brisk clip, both of us anxious to leave dreary Detroit and the hard-nosed judge behind. We wanted to go back to easy-San Diego where politicians and judges had a reputation for going "light" on marijuana cases.

I wondered if I'd ever feel at ease in my own skin again now that my past had been dug up, the hidden dirt and grime uncovered.

I imagined Hunter feeling even worse.

Hunter had "gotten himself locked-up," the prosecutor had told Edward with a snide laugh.

When the first set of indictments came out, the government had had no idea where Hunter was. Then he'd called the prosecutor's office to ask if the indictments were true.

Just by starting a conversation, Hunter had accidently turned himself in.

I was surprised. Hunter always tried to get the best for himself. This seemed like naïveté, or was it stupidity?

The judge decided to release him on bond. Weeks later, he tested dirty for drugs and the government locked him up, along with his movie-star smile.

Now, *that* was stupid.

Even *I* was still randomly tested for drugs, and I'd been on pre-trail for over two years. My Los Angeles pre-trial officer had led me into the bathroom only a month before.

"Do you really have to test me?" I'd asked. "You know I don't do drugs," I called from behind the open door of the stall as I peed.

"That's right. . . . You *just* sell them." She laughed as if her joke was funny, but I gave her a dirty look. I'd *never*.

I didn't *sell* drugs.

After he peed dirty, Hunter was flown to Detroit and placed in a federal holding facility until sentencing. He'd been there for seven months. Not a fun place. I knew. Seventy-two hours had been enough for me.

I didn't wish anyone behind bars, even Hunter, who'd almost put *me* there. Even Harvey, who was locked up immediately when he returned from Greece. Everyone, including the judge, agreed he'd flee.

Didn't Hunter and Harvey know that winners followed the rules?

When the doctor told me to take the tiny white pill a few hours before my procedure, I did. One hour later, the cramps started, at first in predictable waves—a familiar steady rhythm of pain like I was on my period. By the second hour, painful cramps pummeled me like an Ohio tornado.

I doubled over on the bed. Frantic, Ian called the gynecologist, who wasn't worried. But I was, especially when I tried to walk to the car and almost fell over, dizzy and nauseated with pain.

When Ian stopped at a red light on the chic corner of Beverly and Robertson Boulevard, I discarded my dignity, opened the car door and threw up. I arrived at the doctor's office hunched over, shaking from pain, and leaning on Ian's arm. Other patients stared, or at least I thought they did.

"She needs help *now*," Ian told the assistant. The woman shuffled me quickly into a room and onto my back, hiking my feet into stirrups like I had no face and no feelings.

Now the doctor looked worried, her eyebrows downturned.

She'd told me the pill would make the procedure easier, but easier for whom? The doctor?

The pain medication wasn't working.

"Are you addicted to drugs or alcohol?" she asked. I felt judged, but she gave me more medication. In my drug-induced state, I tried to grab Ian as he was rushed, white-faced, from the room by the nurse. No matter how much local anesthesia dripped into my arm, I couldn't block out what was happening.

Now the pain was in my heart.

I broke down on a Friday.

Alone on the outside deck, blanketed only by stars, I crumbled. I drew angry pastel pictures and drank wine, waiting for Ian to come home. The pictures mocked me, each line a margin of my defeat.

I'm weary inside and out—in every cell and the places in between.

For a moment, the hate I felt for myself covered over my past success as a student, as a dancer, as a woman, blackening my life like the gritty dark sky after the recent San Diego fire.

Like a heroine in a melodrama, I contemplated what would happen if I took an entire bottle of Motrin.

I pictured Ian finding my body on the bed. No, that was not the solution.

What I really wanted was permission to go crazy, to lose my cool, to break down.

When Ian came home, I lashed out, unloaded, spewed angry no-nonsense words. His eyes widened, surprised. Then, he changed the rules and danced a two-step I didn't know. His voice escalated and *he* became angry, which I'd rarely seen. Instantly my words stopped, like he'd found my shut-off valve.

Then Ian left, something else that *never* happened. I checked the clock by the quarter hour, knowing he'd return. When he didn't, I clung to my cat and crawled into bed, hopeless and drunk, and cried myself to sleep.

I woke in the morning to shame and regret. My awkward out-burst had been a cry for attention. Instead, I'd pushed Ian even further away.

Ian returned that evening but we still didn't talk about what was wrong or why he didn't want to sleep with me. He said only that he was tired of living with my legal case every day. "Maybe we need more space."

Houses were our business, so it didn't take long for me to find an artsy two bedroom in Topanga Canyon for us to share and, a week later, separate places: A storybook cottage for myself in the Hollywood Hills that was a three-minute drive from a sun-filled apartment for Ian with French windows that opened to trees.

The only difference in our relationship now, besides sex, was location. I still talked to Ian two or three times a day and saw him at work. And he was my weekend date.

The most precious part or our relationship remained. Ian was still my best friend.

The past two years had taught me how important friendship was. Without the support of friends and family, I didn't know how I'd have made it through.

Nights when I was depressed, I'd re-read the thirty-six letters my friends and family had written to the judge on my behalf.

I felt like I'd died, the letters were my elegy, and all my friends had come to my funeral.

I was alive, but so tired—dead-dog tired.

July of 2005—two years and three months since my arrest—I was still waiting to be sentenced.

I was done.

Jack's call surprised me. Stephen had recently hired this young, hip San Diego attorney who wore safari-styled blazers and stream-lined stylish pants.

I applied lip gloss and tightened my ponytail, reinserted my gold hoop earrings. I wanted to look good for this attorney who was in LA and stopping by the office. When he walked in the back door, I stood up and greeted him with a smile.

Did he look away?

I felt uncomfortable as he led me into the conference room where he wanted to sit. He was acting *too official*…rigid and stone-faced, his eyes shifting to mine, then away.

I knew something was wrong.

He's not smiling.

When he first spoke, I was too startled to move or answer. Then the realization sunk in. Stephen had sent Jack to let me go. I didn't want to sign the paper Jack had laid on the table, agreeing to stay on another six weeks. I didn't want to stay another hour.

I wanted to run—far, far away. And *never* talk to Stephen again.

How could he?

Jack was only the messenger, but his words were a dagger through my heart. The heart I'd poured into Westminster Investments. During the past year and a half, Ian and I had worked hard to build Stephen's Los Angeles business: hiring and firing employees; renovating a building that housed our offices plus four apartments; and purchasing, renovating, and selling over eighty homes throughout Los Angeles County.

Besides my legal case, I *breathed* Westminster Investments.

But my soon-to-be criminal status was a liability and an expense. Stephen was paying an extra salary to a woman we'd hired to take my place when or if I had to go to prison.

It had been over six months, and I was still there.

I wouldn't—couldn't—go back to work on Monday.

Most of the employees knew about my pending legal situation. That was embarrassing enough. Now *this?*

I'd lose all respect.

Ian sounded almost as hurt as I did and said he didn't know how the office would survive without me. "We're a team. You *are* the office."

I know. I know.

Ian told me Stephen was livid I'd declined his offer. Elizabeth refused to return my calls.

I sat on the stoop by the Dutch door of my cottage, puzzled.

I'd heard stories of Stephen banishing ex-employees and ex-friends, but I never thought it would happen to me.

I began to have panic attacks—short bursts of fear—that would visit when I woke up, drank coffee at the Coffee Bean on Sunset Boulevard, or visited the dry-cleaners.

Besides Ian, Westminster and Stephen had been my only constants. Stephen had counseled me when I left the spiritual community, hired me when I needed a job, put up a bond for me when I was arrested, kept me on the payroll as I awaited sentencing and, I thought, forgiven me for continuing the marijuana business.

Now he'd taken it all away.

CHAPTER 29

MY GOOD-GIRL SUIT

I was stifled.

Although the owner of the Pilates studio on Larchmont was good-looking and I wished he'd ask me out, I barely said a word.

How could I? I was waiting to be sentenced to prison.

I became a hermit.

At night, I lit candles, wrote poetry, and camped out in front of the bookcase with my ashtray and glass of wine. With my CDs scattered in disarray on the floor, I played songs, from "Kids with Guns" by the Gorillas to "Sweet Jane" by the Cowboy Junkies to "Feels Like Home" by Norah Jones.

I'd scream and cry. If I could get out of my head, I'd dance—anything to get my bottled emotions out. During the day I followed a triangle from my house to Ian's and then to Willetta Street and a few blocks to the craftsman house we'd bought to renovate. Then I followed the triangle back home.

Waiting.

When Edward called with news, fear vibrated up and down my spine like a discord of scales on an out-of-tune piano.

Finally the day arrived. I would be sentenced in the Detroit courtroom. Thirty months after my arrest, the waiting would be over.

My sentencing date—Nov. 11, 2005—was permanent, Edward said.

Two weeks. Anxiety sped through my veins. I knew the participants on the other side—the judge, the prosecutor, and Erick the DEA agent. I knew how to survive my day in the courtroom. I gathered my friends and family, the people who loved me the most and saw me for the good woman I *really* was, a person the judge couldn't seem to see.

Detroit.

I pulled open the closet door. The Nicole Miller suit looked perfect—good-girl perfect—but it mocked me, its dark blue illusion of protection destroyed at my debut in court ten months ago.

The second time I'd worn the suit, I'd had my picture taken for my pre-sentence investigation report that would follow me as I passed through the system.

The report was the condensed bible of my "criminal life."

The probation officer brought the camera out before I knew what was going on, but Edward knew. "Smile," he said.

My photo—with pearls—on the first pages of the report was intended to ease the reader into the personal tale of a-good-girl-gone-bad, a girl gone temporarily "off the rails," as Ian had written in his letter to the judge.

The picture—the smile, the suit, the pearls—was perfect, even in black and white.

One more night and the long-awaited day of sentencing would be here.

I remembered being thirteen at the county fair, seated and strapped in, about to ride the Zipper.

The carnie slammed the mesh door and I was imprisoned. Get me off! What if the door opens? What if I fall?

Once again, there was no turning back.

I'd decided to stay at the Ritz-Carlton, which I knew was a risk, given the twenty or so times I'd stayed there. I was feeling fragile already. Would my past surface? Would my mind glorify successful drug trips?

The luxury of the hotel gave me no emotional comfort. I couldn't cover the pain by drinking a nice glass of cabernet or going shopping. The old tricks had deserted me.

I wanted to be the blue suit in the closet, the flower engraved on the brass doorknob, the chocolate on my pillow.

Anything but me.

How could prison be God's plan for my life? It didn't fit. My mind searched frantically for a back door, but none existed. Edward was my only hope, my only savoir. I called him twice, but he didn't answer.

Ian was in the bathroom, but I knocked anyway, asking him to meet me in the lobby. His voice echoed through the door. "I'll be there, soon."

I needed Ian. I needed Edward. I needed time alone. I didn't know what I needed, or what I wanted.

Except off this ride.

I wanted to believe there was something more Edward could do to prepare my argument, but deep down I knew there wasn't.

Still, I thought I'd get out of it somehow, that I wouldn't *really* go to prison.

As I walked down the long hall, ghosts of Rob and Dane and ten years of my own greed followed me along the ornate carpet. But when the elevator door opened to the lobby, the ghosts disappeared. All I saw was a man clad in the loose white shirt and pants of a spiritual disciple. In the plush setting of the Ritz, the barefoot man looked surreal, but . . . I knew those clothes—that look—from the retreat in India.

Breathe in. Breathe out.

The knots in my stomach relaxed, but only for a moment. As I walked toward the hotel lobby, more barefoot men and women in white walked past me.

I'd been a disciple, too, in San Diego, but we'd worn modern clothes, make-up, and heels.

The Ritz-Carlton was the last place I expected to see a group of disciples, or a guru. But, how could I judge, when my own reality seemed to be falling apart?

I sat on the antique couch in the hotel bar, rubbing my hands together. I barely felt alive, even when my parents stopped by to say good night, even when my mother kissed me.

My brother sat on my left, and I smiled, trying to hold together the perfect-girl image of my childhood. But the facade had shattered.

Everyone smiled, ignoring the dark cloud of dread.

Ian lit my cigarette, and I quickly filled my ashtray. I ordered a second glass of wine and then walked around the corner to the gift shop to buy another pack of cigarettes. As I did, more people in flowing clothes disappeared down the hallway to my left.

When I returned, a woman in white had joined us, invited by my San Diego friend and former roommate Katie. The woman told us she was a devotee of the Indian Amma. The "Hugging Mother" guru had traveled to the States to give *satsang* (a gathering together for the truth) tonight at the Ritz-Carlton, and all the barefoot guests were followers. Some had flown from Australia and Europe to see her.

The woman in white and I exchanged stories, parallel ones, since her son had been incarcerated. I was no longer surprised at the secrets my story unlocked. I'd heard so many that imprisonment had begun to feel like a disease, an American pandemic.

The commonality always touched me.

I was buffeted by two conflicting feelings—both of them intense—fear I might be going to prison and joy at finding a guru at the Ritz-Carlton that evening.

My spiritual and material worlds intertwined. For a moment, my discouragement rolled off like a droplet of water on a lotus leaf, erasing all doubt.

"Here take this," the woman in white said, handing me a token and a flyer for the next day's event at the Hyatt. "You can pray to the mother for assistance."

I knew I wouldn't go, but took them anyway. The clear almond eyes of Amma gazed out at me from her photograph, the truth boring into my soul, reflecting back my own dishonesty.

I know. I know.

I was no longer alone. *I never had been.*

For a moment, I'd only forgotten.

I wanted to cry when I looked at my mom in her black blazer and flowing maroon skirt. She seemed so tiny, so fragile, sitting perfectly still on the edge of the bed. My dad knelt, helping her on with her shoes. Her health had been declining the past few years.

Was her sickness my fault? Had my situation made her worse?

Her sister—my Aunt Joan—was also in the room. She called me "Jenny"—as always. Her large eyes were gentle, her smile genuine.

No one knew how to act or what to do. Neither did I. I had the feeling, though, that everyone was following my lead.

"How do I look?" I twirled, modeling my perfect blue suit and pearls like I was waiting for a homecoming date. The pearls were my mother's favorite, my hairstyle—pulled back into a soft knot—my dad's.

I was desperate for their approval. I was desperate for God's.

"Jenny, you look beautiful, as usual," my mom said.

Once again, I choked back my tears. "Mom, I'm going to be okay." I held onto my big-girl grin and flashed the familiar cheerleader smile, the one that had cheered the Panthers onto victory in high school.

I can't let her see I'm not okay.

My mom needs me to be strong.

At breakfast, Edward pulled out his chair and placed the white napkin on his lap. "We're going to ask for probation only." I looked down at the napkin—crisp, white linen like the waiters' aprons, just like the napkins on my first date with Dane.

Then, I'd been young, naïve, insecure around a seemingly powerful wealthy man. *Is that when I'd thrown my life away?*

I was tired, drained, like I'd driven tons of pot across the US and gotten arrested by the federal government.

Because I had.

I held Ian's hand.

As we drove to downtown Detroit, I looked out the window in time to see the "world's largest tire," originally built as a Ferris wheel for the 1964 New York World's Fair.

How many times have I passed that tire? Twenty, thirty, fifty?

This was the tire that used to make my heart race, knowing we were close to the trip's finish line—drugs unloaded, cash in my hands. It was hard for me to let go of the past, even though everyone and everything in my present life told me it was wrong.

"But, we had fun, right?" Dane had asked a few weeks ago. We had. I didn't want to embellish the good times, but I also didn't want them destroyed.

From the back window of the car, I watched the seven-story-high tire statue grow smaller. In my mind, I slid my hands down the sides of the tire reliving my adventures: the smell of the cash, the sound of the zipper closing a canvas hockey bag, the residue of marijuana on my fingers, fancy dinners, expensive hotels, fine wine . . . until, finally, I touched only air.

This was the end of a very long chapter of my life.

The actual event was over in less than fifteen minutes. The judge walked into the courtroom and slammed her gavel three times.

Guilty. Guilty. Guilty.

According to Edward, the judge had decided my sentence even before she'd entered the courtroom. The court reporter told Edward she'd heard the judge whisper, "I'm giving her three years," to my probation officer.

Maybe she already knew everything about my case, but what about justice? What about fair? The prosecutor talked about my cooperation. Edward—and I—spoke on my behalf. Was all that for nothing?

Why had we come all this way?

I walked out of the courtroom and fell into Susan's arms, the friend who'd counseled me in 1996 after Joeluine died. She'd arrived late with Lane, another good friend from Chicago.

I was shaking as I whispered, "It's not good, Susan. *Three* years."

The day after I returned from Detroit, I moved out of my cottage.

Ian and I had decided I should move into the craftsman house with him while I waited for my "designation letter" to arrive in the mail. The letter would tell me when I was surrendering to prison, and where.

Shocked and dazed, I moved all my belongings with Ian's help.

The day felt hazy or rather, *I* was hazy. I was looking at the city with different eyes, and I was a different girl. I was going to prison.

Almost Christmas—six weeks—and the letter *still* hadn't come. The tension was almost visible in the house . . . in me . . . and in Ian.

Renovations on the craftsman were running late, workmen still pounding, Ian still yelling. I was fried. Everything felt out of my control, waiting to go to prison, not knowing when or where I would be going. Ian kept busy, hiding behind work.

When I'd complained to Ian that we weren't sleeping together, his response seemed unrelated, more of a defense than a reason. "Jen, I never thought you'd be living here this long."

As the weeks passed, the fear came faster, gripped harder, and lasted longer, like I was getting closer to the center of a hot fire.

I barely had time to focus on spirituality now, to read books or meditate—my entire life had become an "intensive"—the biggest spiritual test I'd experienced so far. I felt better when I found prison consultant David Novak on the Internet. In person, he looked professional and normal in white jeans and a navy button-down shirt. I was surprised he'd been in prison, too.

I wanted David by my side.

I wanted to know the rules, the right way to be a convicted felon. I wanted to know what prison was like, to erase the dreadful pictures in my mind that told me it would be an awful, scary place to be.

I feared the unknown.

The scariest place to be.

I'd been concerned I couldn't pay David, but we worked out a trade. He'd be available until I surrendered and I'd give him permission to film me for a pilot he was making for Court TV.

After our meeting at the Marriot Hotel, the valet brought my car and I drove off the hotel lot to the sound of KCRW radio playing Johnny Cash's "Folsom Prison Blues."

I was not alone.

I felt like I was dying, but David assured me I wasn't.

There were lots of *lasts*. My parents visited me for our last Christmas; my Chicago friend Lane flew with me to Hawaii for my last vacation; and I celebrated my last New Year's Eve alone, with the lights off, tucked in my bed, feeling dead.

I dreaded the New Year. I willed 2006 not to come.

The suspense ended January 18, 2006, two months after my sentencing. Smiling, I thrust the letter in Ian's face. "I got Alderson."

Inside my head, I recognized my tone of voice. I sounded just like I had when I received my acceptance letter to Ohio State's dance program: *I got Ohio State.*

I'd *asked* for Federal Prison Camp, Alderson. The West Virginia prison was 252 miles—a five-hour drive—from my parents in Washington Court House, Ohio, and 2,291 miles from California.

My prison consultant had told me it really didn't matter where I went. "Like McDonald's, Jen, all prison camps are alike."

This time, I didn't believe him. I'd seen the pictures. California's only federal prison camp looked barren and dusty with a razor wire fence. Alderson was located in the foothills of the Allegheny Mountains—nature and hills and *trees.*

Maybe there my childhood trees will protect me.

I would surrender in three weeks: February 28, 2006.

I spent my last week as a free woman packing. I'd made it through the first six boxes, but by the seventh, I began to cry. Not because I was sad, but because I felt crazy.

I'd moved a lot, but I usually packed my belongings to go to somewhere new.

Now, my belongings were going to storage, and I was going somewhere without them.

Soon Ian would sell the house so we could make a profit, but then I wouldn't even have a home to come back to.

I focused on tearing down my life, piece by piece, like a deconstruction specialist.

Four days before I left, I visited my pre-trial officer for the last time. Every month for the past year and a half, I'd driven to downtown LA, paid eight dollars to park my car, and jaywalked across the street to meet her. It had felt good to disobey at least *one* rule.

Two days before, I sold my car.

One day before, I completed the accordion file that contained important information for Ian: bills that needed to be paid, procedures on how to write me, contact numbers and names of family and friends. Everything Ian needed to take care of me from the outside, when I was inside.

The day before Ian and I left for West Virginia, I went shopping.

I bought a pair of tall Fry boots I'd coveted for a year, ever since I'd seen Chloe Sevigny wearing them in the Bill Murray movie, *Broken Flowers*. To me, the movie illustrated the sadness of going through life emotionally disconnected. Dead.

I don't want to be like that.

Now, *I* felt broken, disconnected, as I shopped, looking at earrings, wallets, purses, and other items I couldn't take with me, wouldn't need.

What else can I buy?

I was looking for something I couldn't find: control.

Choosing—having a choice—was something I'd be giving up for a long time.

I choose *you*, silk turtleneck the blue of my dad's eyes.

I chose *you*, ribbed thermal shirt the color of green—of healing—as iridescent as forest moss.

I chose *you*, trendy T-shirt, pink and perfect as the princess I used to be.

My shopping spree was comical, manic, maybe crazy. I was headed for prison the next day and everything I bought would go into the eighth packing box.

I'm falling apart.

I wore the boots and the pink T-shirt on the plane and the blue silk turtleneck at dinner that night, my "last supper." I'd wanted steak and fancy wine, but the Hilton's food had seemed tasteless, bland. I don't even remember what I ate as the film crew filmed me under studio lights.

I had one glass of the cheap house merlot in the hotel bar, one cigarette.

My last.

That night I slept in my new silk pajamas, cuddled in Ian's arms.

I remember lying quietly, listening to Ian breathe as he slept. I tried to picture myself in prison the next day, but I couldn't. I willed myself to sleep but instead fell deeper into stillness, a silence I recognized as shock.

I squeezed my Gund bunny, the tiny stuffed animal that I'd hidden behind the pillows for the past five years. I'd washed the dirt from my bunny last night. Nothing felt clean or perfect . . . or good . . . or pretty.

And I was done trying.

I wanted to feel better.

I guessed "better" didn't always mean feeling good.

I wore gray sweats, a white T-shirt, a thick white puffy coat with a hood and two big pompons on the end of each tie. I looked ridiculous, but David told me to dress like a prisoner and maybe the guard would let me keep my clothes.

But, *pompons?* I'd reverted back to the little-girl part of myself who wanted attention, protection.

As David drove, the cameraman sat in the back, filming.

"Are we there yet?" asked my little girl.

He chuckled. "Why, are you in a hurry?"

No, we *weren't* almost there. For a moment, I laughed, too—but off-key and out-of-tune. For a moment, I wanted life to be fun, and everything inside myself to be okay. My laughter quickly faded.

In the town of Alderson, beside the creek, I hugged Ian. Or did he hug me?

With the cameraman out of range, I cried. "I'm sorry."

"I know. I know."

Ian continued. "Remember, God has his reasons. He loves you. *I* love you."

I know. I know.

There it was. The sign. Not a "God sign" but the prison sign.

FPC ALDERSON

I wanted to turn back.

I didn't know what to do. I had my ID and money in my plastic bag, and my book, *A Course of Miracles.* Other than that, nothing.

David punched the intercom button beside the two yellow gates. "I have a two o'clock commit here. Myers."

When the white truck came toward us, I didn't want to leave. I looked back at Ian once more and mouthed the words, *I love you.*

"Jen, your sunglasses," David said.

I'd forgotten. I whipped them off and handed them to Ian.

David looked me in the eyes. "Are you ready?"

"I'm ready."

No more waiting. Still the performer, I stepped out of the van and raised my hand for a final wave and a smile.

Once through the yellow gates, I was on the other side.

I didn't look back.

CHAPTER 30

THE LOST GIRLS

Nothing could have prepared me for the shock of prison.

I thought I was ready when I got into the truck. The officer, Ms. Green, introduced herself in a slow, almost sweet, Southern drawl, and I thought I'd be okay.

Then I was strip-searched, fingerprinted, given physical and psychological health exams and a stack of new clothes—khaki pants, faded brown T-shirt, and black steel-toed shoes. I stashed other clothes in a white mesh laundry bag and slung it over my right shoulder, already missing my Marc Jacobs purse.

I was marked and labeled a felon now: Inmate # 87836-198. My ID hung around my neck like an ugly plastic lei.

An officer had told me where I should go, but I stood stunned and confused in front of an expanse of grass with two brick Colonial Revival buildings on either side. Women walked in various directions, following an invisible pattern, as if they had somewhere to go. Standing there in my turquoise winter coat with the broken snaps and too-long sleeves, I probably looked as lost as I felt.

Another officer waved me in the direction of Range A, a two-story brick building that would be my temporary home. *I don't belong here,* I thought to myself as I shuffled toward the grass oval in my new black shoes.

I didn't know what was coming, and I was afraid.

The noise was deafening as I walked down one side of a room half the size of my high school auditorium. Four rows of open cinderblock cubes divided the room. I was assigned to cube 32 on the second floor—A-4—with other new commits who were running around talking and laughing.

It wasn't quiet. It wasn't private. And nothing belonged to me.

When I realized I didn't have anything but the few drab articles of clothing I'd been given, I felt desolate. I didn't even have a pen. I was told I could shop, but it was 6 p.m. and the commissary—the prison store—was closed until noon the next day.

A skinny, blue-eyed officer sat three of us down in a small room for a brief orientation. "Women will try and hit on you," she said, frowning at me. "Why are *you* so tan? You go to that tanning booth or something."

Singled out, my face turned red. For the first time in my life, I didn't want any attention.

"She's from *California,*" said a young blond, accentuating the state like she was proud to have met someone from such an exotic place.

The girl had round eyes and cheeks like the Cabbage Patch dolls I'd coveted as a child. *Why is she in prison? Is she even eighteen?*

That first night, another inmate gave me a pair of flip-flops for the shower and an empty 11-ounce instant creamer bottle to fill with drinking water.

Someone was nice to me. I felt a tiny glimmer of hope.

"COUNT!"

Jesus. What the . . . ?

The talking ceased in the room except for keys jangling on belts and boots marching on concrete.

From my top bunk, I could see the guard counting us on her nightly prison route, her head moving left to right like she was watching a tennis match. With a final call of "Good count!" the hallway door slammed and the noise escalated again. Cross-legged on the top bunk, I saw the hallway door open at the other end of the room. "I said *quiet!*" the officer commanded.

My plastic mattress crackled when I moved, and my turquoise coat wasn't much of a pillow. I closed my eyes and wished myself to sleep, wished I'd be somewhere else when I opened my eyes.

Cold. But, I couldn't do a damn thing about it. Everything was out of my control.

Noisy. The big girl below me snored like a chainsaw. And my tired metal bedsprings vibrated, keeping me just on the edge of sleep like I was on a 747.

This time I *wished* I were on a plane. But I wasn't going anywhere.

My wings had been clipped.

At mail call the next afternoon, I reached for my letter. "GET your hand off *my* desk," snarled the uniformed woman, the same officer who'd counted us last night.

I pulled my hand back like it'd been burned.

I hadn't been reprimanded like that since I was ten, when my gymnastics coach yelled at me for taking an extra step in the floor routine.

Another inmate stared at me from across the hall, but in a nice way. She was tall, maybe five foot seven, with straight brown hair hanging to her waist. Her big brown eyes seemed compassionate.

Who is she?

Her voice was friendly, too. "Hi, I'm Ericka." She didn't extend her hand or give me a hug, but that didn't hurt my feelings. I already knew inmates weren't allowed to touch.

A whistle blew, signaling it was time for dinner, and women pushed open the door, shoving and running. The mass of running women—all kinds of women—scared me. "Why are they running?" I asked Ericka, as we pressed through the crowd.

They want to be first down the steps, first down the hill, first in line for dinner, she said. The line—and the wait—could be very long. It was another example of the tedium that summed up prison: "Hurry up and wait."

When Ericka told me she'd arrived three days ago and she was scared, too, we bonded. Instantly, we became friends.

We'd walk the track and chat like high school girlfriends, her twang bringing back memories of my childhood in Ohio, even though she was from Kentucky. We needed relationships in prison just as much as we did outside—maybe more so. To fill in for family and friends we were missing, some women adopted mothers, sisters, or *girlfriends*. Others, like Ericka and me, just hung around in pairs.

We became "Jen and Ericka," one rarely without the other.

Other inmates referred to us as "the blond and the tall girl with the long hair who always wears a dress."

Ericka was Pentecostal, so she was prohibited from wearing short sleeves, shorts, or pants. Instead, she wore a prison-issue khaki dress.

She was only eighteen—the youngest a felon could be.

She walked a cute lopsided shuffle, her shoulders drooped like girls do when they try to hide their height. Then she'd suddenly look up, flip her long hair, and flash her dazzling beauty queen smile.

Maybe we were trying to protect each other. I wanted to protect something, or someone. Most of all, I wished I could protect the children whose mothers were locked up on lengthy non-violent drug sentences, sentences so long it seemed they'd *never* find their way back home.

When one woman, who'd been locked up for ten years on a non-violent drug conspiracy charge, claimed she was innocent, I almost believed her. She had three—or was it four?—children. Her husband was locked up, too. She couldn't stop crying, and I didn't know what to say. She was right. Her situation *did* seem hopeless.

Even when a prisoner's loved one isn't literally locked up, her partner might as well be. I soon learned that husbands, boyfriends, parents often tend to the prisoner and the life she's left behind. Some drive hundreds of miles every week for a visit, desperate to keep their connection alive, desperate for the children to know their mother.

Desperate.

Life inside and out becomes a sad and lonely country song, like the poem I wrote in prison:

There's no soup on the stove,
And the house it's getting cold from the loss of power in the kitchen, and
the loss of love that we're missin',
And the bills are piled on the desk,
I guess the electricity's gone missing . . .

A familiar prison joke was that the inmates looked better on visiting days than the visitors, refreshed like we'd "been at the spa," Ian would say.

I told him we spent *hours* preparing for a visit—the only event that took us out of prison and back for a moment into the world we once knew.

Blow-drying, straightening, curling our hair in the hair room located off the shower stalls in every range. The women applied sparkly blue eye shadow, pink blush, and thickening mascara; slathered on cherry-almond lotion, baby oil, and baby powder, all bought at the prison store. Then they'd add a swipe of perfume from a torn-out magazine sample, anything to get rid of that stifling prison smell that even two scoops of detergent and three Downy dryer sheets wouldn't extinguish.

That prison smell made me feel like the outside world had disappeared. After months locked up, I felt discarded, forgotten, like one of the lost girls.

When Ian met me in the visitor's center on his tri-monthly visit, he seemed like someone from another planet. After snacks from the vending machines, we sat side-by-side in gray plastic chairs or walked on the lawn, trying to get reacquainted. Six hours later, the visitors had to leave. The last three hours my stomach would clench. The last hour I'd do everything to hold back my tears. Sometimes, embarrassed, I'd cry.

The children *would* cry, and I'd look away.

I wanted to cover my ears when they screamed and reached for the mother they had to leave over and over again.

In a small, enclosed room inside the visitor's center, the same humiliating ending to visiting day:

"Drop your pants, bend over, cough."

Sure, officer, no problem. I'm a veteran—used to exposing my tush. I ain't hiding nothing—no hoop earrings, no cigarettes, no drugs.

Then we'd climb back up the hill to join those who were worse off than we were—the ones who had no visitors, ever.

In the evenings, I'd wear my Bose radio headset and circle the compound. I'd walk a brisk clip down the hill past the education building, the dining hall, the deserted cottages, and then back up past the chapel, the recreation building, and finally Range B-2, the building I'd moved into after eight months.

Like the others inmates my "bunkie," Lamont, and I shared an open five-by-seven cinderblock cube with one trashcan, one bulletin board (no tacks), and two bunk beds, mine *the top*. Each of us had a locker, a metal desk, and a stool.

I was mortified the evening I found out Lamont was assigned to my cube.

Why, God? I thought you'd protect me.

I'd been scared of the black, older gay woman from Chicago with red braided hair.

I was on the top bunk when she appeared in the doorway with a big smile. "Hey, friend," she said.

Immediately, I was disarmed. Lamont became my friend, my protector. One out of three women who practiced Nichrin Buddhism, she was the best bunkie I could have had.

God *hadn't* left my side.

I cried only a few times during my fourteen months in prison, usually in the relative privacy of my nighttime walk. I'd keep my head erect, wiping away my tears before anyone could see that, inside, I was barreling through my pain. With each stride, each pump of my arms, I felt stronger, like I could propel myself through the prison gates and out into the West Virginian prison sky . . . into a universe of forever I couldn't see but knew was there.

One night, after one of those walks, I sat alone at a metal picnic table and looked up at the moon, a huge orange ball the color of a Creamsicle. I counted the stars one by one as they appeared in the dark, clear Virginia sky, like I counted the days until my release.

As I looked at the moon I thought of Ian, how he hadn't deserted me like I feared he would. Every month, he sent me money from my share of the sale of our craftsman house, which I used for phone calls and commissary purchases. He sent letters every week and, later, e-mails every day. He paid my bills; communicated with my attorney, my parents and my brother; and supplied me with books, newspapers, and magazines.

I wrote and rewrote in the margins of books odd calculations that only another prisoner could understand: my yearly fifty-four good-time days—if I were good; the drug-program reductions—if I got in; the halfway-house time; and my reduction—if I got one. *Please, God, just get me out.*

Like everyone else, I was obsessed with getting out and counted every day like a personal victory, knowing when I woke each morning I was one day closer to going home.

That night at the picnic table, though, I felt close to the world beyond the fence. The world I couldn't see. The stars I'd seen in Chicago, Florida, San Diego, Hawaii—even India—were the same as these prison stars that hung like flashlights in the sky lighting the way back home for us—the 1,300 women on the compound.

The stars guaranteed we weren't forgotten.

For a moment I knew, whether I was a name or a number—a dancer, a prisoner, or a professional—we were *all* the same.

And, I was not alone.

The next day I broke down.

I never felt anything like this before or after. I was frustrated—prison frustrated—confronted by all the things I couldn't do and couldn't have. I didn't want to be there.

No one did.

The phone restrictions tipped me over the edge, those damned fifteen-minute phone calls and the 300-minutes-per-month limits. Five measly hours had to be stretched over thirty days.

Ian and I had gotten into a fight over the phone, and he'd hung up.

The call to my brother didn't go well either. The next call to Kelly, my best friend from Chicago, went even worse.

Everyone sounded angry at me. And, with my monthly minutes spent, I couldn't call them back. During my last fifteen-minute call to Kelly, the phone had given me the familiar "beep-beep" warning only I could hear. I had three minutes before it cut me off. Not only could I *not* resolve this awful web of conflict with Ian and Kelly, but I had two long, empty weeks when I couldn't use the phone at all.

As the weeks ground by, dread and anxiety threatened to overcome me, and cover my sanity with their dark cloak. Being locked up is awful, but not being able to speak to anyone on the outside is worse. A few months later, we finally got access to e-mail, which was an un-limited luxury, as long as we paid five cents a minute.

A voice—any voice outside of prison—kept me connected,

grounded to "the real world" like an invisible thread as strong as a nylon tie-down.

The real world—that's what we called everything outside of prison.

I wanted to call our time at Alderson a mistake—a fairy tale gone sour. Later, I wondered if inside prison was the most real I'd ever lived.

When I couldn't call anyone back, I felt more trapped than ever before.

I wanted a glass of wine. I wanted dim lights, incense, and candles. A hot bath, a soft touch. McDonald's, Starbucks, and Nordstrom.

I wanted privacy.

But the florescent lights were bright and wouldn't be turned off until 10 p.m. Six weeks into my sentence, I'd been moved into the smelly room nicknamed "the Fishbowl" because of the large interior glass window. So, fully clothed in my after-work attire—gray sweats and an old pink T-shirt I'd scored from a friend—I covered my head with a scratchy wool blanket, sat on my bunk facing the wall and sobbed. But the lump in my stomach wouldn't go away.

I don't want anyone to see me cry.

But I was in the Fishbowl with eleven other women. Everyone could see us.

After four months in prison, I felt like I did belong here— *almost*—and that scared me.

I'd become used to the prison routine:

6 a.m. wake up and breakfast;

9 a.m. work;

11 a.m. lunch and then back to work;

4 p.m. count followed by mail call;

Free time—do crochet or crafts, work out, walk with a friend, write on the library typewriter, make collages in my cube;

10 p.m. count.

Other times, I had to work in the evenings.

I never got used to the starchy diet with barely any protein—most of that chicken, chicken, and chicken. Or, to the dizzy spells I tried to cure by taking three vitamins a day. Worst was the touch of male guards during the nighttime counts. They weren't *intimate* touches—usually—but still an invasion.

We all agreed—their touch made our skin crawl.

I walked prison routine as though it were an unwanted labyrinth with no center, no exit. I developed my own routines within the confines of the Alderson schedule:

Tuesday aerobics with Ericka;

Saturday dinner and church with April and Ericka;

Sunday dinner with Marcie, Shelia, Leah, Ericka, and Denease on a picnic table outside. The food we prepared in the microwaves—wraps with spam or vegetables from Shelia's garden, macaroni with tuna as a luxury; and unique prison desserts like cheesecake made with pudding, instant creamer, and lemon—was much better than food from the dining hall.

I wanted to fit in, but not so much that I'd disappear.

The beauty of Alderson—its crab apple trees, chipmunks that ate Jolly Ranchers out of our hands, and the West Virginia hills—were as seductive as a mother singing an off-tune lullaby. I was afraid I'd drift to sleep and get lost like Hansel and Gretel but never find my way back home—like the women with long sentences.

The inmates knew. After you've been locked up for ten years, you risk becoming institutionalized like the women who become so obsessed with cleanliness in their cube they won't even throw trash in the cube's trashcan.

Could these women operate on the outside—a world where you create your own routine and structure, a world where you once again have choice?

I wasn't in physical danger, though I'd been threatened early on when a girl took my fresh mattress and replaced it with a smelly one from the Fishbowl.

Another inmate had warned me my new roommate wouldn't like the exchange. "Girl, Ms. Johnson ain't going to like that smelly mattress in her room. You gotta get it out." Ms. Johnson, an old-timer and church-going woman who'd been in prison for ten years, had a following that looked out for her.

And I was new. I didn't know what to do. Shakira—the girl who'd stolen my mattress—scared me. She was young, solid, and hung out with a rough bunch from DC.

Later that evening—with the help of Ms. Johnson's friends—I went back for my soft mattress, a coveted item. I'd gawked as two hefty women dragged the smelly mattress across the floor and dumped it in front of the officer's station.

Let the officer—the police—deal with it.

My battle had been won. With some help, I'd stood up for myself in prison.

My pride was short-lived. After dinner Shakira caught me on the stairs. "White bitch, it ain't over."

I wanted to disappear. She was tough. I wasn't. With my ponytail pulled high, my gray shorts rolled up at the waist and my white anklets neatly folded down, I looked neat—even prissy.

I never liked conflict, but especially not in prison with a scary-looking woman. The real danger, though, was something I felt rather than saw. A dark cloud of victimizing, complaining, blaming—a general "I'm not okay" feeling—hovered over the compound like a disease.

Ian noticed.

We'd end our nightly ten-minute phone calls with a sweet good night, and the next morning he'd open my e-mail that listed all the wrongs in my life: books I hadn't received, communications I wanted Ian to make, concerns about our relationship. I even went back to "What are we? Why don't you want to sleep with me? Is there an *us*? What is going to happen to us when I get out?"

I'd brood on all this and feel hurt and misunderstood when Ian pointed out I was caught in the grips of the compound's negativity.

I'd whine in response. "No one understands."

But he was right and, after a while, I developed an inner sense—like a light on a miner's hard hat—that lit my way when I was out of balance.

It was a matter of survival. I couldn't afford to be *down* in prison where I had few distractions. I couldn't look forward or back. To stabilize myself, I had to take "one day at a time," which was the best advice veteran inmates give the new commits.

I learned to take responsibility for my emotions, no matter my discomfort.

Some evenings I wanted to escape the eyes of other inmates and cry or take the 800 Motrin my friend had in her locker to deaden my pain, but I didn't.

I wanted to experience prison *alive*.

Some woman didn't stabilize, couldn't normalize.

The daily pill lines for prescription medication were long, and some women slept their time away. Or, worse . . .

That's why we had suicide watch. That's why I volunteered.

"Myers, get up." Although I was supposed to wake up on my own, the male guard tapped my leg.

I looked at the clock—2 a.m.—time for my three-hour shift.

The compound was eerily beautiful with no one around as I walked past the trees down to the lower compound, my way lit by old-fashioned street lamps that made prison appear to be a tiny village or a town.

Once inside, I sat down facing the silent inmate across from me.

We couldn't read. We couldn't crochet. All we were supposed to do was watch the woman through the bars, in her enclosed cell.

I was assigned to a dark-skinned, plump woman who seemed happy, almost pleasantly content. I'd heard rumors that some woman faked depression to escape to a private, quiet cell as though they were retreating to a five-star hotel room. The woman sang to music only she could hear. Not rap, but country music.

I wanna drink that shot of whiskey.

I wanna smoke that cigarette.

I wanted to fall into her country music dream where hearts were aching, beer bottles breaking, and Chevys driving down clover-lined roads.

She began dancing. As she cross-stepped toe to heel, I wondered if our roles should be reversed. Maybe this cheery woman should be watching over me.

"I slept with a guard when I was in Florida, at Coleman," Lucy told me when I moved into her range. She'd been in prison for seven years and seemed comfortable here. She snuggled cat-like under her crocheted blanket, leaning against two pillows. "Six months. He was transferred, so it ended."

I tried not to judge.

"It goes on here too, Jen," she said coyly and wrapped a strand of surfer blond hair around her finger. She changed topics and made me an offer. "Do you want me to soak your tennis shoes?" She seemed to want to win my attention. I looked down at the stains on my white shoes, ashamed, noticing for the first time how dirty they were.

I thought of Lucy and *her* guard when I talked to the guard on staff that evening. The guard I was attracted to.

"Can I go to church?"

"Yeah, sure, Myers," he responded. The only way an inmate could get out of work was to attend a religious service.

It unnerved me to be attracted to him, left me feeling vulnerable. His eyes shifted behind his glasses, looked back at me and then away. He'd noticed me. This was dangerous territory. I was a woman. I was deprived, hungry for touch and attention from a man. He was a man, and he was a guard.

I looked down at the set of keys that hung off his belt. He counted us—me—every day at 4 p.m. as we stood at the front entrance of our cubes. He locked us—me—inside at 10 p.m. every night.

He has power over me, I thought, as I eyed the handcuffs attached next to the keys. At Alderson, I mourned the erotic thoughts and desires I'd left behind. I forgot sensual intertwined legs and arms and focused on making women friends and crocheting stuffed animals.

Now, *sex* threatened to emerge.

"Did you check the bathroom?" he asked. In addition to teaching four Pilates classes per week, I was supposed to clean the bathroom.

"Yes. I'm finished. Can I go now?"

As he watched me toy with my ID tag, I fantasized about kissing him. I was embarrassed, disgusted, by my desire.

"Sure, Myers." And I was dismissed . . . back to my isolation.

Alone in my cube, my isolation leaves me breathless.

I am chosen. Plucked by life's hand, and taken away from everything familiar, from everyone I love. The prison walls tower like skyscrapers in my mind. With every shift of my internal kaleidoscope, existence slides further away. The pain moves deep and to my core. Tumbling blue stars banish me to my bedroom, saffron grows into green diamonds grounding me with no dinner. Yet, this time no one will arrive to open the door. The pain is my mother lost in a sea of psychedelic design . . . my lover gone, never to return.

In the main sanctuary, I found a seat near the middle aisle, where I could see. The room was already hot and steamy, overflowing with women. The air felt thick with unspent devotion. The preacher began with a soft whisper, his voice hypnotic. "Take your cup, God's cup. . . ."

I'd never gone to the Beauty for Ashes service, but Ericka and I had watched from outside the door. Sometimes the women danced and cried; sometimes they wailed and slithered on the floor as the preacher passed out options and hope like candy.

I closed my eyes and swung my feet back and forth under the pew. My feet and my heart kept time with the preacher's words.

"Praise Jesus!"

I opened my eyes just enough to see the woman who had spoken. She held her hands high above her lowered head, and said again, louder, "Yes, Jesus!"

Painful moans of hope echoed throughout the room.

"God wants you to drink!" the preacher shouted. "Now raise this cup to your lips and taste the gift of God. Let Him wash over you."

I lifted my imaginary cup and tilted my hands to pour God's gift into my mouth, swallowing imaginary gulps. The heat of devotion burned inside my chest. For a moment everything—even prison—magically disappeared.

"Come together now, come to the front and drink in God's love."

I followed the stream of inmates. Someone's warm fingers interlaced with mine. I looked over at the woman on my right and extended my hand to her.

I feel God's love.

Tears streamed down my face and I reached forward, following the preacher's admonition to grasp God's cup. "Fill your cup," he bellowed again.

With all my passion and trust, I reached—reached for a deeper purpose, a plan for my life. Eyes closed, I dropped into a deep inner abyss familiar from my five-hour meditations with the San Diego spiritual community.

I was bawling in glorious release.

God filled that room.

God filled many rooms in prison, and I visited them all. I attended my first sweat lodge with Native American inmates, chanted *nam-myoho-renge-kyo* in front of the Gohonzon (a Nichrin

Buddhism devotional scroll) and devoured *A Course of Miracles,* the book I'd brought with me.

Was my faith stronger because I had so little control here?

Or was I feeling so alive because prison was the grand finale and something spectacular waited outside.

In prison two choices were under my control: my perspective and how I spent my time.

I could have checked out on medication. I could have criticized and blamed the Bureau of Prisons or Dane for my predicament. I could have wasted my time on idle chatter, gossip, and unhealthy relationships.

Instead, I began to look at the tools I had. From my spiritual search, I'd learned to change my attitude and shift my awareness: Don't make assumptions. Don't fall into discouragement. Don't get attached to emotions. Pray, pray, pray.

Gifts I'd discarded in junior high appeared like childhood friends helping me through the darker days. I returned to writing and making art.

Despite the constant pain, I faced prison head-on.

After the Beauty for Ashes sermon, I wrapped my sweatshirt around my waist and hung my radio headset around my neck, stabilized by the routine. My bag was heavy with the meager belongings I transported everywhere.

We all kept these bags close, but they weren't really ours. The manual made that clear, stating that *everything* was Bureau of Prisons (BOP) property.

Our bodies belonged to the BOP, so we weren't even allowed to sunburn when we lay on our towels on the grassy grounds to tan during the hot summer months.

This was a rule.

"Pass me the Hot 6." April, another inmate and new close friend, tipped the bottle of African oil toward me.

I loved its smell.

Did it exist before prison?

I inhaled coconut. "They're looking. Don't get too red," she said, as I lathered myself with the slippery oil, ignoring her words. "I heard a rumor someone got a shot (an incident report) yesterday." The BOP didn't want to deal with a sick inmate who'd gotten sunburned, an extra liability.

It was always a rumor.

But we saw the woman the next day. You couldn't miss her. She looked defeated, sunburned, red all over.

She'd broken the rules.

By my thirteenth month at Alderson, I could fully appreciate the beauty of a West Virginia spring. Achingly beautiful, expansive, the basin we lived in was surrounded by majestic mountains on all sides. We were tucked away in our own tiny world, apart from everyone we knew.

The beauty never failed to surprise me, and the pain never left.

I walked outside, the clear dark sky looming overhead. Feeling cleansed, I stood close to the chapel building, before I began my nightly walk. The compound's lights illuminated the grassy knoll in front of me, the track wrapped its concrete arms around.

The women's silhouettes were haunting as they walked, the picture timeless—a mirage I wished had never materialized. Mostly in pairs, the women completed endless rotations, round and round, circling like my thoughts as I went to sleep in the Range at night.

It was after nine, and the newest rule prohibited walking the lower compound after eight o'clock, so nearly 1,000 women were on the track. I stood at a distance, watching the eerie dance, feeling oddly comforted. The track seemed alive with a rhythm that held our pain, discouragement, and complaints.

I kept my head straight, my route direct as I walked past the REC building. Living in such close quarters, the inmates had their own rules: Don't look, don't listen. *No ear hustling.*

"Hey," I said in passing, responding to each woman I knew with a nod. "Hi, Mandy."

Walk.

"How are you, Kathy?"

Nod.

Walk.

Stephanie . . . Joanne . . . Denease . . . Gail . . . Suzanne . . . Marcie . . .

I pulled the headset over my ears for privacy.

My earlier restlessness had gone, leaving a precious jewel of calm in its place. The solitude felt like strength.

I was alone but connected, and I wanted to hold onto this connection.

Stay steady, Jen.

Rap music blared from doors and windows of the recreation building, fading as I walked away.

Then I opened the door into chaos—the blinding lights and deafening noise of Range B-2 where I lived.

In twenty minutes, the whistle would blow, signaling the compound was closed for the night. I rushed to complete my nightly routine so I could be on my bed before count. I opened my locker and dislodged the blue pajama pants that were folded and stacked underneath my T-shirts. I found my slippers on top of the dark gray bin underneath my bed.

With these nighttime items and nighttime routines, I felt safe.

Next I'd take peanuts and red and yellow Gummi bears from my locker, pour them into a bowl and illegally shimmy up the bar at the end of the bed like monkey bars from the fifth grade. Surrounded by five magazines, two books, a mug of Sleepytime tea, and my bowl of treats, I'd settle back and wait for count. With these nighttime items, I was comforted in my temporary home. The whistle would shriek and the door shut. We were locked inside, counted at 10 p.m., and tucked in bed with the guard's cry, "Good count!"

"Good night, Shelia," someone would whisper a few cubes from mine. Wide-awake voices would echo around me as I pulled my crocheted blanket over my head.

Good night, Ian.

Good night, God.

Good night, my sweet Zoey.

Every night, I closed my eyes, wishing away the lights overhead and yearning for darkness.

Dark knight, save me.

No one comes.

The dim hum around me slowly faded into the silence I yearned for during the day. I'd feel alone, even though I was surrounded by hundreds of sleeping women, even though a guard would come in the night, counting us as we slept.

As I sleep my dreams tap on the window of our cube, begging to be released. Lamont sleeping below, does not hear.

I'd hold onto the fragile peace I felt inside, knowing it would vanish in the morning when I'd touch the metal bar of my bed and think, as always:

I'm still here. Still in prison.

Fourteen months into my sentence, at 9 a.m. on April 27, I was given immediate release. My sentence had been reduced.

Immediate release were magic words at Alderson. For one day I was a superstar, living the dream that inmates wanted to believe could come true.

The rumor didn't take long to infiltrate the compound. By lunchtime, the inmate behind the salad bar whispered, "Did you hear? Jennifer Myer's got *immediate release.*"

"Yes, I heard. It's me."

My immediate release wasn't as mysterious as they thought. "I worked hard for the reduction," I told the inmate in the e-mail room who asked. Ian had worked hard, too, and so had my attorney and his partner, Julia.

I'd cut a deal. By now, all of my fellow marijuana conspirators had made the same choice. It was the only thing we could do.

The only provision was I had to be off the prison grounds in twelve hours.

The justice system had taken forever—two-and-a-half years—to put me in prison. The Federal Bureau of Prisons gave me seven hours to get off the prison grounds. As I waited, I crocheted a periwinkle shawl, and I dreamed. In twenty-four hours, I'd be back in San Diego, walking the boardwalk by the ocean and shopping boutiques for something to wear. A shadow passed through. *How will I live? I have no home, no car, no job.*

I kept crocheting, knowing somehow, my life would work out. The hours passed, and with the last stitch, I said good-bye to this chapter of my life—and to the pain of belonging to the government and Alderson.

I belonged to myself now.

I was free.

It's been four years, but I still dream that I'm in prison. In one dream, Tim grips my hand through steel bars and says good-bye. I want to hug him, but I can't. I cry as I watch him walk away from my locked cell.

Come back soon, okay?

I'm sweating.

I fear I'll be forgotten.

The dream has twisted the facts. I barely knew Tim when I was in prison. Our relationship began several months after my release. I roll over and pull him close to me, grateful I can touch him.

"If I'm moaning in my sleep, wake me up," I say.

April and Ericka tell me they have these dreams, too, even though we've all been out for four years.

The dreams are a part of my life now, like my collection of boxes.

There's the box my mother packed of old childhood toys: the Raggedy Ann who was by my side when I had scarlet fever, my favorite orange pinafore dress with the zigzag white stitch.

Soon, I'll get rid of the box with my prison clothes: the gray Champion sweatshirt, white T-shirt, gray sweats, and one pair of white granny underwear. The other day, by mistake, I opened the box. When I held the T-shirt to my nose, I swore I could still smell prison.

The Staples copy paper box in my office looks unimportant, but it's a trophy as significant as the ones I won for gymnastics. My entire legal case is in that box, an experience as precious as a college diploma.

I may keep it—like the cards Tim gave me for birthdays and Valentine's Day and the fragile broken shell he brought back after his vision quest last year.

For, despite the pain and the loss, prison is a part of me now, as much as the silent, beautiful spaces in between—those spaces that used to terrify me. I can almost hear the beauty in the struggle like a distant, steady hum of a bee's wings fluttering as they touch the air, some flapping 250 times a second. The number resonates inside me. *Two hundred and fifty.* The number of miles I used to drive in one stretch on one of our trips, the cash I'd pack in my suitcase. My mind plays with numbers, thinking back to the number of choices I'd made, the number of times I chewed my nails waiting to surrender to prison, the pairs of women walking the track at Alderson, the people I may have hurt through my trafficking. I think of the milliliters of flax I poured into the trough for my 4-H steer, the stat class my mom took in college, the number of hours I'd rehearse for a show. *Two hundred and fifty.* The stars I still count in the night sky, just like I did at Alderson, just like I did with my back against the barn as a child, realizing the universe is so much *bigger* than me.

Despite the pain, my journey sometimes seems sweet, beautiful like a symphony with 250 violins. Sometimes, if I'm still, I hear their melody. Sometimes within the empty spaces of "not knowing," I hear a voice that has always been there, a voice that cannot be counted, or touched. The voice is unlimited.

It calls me home.

EPILOGUE

I never counted my money, but I think I must have made—and lost—a million. The money seems surreal now, but the consequences were very real. I wish no one had to spend even *one* day locked up. But in my federal case, no one was saved. Eventually, everyone went down, all twenty-one of us in Detroit's case, and eight in New York's. The sentences ranged from one to twenty-five years, those with previous crimes hit the hardest. Sometimes at night, lying in bed, I think about those people I know who are still in prison. I squeeze my eyes shut, trying for the nothingness of an inner dark void, but I can't stop the pain in my gut. I can't make this one go away, and I'm done trying.

Although I don't yet understand all that I've learned from my experiences, I know that prison was one of my greatest teachers. There, I was confronted with myself like I never was before. With nothing to distract me, I had no choice but to surrender to my inner torment—and breathe. Is it possible that prison doesn't just take away, but also gives? Did lockdown unlock my heart?

Ultimately, I realize freedom is "inside." But, sometimes we need a spiritual teacher, and most of the time we need a spiritual practice. If it hadn't been for the transformational work I participated in before prison—some admittedly paid for with marijuana money—I could have been broken by the arrest, the two-and-a-half year wait to be sentenced, and the fourteen-month imprisonment. I saw others shut down, get depressed, and stop participating in life. It wasn't easy, but I chose life. I wanted to continue to grow, to feel *alive*. Beauty was hidden in this struggle.

Without a deepening of my faith, I don't know if I could have maintained my balance. I don't know if I would have been able to see prison as a gift, an opportunity to improve my life. And I'm not sure I'd be able to share my story, or work with people going in and coming out of prison. Most prisoners with a background like mine wanted to forget about the experience when they were released; prison just didn't fit into their lives, families, or friends. It's easy to forget about prison when you come home to a loving, supportive family. But what about the women who don't have any support system at all?

When I was released, I was still working through the shame of my crime. I thought a lot about marijuana. Some people consider it a gateway drug. Is it?

Possibly. I'm not sure. The debate continues.

But I do know people have been hurt by this drug, and I'm sorry to have contributed to their pain.

Yet I am proud of my prison experience. I survived and emerged determined to tell my story. Maybe I'm paying "karmic debt" with the telling; maybe it's my way of "paying it forward." Certainly, it's my mission. Through LA Myers Consulting, my prison consulting business, I work with men and women who are facing prison for the first time, like I did. I want to help.

People contact me for practical advice on logistics, paperwork, sentencing, surrender, prison facilities, and communication with family, once they're incarcerated. But what they really want is for someone who's walked in their shoes to listen, understand, and support them. Someone who can alleviate their fears.

I'm working with designer Amy Hall and York Prison in Connecticut to train women inside prison to make her handbags, once they're released. I recently joined the board of Action Committee for Women in Prison (ACWIP). We're working with Amy Hall to start a pilot program that will employ women when they get out of prison in an environment where they can integrate more gracefully back into the world. I'm fulfilling the dreams that eluded me before prison. Incarcerated, I had time to review my life. I saw how I'd allowed fear to run me. Now, I know it's possible to live the life I want to live, to listen to the soft voice inside. After my release, I didn't go back to real estate, or get a full-time corporate job. I had to keep moving toward my vision even if no one else believed or understood.

Now I want to shout out my story so others can see the beauty in their own stories, so they can see the possibility of growing through pain, so they can see their potential.

In part because of my choices and because of my experiences in prison, I've grown up to be a woman with a mission, a woman with a voice. I fight against the injustice I witnessed. I fight for the women locked up on lengthy drug sentences. I fight for the next generation to make conscious choices, unlike the ones I made.

I fight for our prisons inside, and out, to crumble.

I fight to be the woman I was meant to be—for the woman I chose to become.

BOOK CLUB QUESTIONS

1. As a child growing up on the farm, the author dreamed of "bright city lights." How did this ambition escalate, once Dane gave her a taste of "the good life"? What dreams and ambitions did you hold in childhood? In what ways have they come to pass? Which ones are yet to be realized? If some have been discarded, explain why.

2. The author's parents raised her to be a "good girl" and she let them down. What did they expect of her? Has she redeemed herself? What values were instilled in you? Did you ever rebel against them? Have those values remained the same or have they evolved over the years?

3. The author gave in to three temptations. What were they, and how did they affect her life? How did she learn to withstand temptations by looking at future consequences of such actions? What temptations have you faced? How did you respond? How have you learned to deal with them?

4. Themes of love and heartbreak weave throughout the book. What patterns did the author see in her relationships? If you have shared or observed a similar experience, what was the outcome? How did the experience deepen future relationships?

5. In the book, the author's friend Joeluine dies suddenly. How was the author affected by this loss? What new direction did she take? Discuss a major loss in your life. How were you affected?

6. What did the author learn on her spiritual journey? Who were her teachers? If you have taken such a journey, how did it begin? What were your most valuable lessons? In what way was your life changed?

7. The author wanted to appear attractive, even in prison. Is this typical among both women and men? Are attractive people treated differently in the marketplace and in relationships? How have your positive or negative feelings about your looks impacted you? Do you judge the attractiveness of other people or feel judged by them?

8. A series of quick decisions set the author on a path to prison. What were they? Have you ever made a decision that led you down the wrong road? What consequences did you suffer? What did you learn?

9. To the author, marijuana was a popular recreational drug, nothing more. She was shocked when DEA agents told her it was a gateway drug. What does this mean? Do you agree? Why? Why not?

10. According to the author, once members of the marijuana conspiracy were charged with a crime, everyone—even those she considered friends—conspired to betray one another. Under what conditions would you tell authorities of a crime committed by a friend or a family member?

11. The author experienced betrayal in romance, friendship, employment, and crime. In what way have you been betrayed, betrayed someone else, or betrayed yourself? Did you learn from the experience? If you could replay one of these scenarios, what would you change? Would it alter the outcome?

12. What life lessons has the author gained from her crime and punishment? What is the biggest lesson you learned from a misdeed, large or small? What good that came of it, if any?

13. In the book, the author often judges and defines herself by what others say about her. Do other people's opinions define you? If so, what do they say? Do you agree with their definition? If you set aside their ideas, how would you define yourself?

14. In the book, the author made friends wherever she was: in the dance world, in the marijuana conspiracy, in a spiritual community, in real estate, and even in prison. What, in her character, allowed her to assimilate? Is it more common in women? Is this one of your attributes? If so, how do you explain this ability?

15. When the author first meets Dane and his unlimited bank account, she sees money as freedom. When does she finally understand true freedom? How would you define it? What, in your life, taught you the meaning of freedom?

ABOUT THE AUTHOR

JENNIFER MYERS is a federal prison consultant, artist, and speaker who lives in San Diego. Her poems and short stories have appeared in the anthology *Razor Wire Women* and the online literary journal *Qarrtsiluni*. *Trafficking the Good Life* is her first book.

To contact Jennifer: www.jennifermyers.co.

Other Books by
Bettie Youngs Book Publishers

On Toby's Terms
Charmaine Hammond

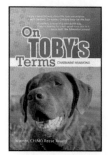

On Toby's Terms is an endearing story of a beguiling creature who teaches his owners that, despite their trying to teach him how to be the dog they want, he is the one to lay out the terms of being the dog he needs to be. This insight would change their lives forever.

Simply a beautiful book about life, love, and purpose. —**Jack Canfield, compiler,** *Chicken Soup for the Soul* **series**

In a perfect world, every dog would have a home and every home would have a dog like Toby! —**Nina Siemaszko, actress,** *The West Wing*

This is a captivating, heartwarming story and we are very excited about bringing it to film. —**Steve Hudis, Producer**

Soon to be a major motion picture!
ISBN: 978-0-9843081-4-9 • $15.95

Diary of a Beverly Hills Matchmaker
Marla Martenson

Marla takes her readers for a hilarious romp through her days in an exclusive matchmaking agency. From juggling the demands of out-of-touch clients and trying to meet the capricious demands of an insensitive boss to the ups and downs of her own marriage with a husband who doesn't think that she is "domestic" enough, Marla writes with charm and self-effacement about the universal struggles of finding the love of our lives—and knowing it.

Martenson's irresistible quick wit will have you rolling on the floor. —**Megan Castran, international YouTube Queen**

ISBN: 978-0-9843081-0-1 • $14.95

The Maybelline Story—And the Spirited Family Dynasty Behind It

Sharrie Williams

Throughout the twentieth century, Maybelline inflated, collapsed, endured, and thrived in tandem with the nation's upheavals. Williams, to avoid unwanted scrutiny of his private life, cloistered himself behind the gates of his Rudolph Valentino Villa and ran his empire from a distance. This never before told story celebrates the life of a man whose vision rocketed him to success along with the woman held in his orbit: his brother's wife, Evelyn Boecher—who became his lifelong fascination and muse. A fascinating and inspiring story, a tale both epic and intimate, alive with the clash, the hustle, the music, and dance of American enterprise.

A richly told story of a forty-year, white-hot love triangle that fans the flames of a major worldwide conglomerate. —**Neil Shulman, Associate Producer, *Doc Hollywood***

Salacious! Engrossing! There are certain stories, so dramatic, so sordid, that they seem positively destined for film; this is one of them. —*New York Post*

ISBN: 978-0-9843081-1-8 • $18.95

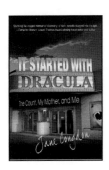

It Started with Dracula
The Count, My Mother, and Me

Jane Congdon

The terrifying legend of Count Dracula silently skulking through the Transylvania night may have terrified generations of filmgoers, but the tall, elegant vampire captivated and electrified a young Jane Congdon, igniting a dream to one day see his mysterious land of ancient castles and misty hollows. Four decades later she finally takes her long-awaited trip—never dreaming that it would unearth decades-buried memories, and trigger a life-changing inner journey. A memoir full of surprises, Jane's story is one of hope, love—and second chances.

Unfinished business can surface when we least expect it. *It Started with Dracula* is the inspiring story of two parallel journeys: one a carefully planned vacation and the other an astonishing and unexpected detour in healing a wounded heart. —**Charles Whitfield, MD, bestselling author of *Healing the Child Within***

An elegantly written and cleverly told story. An electrifying read. —**Diane Bruno, CISION Media**

ISBN: 978-1-936332-10-6 • $15.95

The Rebirth of Suzzan Blac

Suzzan Blac

A horrific upbringing and then abduction into the sex slave industry would all but kill Suzzan's spirit to live. But a happy marriage and two children brought love—and forty-two stunning paintings, art so raw that it initially frightened even the artist. "I hid the pieces for 15 years," says Suzzan, "but just as with the secrets in this book, I am slowing sneaking them out, one by one by one." Now a renowned artist, her work is exhibited world-wide.

A story of inspiration, truth and victory.

A solid memoir about a life reconstructed. Chilling, thrilling, and thought provoking. —**Pearry Teo, Producer,** *The Gene Generation*

ISBN: 978-1-936332-22-9 • $16.95

Blackbird Singing in the Dead of Night
What to Do When God Won't Answer

Gregory L. Hunt

Pastor Greg Hunt had devoted nearly thirty years to congregational ministry, helping people experience God and find their way in life. Then came his own crisis of faith and calling. While turning to God for guidance, he finds nothing. Neither his education nor his religious involvements could prepare him for the disorienting impact of the experience.

Alarmed, he tries an experiment. The result is startling—and changes his life entirely.

In this most beautiful memoir, Greg Hunt invites us into an unsettling time in his life, exposes the fault lines of his faith, and describes the path he walked into and out of the dark. Thanks to the trail markers he leaves along the way, he makes it easier for us to find our way, too. —**Susan M. Heim, co-author,** *Chicken Soup for the Soul, Devotional Stories for Women*

Compelling. If you have ever longed to hear God whispering a love song into your life, read this book. —**Gary Chapman,** *NY Times* **bestselling author,** *The Love Languages of God*

ISBN: 978-1-936332-07-6 • $15.95

DON CARINA
WWII Mafia Heroine

Ron Russell

A father's death in Southern Italy in the 1930s—a place where women who can read are considered unfit for marriage—thrusts seventeen-year-old Carina into servitude as a "black widow," a legal head of the household who cares for her twelve siblings. A scandal forces her into a marriage to Russo, the "Prince of Naples."

By cunning force, Carina seizes control of Russo's organization and disguising herself as a man, controls the most powerful of Mafia groups for nearly a decade. Discovery is inevitable: Interpol has been watching. Nevertheless, Carina survives to tell her children her stunning story of strength and survival.

ISBN: 978-0-9843081-9-4 • $15.95

Living with Multiple Personalities
The Christine Ducommun Story

Christine Ducommun

Christine Ducommun was a happily married wife and mother of two, when—after moving back into her childhood home—she began to experience panic attacks and a series of bizarre flashbacks. Eventually diagnosed with Dissociative Identity Disorder (DID), Christine's story details an extraordinary twelve-year ordeal unraveling the buried trauma of her past and the daunting path she must take to heal from it. Therapy helps to identify Christine's personalities and understand how each helped her cope with her childhood, but she'll need to understand their influence on her adult life.

Fully reawakened and present, the personalities compete for control of Christine's mind as she bravely struggles to maintain a stable home for her growing children. In the shadows, her life tailspins into unimaginable chaos—bouts of drinking and drug abuse, sexual escapades, theft and fraud—leaving her to believe she may very well be losing the battle for her sanity. Nearing the point of surrender, a breakthrough brings integration.

A brave story of identity, hope, healing and love.

Reminiscent of the Academy Award-winning *A Beautiful Mind,* this true story will have you on the edge of your seat. Spellbinding! —**Josh Miller, Producer**

ISBN: 978-0-9843081-5-6 • $16.95

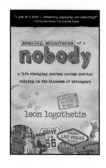

Amazing Adventures of a Nobody

Leon Logothetis

Tired of his disconnected life and uninspiring job, Leon leaves it all behind—job, money, home even his cell phone— and hits the road with nothing but the clothes on his back. His journey from Times Square to the Hollywood sign relying on the kindness of strangers and the serendipity of the open road, inspires a dramatic and life changing transformation.

A gem of a book; endearing, engaging and inspiring. —**Catharine Hamm,** *Los Angeles Times* **Travel Editor**

Leon reaches out to every one of us who has ever thought about abandoning our routines and living a life of risk and adventure. His tales of learning to rely on other people are warm, funny, and entertaining. If you're looking to find meaning in this disconnected world of ours, this book contains many clues. —*Psychology Today*

ISBN: 978-0-9843081-3-2 • $14.95

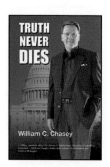

Truth Never Dies

William C. Chasey

A lobbyist for some 40 years, William C. Chasey represented some of the world's most prestigious business clients and twenty-three foreign governments before the US Congress. His integrity never questioned.

All that changed when Chasey was hired to forge communications between Libya and the US Congress. A trip he took with a US Congressman for discussions with then Libyan leader Muammar Qadhafi forever changed Chasey's life. Upon his return, his bank accounts were frozen, clients and friends had been advised not to take his calls.

Things got worse: the CIA, FBI, IRS, and the Federal Judiciary attempted to coerce him into using his unique Libyan access to participate in a CIA-sponsored assassination plot of the two Libyans indicted for the bombing of Pan Am flight 103. Chasey's refusal to cooperate resulted in the destruction of his reputation, a six-year FBI investigation and sting operation, financial ruin, criminal charges, and incarceration in federal prison.

A somber tale, a thrilling read. —**Gary Chafetz, author,** *The Perfect Villain: John McCain and the Demonization of Lobbyist Jack Abramoff*

ISBN: 978-1-936332-46-5 • $24.95

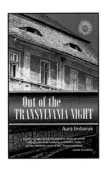

Out of the Transylvania Night

Aura Imbarus

A Pulitzer-Prize entry

"I'd grown up in the land of Transylvania, homeland to Dracula, Vlad the Impaler, and worse, dictator Nicolae Ceausescu," writes the author. "Under his rule, like vampires, we came to life after sundown, hiding our heirloom jewels and documents deep in the earth." Fleeing to the US to rebuild her life, she discovers a startling truth about straddling two cultures and striking a balance between one's dreams and the sacrifices that allow a sense of "home."

Aura's courage shows the degree to which we are all willing to live lives centered on freedom, hope, and an authentic sense of self. Truly a love story! — **Nadia Comaneci, Olympic Champion**

A stunning account of erasing a past, but not an identity. —**Todd Greenfield, 20th Century Fox**

ISBN: 978-0-9843081-2-5 • $14.95

Universal Co-opetition
Nature's Fusion of
Co-operation and Competition

V Frank Asaro

A key ingredient in business success is competition—and cooperation. Too much of one or the other can erode personal and organizational goals. This book identifies and explains the natural, fundamental law that unifies the apparently opposing forces of cooperation and competition. By finding this synthesis point in a variety of situations—from the personal to the organizational—this is the ultimate recipe for individual or group success.

"Your extraordinary book has given me valuable insights." —**Spencer Johnson, author, *Who Moved My Cheese***

ISBN: 978-1-936332-08-3 • $15.95

The Morphine Dream

Don Brown with Boston Globe Pulitzer nominated Gary S. Chafetz

At 36, high-school dropout and a failed semi-professional ballplayer Donald Brown hit bottom when an industrial accident left him immobilized. But Brown had a dream while on a morphine drip after surgery: he imagined himself graduating from Harvard Law School (he was a classmate of Barack Omaba) and walking across America. Brown realizes both seemingly unreachable goals, and achieves national recognition as a legal crusader for minority homeowners. This intriguing tale of his long walk—both physical and metaphorical—is an amazing story of loss, gain and the power of perseverance.

"An incredibly inspirational memoir." —**Alan M. Dershowitz, professor, Harvard Law School**

ISBN: 978-1-936332-25-0 • $16.95

Hostage of Paradox: A Memoir

John Rixey Moore

A profound odyssey of a college graduate who enlists in the military to avoid being drafted, becomes a Green Beret Airborne Ranger, and is sent to Vietnam where he is plunged into high-risk, deep-penetration operations under contract to the CIA—work for which he was neither specifically trained nor psychologically prepared, yet for which he is ultimately highly decorated. Moore survives, but can't shake the feeling that some in the military didn't care if he did, or not. Ultimately he would have a 40-year career in television and film.

A compelling story told with extraordinary insight, disconcerting reality, and engaging humor. —**David Hadley, actor, *China Beach***

ISBN: 978-1-936332-37-3 • $24.95

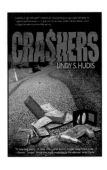

Crashers
A Tale of "Cappers" and "Hammers"

Lindy S. Hudis

The illegal business of fraudulent car accidents is a multi-million dollar racket, involving unscrupulous medical providers, personal injury attorneys, and the cooperating passengers involved in the accidents. Innocent people are often swept into it.
Newly engaged Nathan and Shari, who are swimming in mounting debt, were easy prey: seduced by an offer from a stranger to move from hard times to good times in no time, Shari finds herself the "victim" in a staged auto accident. Shari gets her payday, but breaking free of this dark underworld will take nothing short of a miracle.

A riveting story of love, life—and limits. A non-stop thrill ride. —Dennis "Danger" Madalone, stunt coordinator for the television series, *Castle*

ISBN: 978-1-936332-27-4 • $16.95

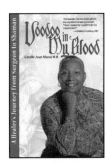

Voodoo in My Blood
A Healer's Journey from Surgeon to Shaman

Carolle Jean-Murat, M.D.

Born and raised in Haiti to a family of healers, US trained physician Carolle Jean-Murat came to be regarded as a world-class surgeon. But her success harbored a secret: in the operating room, she could quickly intuit the root cause of her patient's illness, often times knowing she could help the patient without having to put her under the knife. Carolle knew that to fellow surgeons, her intuition was best left unmentioned. But when the devastating earthquake hit Haiti and Carolle returned to help—she had to acknowledge the shaman she had become.
This mesmerizing story takes us inside the secret world of voodoo as a healing practice, and sheds light on why it remains a mystery to most and shunned by many.

"A beautiful memoir." —Christiane Northrup, M.D.

"A masterpiece! Truly enlightening. A personal story you won't soon forget." —Adrianne Belafonte-Bizemeyer

ISBN: 978-1-936332-05-2 • $24.95

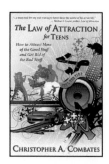

The Law of Attraction for Teens
How to Get More of the Good Stuff, and Get Rid of the Bad Stuff!

Christopher Combates

Whether it's getting better grades, creating better relationships with your friends, parents, or teachers, or getting a date for the prom, the Law of Attraction just might help you bring it about. It works like this: Like attracts like. When we align our goals with our best intentions and highest purpose, when we focus on what we want, we are more likely to bring it about. This book will help teens learn how to think, act, and communicate in the positive way.

ISBN: 978-1-936332-29-8 • $14.95

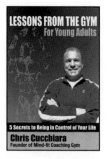

Lessons from the Gym for Young Adults
5 Secrets to Being in Control of Your Life

Chris Cucchiara

Do you lack self-confidence or have a difficult time making decisions? Do you ever have a tough time feeling a sense of purpose and belonging? Do you worry that you don't measure up? Or that you're doing what other people want of you, instead of what you want?

Growing up, Chris Cucchiara felt the same, until he joined a gym. The lessons he learned helped him gain the confidence he needed to set and achieve goals. In *Lessons from the Gym for Yourg Adults,* Chris shares his experiences and powerful insights and shows you how to:

• develop mental toughness (a life without fear, stress, and anger);
• develop an attitude to get and stay healthy and fit;
• build an "athlete for life" mentality that stresses leadership and excellence as a mindset; and,
• stay motivated, and set and achieve goals that matter.

ISBN: 978-1-936332-38-0 • $14.95

The Tortoise Shell Code

V Frank Asaro

When renowned attorney Anthony Darren is wrongfully accused of participating in a high seas crime that ends in death, not only is his freedom at stake, but also at risk is his reputation, and most of all, the budding relationship he prizes the most: the daughter he only recently came to know. He breaks out to prove his innocence—and turns the tables on those who framed him.

"One of the most interesting and exciting books I've read. This will have you on the edge of your seat." **—Ron Russell, author of *Don Carina***

ISBN: 978-1-936332-60-1 • $21.95

Bettie Youngs Books

We specialize in MEMOIRS
. . . books that celebrate
fascinating people and
remarkable journeys

In bookstores everywhere, online, Espresso,
or from the publisher, Bettie Youngs Books.

VISIT OUR WEBSITE AT
www.BettieYoungsBooks.com

To contact:
info@BettieYoungsBooks.com